Acts of Naming

THE FAMILY PLOT
IN FICTION

Michael Ragussis

New York   Oxford
OXFORD UNIVERSITY PRESS
1986

Oxford University Press

Oxford   New York   Toronto
Delhi   Bombay   Calcutta   Madras   Karachi
Petaling Jaya   Singapore   Hong Kong   Tokyo
Nairobi   Dar es Salaam   Cape Town
Melbourne   Auckland

and associated companies in
Beirut   Berlin   Ibadan   Nicosia

Published by Oxford University Press, Inc.,
200 Madison Avenue, New York, New York 10016

Oxford is a registered trademark of Oxford University Press

Library of Congress Cataloging-in-Publication Data
Ragussis, Michael.
Acts of naming.
Includes index.
1. English fiction—History and criticism.
2. Names, Personal, in literature.
3. Family in literature.
4. American fiction—History and criticism.
5. Plots (Drama, novel, etc.) I. Title.
PR830.N35R3   1986   823'.009'24   86-728
ISBN 0-19-504070-8 (alk. paper)

2 4 6 8 10 9 7 5 3 1
Printed in the United States of America
on acid-free paper

*To my mother
and to my son*

Where thou goest, Daniel, I shall go. Is it not begun?
Have I not breathed my soul into you? We shall live
together.
GEORGE ELIOT, *Daniel Deronda*

Acknowledgments

After completing a book on naming, it is with a deepened understanding of naming as acknowledging that I place at the head of this book the names of those people who helped me write it. The following friends and colleagues read large portions of my manuscript and made invaluable suggestions: Jim Maddox, Lucy Maddox, Leona Fisher, and Garrett Stewart. Eric Cheyfitz, even while on sabbatical and many miles away, took time from his own work to comment on my manuscript; the seriousness with which he takes his own work, and with which he generously greeted mine, inspired me. Andrew Collin, Jim Gardner, and Archie Gittes gave support of different kinds; they understood the varied contributions that help make a book. Two people oversaw the entire project, reading it from the first word to the last, making themselves available at every turn in the journey, assuring me that the end was in sight. Joe Sitterson read every page with the scrupulous intellectual care that keeps an author honest. Sue Lanser brought to the project her immense powers of head and heart, ironing out the snags in my logic, reminding me to honor my contract with my reader, and renewing my enthusiasm and delight when I no longer could find them. Finally, my dedication makes plain the kind of family debt that goes beyond words. In a book so critical of the politics of the family, I wanted to acknowledge the kind of blessing I have known.

The National Endowment for the Humanities gave me a year in which to think and write; during that year the major idea of this book was born. Georgetown University made possible a summer of uninterrupted study. I would also like to thank the editors of *Nineteenth-Century Fiction* and *ELH* for permission to reprint (in altered form) essays that first appeared in the pages of their journals.

Contents

Acts of Naming

Introduction:
In the Name of the Child

> The word ["name"] seems to be a compressed sentence signifying
> that the object for which there is a search, is a name.
>
> PLATO, *Cratylus*

I take as my subject in the following pages those acts in fiction that have
as their object a name. To bestow, find, reveal, or earn a name; to take
away, hide, or prohibit a name; to slander and stain or protect and serve
a name—I will argue that such acts are the means and ends of the
characters in fiction, and as such lay bare a novel's deepest levels of plot.

I have begun with a quotation from Plato because the *Cratylus* is
generally ackowledged as the point of departure for the study of naming.
This fact alone may serve to remind us that from the beginning the
question of names proceeds under the aegis of philosophy. How, then, do
the acts of naming that I have enumerated become the subject of fiction?
At what point and in what way does fiction take over the concept of the
name as the end of a search—a search that is typically characterized as
the subject of a specifically philosophic inquiry? To begin to answer this
question, let us look at the novelist pondering the question of names
through the eyes of the philosopher. While writing *Tess of the d'Urbervilles*, Hardy recorded his reaction to Plato's dialogue in the following
words: "After reading Plato's 'Cratylus': A very good way of looking at
things would be to regard everything as having an actual or false name,
and an intrinsic or true name, to ascertain which all endeavor should be
made. . . . The fact is that nearly all things are falsely, or rather inadequately, named."[1] Does Hardy's approving gloss on Plato's text enter the
novel that he is writing at the time? Beginning with the revelation that
things are inadequately named, Hardy puts before us in *Tess* the further
problem that we may not know how to name persons at all. Hardy bases

the tragedy of *Tess* in those acts of naming that fix the identity of people through false names, and in this way the general inadequacy of the names for *things* becomes specified as the failure to know how to name *persons*. In fact, when we recall "the philosopher's regard" with which Angel inspects Tess, and the ways in which he insists on naming her, we begin to realize that Hardy exposes in *Tess* the tragic consequences of applying to persons the philosophic method of naming things. Despite its persistent search for the right name, philosophy offers us no genuine model for naming people. Therefore, like Hardy in this initial example, the novelist typically reimagines philosophy's search for the names of things. From the eighteenth century to the present, the novel in England and America develops as a coherent tradition in search of the way to name persons. In crossing the border from philosophy's names for things to people's names for each other, fiction constitutes itself as that field of discourse which defines what it is to be "human"—the final name toward which fiction directs its search.

I have begun with the *Cratylus* for a second reason. It reemerges as a fundamental document during the Enlightenment when philosophy rediscovers naming as a crucial subject of inquiry—and when the novel emerges as a genre by organizing its plots around acts of naming, in response to the view of names held by such a philosopher as Locke. On this first point, scholars have recently argued for a remarkable proximity between Plato and Locke: "It might be no exaggeration to claim that when Locke's *Essay* first appeared it constituted the most detailed investigation of semantic theory in western philosophy since Plato's *Cratylus*."[2] I wish to emphasize the way in which these two texts concentrate philosophic inquiry on the name as the central locus of meaning. Locke attempts to put an end to the *Cratylus*'s seminal debate over whether names are conventional or natural when he issues his influential dictum that while names are often believed to stand for the reality of things, they "signify nothing but the Ideas, that are in the Mind of the Speaker."[3] He argues for the conventional nature of names by explaining the way in which we come to have general terms when all things are particular: communication would simply be impossible if everything had its own name. Therefore, Locke argues, language makes a crucial compromise from the start: it creates the convenient fiction of general names—those names that are Locke's subject in the third book of his *Essay*. Hobbes anticipates this crucial moment in English nominalist philosophy when he exposes the peculiarity of names and the reason we should mistrust them: "There being nothing in the world universal but names, for the things named are every one of them individual and singular."[4]

Locke's critique does not simply dismiss the significance of names. English Enlightenment philosophy, precisely insofar as it adopts the notion of conventional names, ultimately refashions the sign as the crucial tool of science. If names are man-made, arbitrary signs, they have the capacity to become the perfect instrument of knowledge. As Hobbes puts it, "in the right definition of names lies the first use of speech, which is the acquisition of science"; and again, "By the advantage of *names* it is that we are capable of *science*."[5] Hence the classificatory systems of the Enlightenment and the development of the science of taxonomy. By seeking the name as the means whereby science can classify and reveal all things in perfect clarity and order, English empiricism fulfills the Platonic notion that defines the name as the object of a search.

But what about proper names? They are lost in a parenthetical aside: "all (except proper) Names are general"[6]—that is, lost in philosophy on its way to becoming science. But they are rescued and adopted by a rival discourse, the new genre of literature that arises in the same period, as if to show us that the names we seek are not simply those that will name things.

The difference between naming in philosophy and in fiction may be tentatively summarized along the following lines. From the point of view of the novel, the mistake in the *Cratylus* is that it draws no essential distinction between the names of things and the names of persons; when Socrates, in the first part of his argument, defends the natural meaning of names, he employs a method of etymological analysis that makes all names the same, so that, for example, "air" is etymologically deciphered as "the element which raises things from the earth," while in a similar vein "Agamemnon" is deciphered as "admirable for remaining."[7] Again from the point of view of the novel, the mistake in Locke's *Essay* (and the philosophic tradition that derives from it) is that it neglects not simply this distinction but the entire issue of proper names. In short, philosophy seeks general names, for things and ideas, while fiction seeks proper names, for individual persons.[8]

To understand more precisely why fiction historically takes as its field of interest the naming of persons, we must recognize a profound anomaly in Enlightenment culture: the Enlightenment is at once the epoch of the general name and the individual person. Historians typically point to the emergence of the individual during the Enlightenment, and in fiction this is of course the epoch of the orphan, the bastard, the criminal, the shipwrecked—or outcast—self. From one angle, such a view is in fact supported in the language philosophy of the time. When, for example, Locke moves the locus of meaning in naming from the thing itself to the mind of the speaker, he signals that era of subjectivity that we equate with the novel, both as a genre of private consumption and as a genre whose theme is the individual self. But the program Locke initiates for philosophy—the demystification of names so they can become the tool of science—neglects the naming of persons. One could even argue that the perfection of a scientific discourse of general names becomes philosophy's protection against the threat of subjectivism. In this light philosophy's program of general names does not simply neglect proper names. It is meant to disenfranchise and, ideally, to erase the individual and the name for the individual, the proper name. The naming of the individual, then, was necessarily excluded from the enterprise by which philosophy used general names to order all things into classificatory systems.

The novel's exploration of the naming of persons does not develop simply in response to a gap in philosophical discourse. It would be more accurate to say that the novel responds to a critical disjunction in Enlightenment culture: the neglect of the proper name within Enlightenment philosophy versus the new value of the proper name within the domain of the eighteenth-century family. During the eighteenth century in England significant changes occurred in family life that gave a new prominence to the child's name. For example, the omission from genealogies of the names of short-lived infants drops significantly between the sixteenth and the mid-eighteenth centuries, and the practice of giving a newborn infant the same first name as an elder deceased sibling, common in the Middle Ages and the Renaissance, similarly drops sharply by the middle of the eighteenth century.[9] Such changes, of course, signal the growing belief in the uniqueness of the individual, in the belief that one child cannot simply replace another. I wish to emphasize the way in which the child emerges during the Enlightenment as the carrier of the proper name, and the way in which in the same epoch the novel arises to record and explore the urgency of the child's role. It is the child who takes the question of naming out of the hands of the philosopher and turns it over to the novelist.

The naming of the child within the domain of the family by no means presents the novelist with an entirely successful model for the naming of persons. To the contrary, it is the family's system of naming that produces the immediate crisis to which fiction responds with what I will call naming plots. Precisely insofar as the child is recognized as an individual, he or she arrives on the scene as a challenge to the family's attempt to fix the child's identity through naming.[10] To understand how this happens, we must realize first that the family name constitutes something like the general name in philosophy or the species name in natural science.

Socrates tells us in the *Cratylus* that "the offspring of every kind, in the regular course of nature, is like the parent, and must therefore have the same name" (394a). But in his etymological analysis in proof of the natural meanings of the name, only the names of human beings (as opposed to those of things, or ideas, or gods) are "apt to be deceptive because they are often called after ancestors with whose name . . . they may have no business; and they are the expression of a wish . . ." (397b). One could argue that philosophy throws up its hands in frustration at human names because the child, unlike the thing or the idea, is potentially powerful enough to resist the name. The child enters the naming system as the unpredictable, the unfixable, the power that threatens to resist our will or wish. The child is always potentially the deviant, the break in the chain, the hole in history, for the philosopher as well as for the family. For this reason the family name functions to classify—and thereby nullify—the individual, while the proper name exerts the power of a magical wish which expresses the will of the family. No names better illustrate this latter point than those which Puritan parents commonly gave: "Roger Clapp's children were named Experience, Waitstill, Preserved, Hopestill, Wait, Thanks, Desire, Unite and Supply. Other appellations included Rich Grace, More Mercy, Relieve, Believe, Reform, Deliverance and Strange."[11] Both the family name and the proper name form part of a system whose function is to determine and fix the child's identity, to make the child serve the will of the family.

The special irony of Enlightenment culture, then, makes the naming systems of the philosopher and the family a cooperative effort: the neglect of the proper name in favor of the general name in philosophy becomes, within the family, the use of the proper name to serve the family name. It is in this sense that the naming plots of fiction take as their broadest setting the philosophical inquiry into names, and as their most immediate setting the family's practices of naming. And it is especially within the domain of the family that we see the way in which the procedures of personal naming charge the child with an extraordinary weight of meaning. We begin to realize that what is at stake in the naming process is no less than an act of possession. In a ceremony like baptism, for example, the giving of a name is just such an act: "The naming of a person had the meaning of attaching the baptized to this person so that the baptized belonged to him. This is confirmed by exegesis; for the consequence and the effect of baptism 'in the name' of Christ may be gathered from a consideration of Paul's assertion, 'you belong to Christ.'"[12]

In most cultures one of the primary functions of human names is to order the flux of the generations by bringing the new individual inside the cultural system. In our culture this is managed through the family name, and sometimes extends to giving the child even the proper name of the father (as in *Pierre*), thereby making the proper name a family name. Lévi-Strauss argues that there is no such thing as a proper name because all naming is at bottom classifying, a way of placing the individual in a classificatory order. And this is certainly true of such names as Pierre Glendinning IV, or of such Puritan names as Waitstill or Believe. But whereas Lévi-Strauss sees such a process unequivocally as a positive integration of the individual into the community, the novel typically dramatizes the child as the victim of such a system, lost in any number of family or class names.

Lévi-Strauss tries to disprove the significance and value of proper names by showing that even when such names do exist, they occupy an inferior position in the naming system: "It is only children who overtly bear their names, either because they are too young to be structurally qualified by the family and social system or because the means of qualification have, for the time being, been suspended in favour of their parents. Proper names thus undergo a truly logical devaluation. They are the mark of being 'unclassed.'"[13] Despite his claim that anthropology is a rival discipline to philosophy (not unlike my claim for fiction), Lévi-Strauss's view of naming sounds like that of an Enlightenment philosopher: the individual must be classified—a contradiction in terms that kinship-based societies solve by devaluing the status of the individual, and that Western culture, especially from the eighteenth century on, makes the subject of a tragic vision. Isn't the dark suggestion of Hardy's title not that Tess of the d'Urbervilles is in possession of a family name (what Lévi-Strauss would claim is the preferred position), but just the opposite—that Tess is tragically possessed in the name of the family?

The family's attempt to fix identity through the name has its parallel in the critic's most characteristic approach to names in fiction. The critic elucidates character through the name, sometimes even making an equation between name and person that fixes character once and for all. Such a method extends Cratylus's argument to the names of persons in fiction: the name designates character ("Agamemnon" means "admirable for remaining"). In this context the typical analysis of names in fiction extends an already long line of etymological analysis of personal names, from the "speaking names" in the *Iliad* (with Hector as "the shielder," for example), to the Old Testament practice, "As his name is, so is he" (I Sam. 25:25), to the passage in Matthew in which the exegesis of the name Peter authenticates the natural meaning of names. Such examples support a long tradition that lasts at least through the Middle Ages and the Renaissance.[14] And one could, of course, supply ample cases of telling names in English and American fiction (Lovelace and Chillingworth and Angel Clare). From Dickens the examples would be legion (Pumblechook and Gradgrind, Boythorn and Skimpole, and so on).

Science is the great demystifier of such a view. As part of its claim that names are conventional, science appeals to the idea of the natural name only to deflate it, and we find especially at the beginning of the twentieth century, in philosophy, psychology, and anthropology, a demystification of what is seen as the savage or neurotic view of the animism of names.[15] At the same time it is not difficult to find this idea of the natural name haunting even the modern mind. After all his arguments against the verifiability of the magic power of the name, Jung, for example, still finds a certain power in the "compulsion of the name":

> Herr Gross (Mr. Grand) suffers from delusions of grandeur, Herr Kleiner (Mr. Small) has an inferiority complex. The Altmann sisters marry men twenty years older than themselves. Herr Feist (Mr. Stout) is the Food Minister, Herr Rosstauchsher (Mr. Horsetrader) is a lawyer, Herr Kalberer (Mr. Calver) is an obstetrician, Herr Freud (joy) champions the pleasure principle, Herr Adler (eagle) the will-to-power, Herr Jung (young) the idea of rebirth, and so on. Are these the whimsicalities of chance, or the suggestive effects of the name, as Stekel seems to suggest, or are they "meaningful coincidences"?[16]

While acknowledging that our imaginations find the idea of the natural name irresistible at some level, can we in fact say that fiction is predicated upon a theory of natural names—the kind of theory that lies at the heart of the critic's equation between person and name? Fiction undermines such a theory by exposing the way in which it comes dangerously close to reducing people to things, to assigning a "meaning" to a person and thereby neglecting what I take to be the tacit goal of the novel—the telling of a complicated and varied individual life story. The farthest extreme of the theory of the natural name would require of a character the predictable reenactment over and over of a central trait—what Dickens's minor characters often produce, in the background of the primary action. Reducing a major character to the name he or she bears would shrink the entire plot of a novel to a simple, quasi-scientific verification, in deeds, of what the name means. The view that equates name and person, then, offers little possibility for expansion in fiction, and has perhaps its broadest usefulness in the fatalistic plot in which the name shapes the destiny of the character. Such an idea does enter the novel at its earliest stages, but as a comic hobgoblin, as one of the prime Shandy-

isms in *Tristram Shandy*. Mr. Shandy thinks "a great deal more depended than what superficial minds were capable of conceiving" on "the
choice and imposition of Christian names," that, in fact, "there was a
strange kind of magick bias, which good or bad names, as he called them,
irresistibly impressed upon our characters and conduct": "*Andrew* was
something like a negative quantity in Algebra with him;—'twas worse,
he said, than nothing:—*William* stood pretty high:—*Numps* again was
low with him:—and *Nick*, he said, was the DEVIL. But, of all the names in
the universe, he had the most unconquerable aversion for TRISTRAM."[17]
Mr. Shandy's view stands behind one of the crucial errors that characters
commit inside the novels I will be examining—that is, to reduce another
human being to a name, to a single and fixed value.

The special feature of fiction that warns us most emphatically against
such a view bestows several names on a single person. This persistent
renaming problematizes the idea that a single name fixes a character's
meaning, and begins to suggest how entire plots are organized around a
series of renamings. In *The Member of the Wedding*, for example, the
title character is alternately named Frankie, F. Jasmine, and Frances, so
that each of the three parts of McCullers's novel opens with a paragraph
in which the narrator names the central character differently, while the
title names her again. That a character bears many names suggests that
an individual's history requires a set of names, or a series of renamings
that signal the different stages of a life story or fictional plot. The "true"
name, then, often functions as a series of names, a composite name, as if,
instead of shedding one name after another as Natty Bumppo does in
Cooper's novels, one must take them all, to have one's history as Nathaniel (or Natty) Bumppo Straight-Tongue Pigeon Lap-ear Deerslayer
Hawkeye. The extraordinary number of names a single character lives
through allows us to revise Plato's remark by pushing it to the limit:
fiction shows us that for persons the name is what is always sought and
never (or at least rarely) found. The plots of fiction are rarely resolved
through the successful completion of a search for the single name, though
sometimes a plot seems designed along such lines.

The name in fiction, then, does not fix identity and hold it still. Quite
the contrary, the name is a significant variable throughout the text,
perpetually rewritten and recharged with varying meanings. Who, for
example, is Harriot Lucas? Miss Laetitia Beaumont? Rachel Clark? Mrs.
Dorothy Salcomb? Mrs. Mary Atkin? Each is a name that Clarissa
Harlowe invents for herself at different points in her story. Who is
George Jackson? Sarah Williams? George Peters? And the last, and
perhaps most teasing clue: who is Tom Sawyer? Huck, in *The Adven-*

tures of Huckleberry Finn. We will see that the characters in such novels as *The Scarlet Letter, Bleak House,* and *Tess of the d'Urbervilles* bear a similarly elaborate list of names, but, unlike Clarissa and Huck, not by their own choice—such names are assigned to them by others—while Natty Bumppo marks the different stages of his life by a series of different names in a plot where the name is not arbitrarily invented by oneself or another, but is earned through deeds. In such cases the single name hides within it a cluster of other names.

On the title page such names as Clarissa or Deerslayer or Huckleberry Finn appear single and clear, as if a fixed certainty, but in fact they invite us into the text of fiction, where the title-name is made a literary intertext (as in *Ulysses* or *Absalom, Absalom!* or in Durrell's *Justine,* in which the author's epigraph is a quotation from Sade's *Justine*); or where the title-name is the false or fictitious name that the course of the plot must expose and replace (as in *Tom Jones* or *Oliver Twist*); or where the title-name openly admits the variability of names (as in *The Unnamable,* in which no name becomes a special kind of name).

Such examples of the variable name stand behind my claim that the most fruitful approach to names in fiction is not the exegesis of a single name, the so-called proper name. Instead, I wish to allow the different names a character bears to write up a life story, and to understand the way in which various acts of naming organize entire plots.

While fiction recharges with power the names of people, it does so most profoundly by claiming not that names are natural or that destinies are shaped by a powerful name, but that people shape destinies—others' and their own—by the immense power they accord to names. Fiction shows us that we so value names that they become the center of both symbolic and literal acts of recognition, abandonment, rape, suicide, and murder. Even characters whose names do reveal a side of their nature (Lovelace or Chillingworth or Angel Clare) are far more deeply portrayed by the complicated acts of naming they perform. In this light, the name functions most profoundly in fiction not as a static standard-bearer that reveals character from the beginning, but as the center of a matrix of action, at the center of the plots of fiction.

I have been claiming that fiction represents the naming of persons through a complicated series of acts of naming, or a naming plot. In this way fiction upsets the family's (and the critic's) attempt to fix the identity of a character (especially a child) through a key name. When this attempt fails, the family retaliates by withholding the name instead of bestowing it. The child who fails to be equal to the family name becomes dispossessed of that name. I am thinking, for example, of the way in which children are literally disinherited, so that Pierre discovers that there is not the "least mention of his own name" in his mother's will.[18] Mrs. Compson in *The Sound and the Fury* uses a special method of withholding the name: as part of her pride in her own name, she divides her children into Compsons, or "strangers" (all but Jason), and Bascombs (she tells Jason, "you are a Bascomb, despite your name"). At its farthest reaches such a system literally becomes a kind of unnaming. Mrs. Compson prohibits the use of her daughter's name within the household, and even Caddy's own daughter is kept from hearing the unspoken name Caddy: "She must never even learn that name." In a similar vein, she bestows her brother's name on her son ("Maury"), but then takes it away to keep the stigma of the child's idiocy from her own family, finally bestowing on him the biblical name that publishes her own sorrow and suffering: "Benjamin the child of mine old age bellowing."[19] Even withholding a name (a kind of orphaning by unnaming that can occur inside the family) may add to the multiplication and variability of the names a character bears (as in Maury/Benjy, or Jason Compson/Jason Bascomb).

The refusal to allow the child the proper name or the family name has its broadest variation in not allowing the child the species name. In this way the adult world attempts to turn to its own advantage the unknown nature of the child. By withholding the name "human" from the child, the adult makes the child a useful test case. The child is imagined on a series of borders, providing the adult with a relatively safe access to primitivism, bestiality, madness, the supernatural, and so on. The child who is given the proper name of "Strange" signifies this potential function. In eighteenth-century America "Infants . . . were sometimes referred to as 'strangers,' not immediately accepted as full-fledged human beings."[20] The child becomes the questionable subject of endless debate in a world of adult human beings. In short, the child takes up his value as "The Young Experiment," as he is named by his father in Meredith's *The Ordeal of Richard Feverel.*

During the Enlightenment the child's usefulness in scientific experiments is fueled by the remarkable cases of the wild children, captured and incarcerated, studied and tested and analyzed—in short, made the object of naming and classifying. In their preoccupation with the question of human nature, eighteenth-century philosophers used the child as an instrument to philosophize about the borders along which to position human beings, monsters, and wild men (a new species that Linnaeus christened *homo ferus*). At the end of the eighteenth century, in the case of the Boy of Aveyron, for example, we see that the child has his significance and value as a sign in what I am calling, for the novel, a naming plot.

Once captured, the nameless child is first called "Joseph," then renamed "Victor," and while the philosophers and scientists are debating whether to classify him as an "idiot" or "*homo ferus*," most people know him as nothing but the "Savage," and even upon his death no one knows his family name (though most assume that for the "Savage" there is no such thing).[21]

It is no accident that a similar example occurs in Enlightenment philosophy in the crucial text on naming that we have been consulting. In Locke's *Essay* the problem of how to classify human beings (not how to name individual persons) is crystallized in the case of a child whose identity is questionable to those in charge of naming him:

> When the Abbot of St. Martin . . . was born, he had so little the Figure of a Man, that it bespake him rather a Monster. 'Twas for some time under deliberation, whether he should be baptized or no. However, he was baptized and declared a Man provisionally [till time should show what he would prove]. Nature had moulded him so untowardly, that he was called all his Life the Abbot Malotur, i.e. Ill Shaped.[22]

Locke uses this example to expose the pure conventionality of names, to show that for us it is not nature that declares what a man is, but our own verbal classificatory systems—in this case, a series of definitions that we demand of anyone who wishes to be known by the name "man": "to be of any Species, and to have a right to the name of that Species, is all one. As for Example, to be a *Man*, or of the Species *Man*, and to have the right to the name *Man*, is the same thing."[23] Here we can begin to imagine the farthest reaches of the power of the (species) name, and the way in which human beings are divided between those who rule by naming and those who are ruled by being named.[24]

These cases of the monster-man (the Abbot Malotur) and the "man-plant"[25] (the Wild Boy of Aveyron) do not take us very far afield from the novel. In the novels we will be looking at, one could even say that each character (but especially the child) is only provisionally worthy of being named human,[26] and that the name "human child" is not a harmless tautology but a classification in need of proof. In this light Mary Shelley's *Frankenstein* is a literalization of the psychological and political issues raised by such species names as "human" and "monster," dramatized significantly through the familial roles of parent and child—where, one might add, both class names are problematized in the course of the plot, as both "creatures" live beyond their names at significant moments in their histories (the filthy progeny is, of course, never granted a proper name). In such ways *Frankenstein* exposes the problem of the child's ontological status by exaggerating the question that asks if the child is human, a question that especially tags the bastard or outcast child. In *The Scarlet Letter*, for example, the mother herself "could not help questioning, at such moments, whether Pearl was a human child," as if the mother had "evoked a spirit . . . in the process of conjuration," while in *Absalom, Absalom!* Faulkner repeats Hawthorne's theme: "as if he had not been human born but instead created without agency of man or agony of woman and orphaned by no human being."[27] The question addressed to Pearl—"What art thou?"—reverberates throughout the pages of fiction, in *Oliver Twist*, in *Pierre*, in *Tess*, in *Absalom, Absalom!* and so on. Such a question supersedes the question we ask human beings—"Who are you?"—and the difference between the two questions measures the distance the bastard or outcast child must travel in order to be called human. In knowing neither father nor mother, and in finding that others do not receive him as a human being, the monster in *Franken-stein* asks the double question of himself, unable to know what to name himself: "Was I, then, a monster. . . ?"; "Who was I? What was I?"[28] Such is the dehumanizing question addressed to the unknown child, the child beyond classification: "He is of no order and no place; neither of the beasts, nor of humanity," as the narrator of *Bleak House* says of Jo.[29]

The "plot" of the *Alice* books is shaped by the continual unnaming and renaming of this problematic figure, "a human child" (137).[30] And here "human" neither integrates the child into a community nor authorizes her power, for the *Alice* books subversively deanthropomorphize the world not simply by renaming it, but by reimagining who is empowered to name. In a radical move, human beings are no longer in charge of naming. The creatures of the *Alice* books are freed from the captivity of silence and assume the power of naming. In this way Alice's "fall" (8) and her persistent search for the garden rewrite Adam's fall; Alice enters an ironic Eden where the human being is not the master namer. To chart the plot of the *Alice* books is to follow the successive displacements of Alice's names. First, there is the displacement of Alice's proper name, so that Alice becomes "Mabel" (17) and then "Mary Ann" (27). Then, after attempting to name herself through simple pronominal equations—"She's *she* and I'm *I*" (16)—Alice is forced to admit, "I'm not myself" (35). Finally, Alice's species name is displaced: in countless passages the creatures seize the Adamic power to unname and rename the child. The child is seen by the flowers as no more than an inferior specimen of their own kind, and by others (and sometimes by herself) as a "thing" (70) or, worse yet, as "Nothing" (136). The Unicorn and the Lion turn the tables completely by naming Alice "Monster" (177). In this way the contour of plot moves from asking "Who are *you*?" (35) to asking "*What* are you?" (43), the double question that I have suggested lies at the center of naming as a dehumanizing process.

In the *Alice* books the child learns the arbitrary and exorbitant power the human exercises over the nonhuman. When Alice is asked, "Are you animal—or vegetable—or mineral?" (176), the game by which the child learns to master things through names is turned against the child herself. At the same time, the radical reversal that gives the nonhuman the power to name the human suggests an even more subversive lesson: the ways in which the adult works the same system against the child. When the child in this fantasy world is tested, catechized, and made the object of scrutiny, in order to be named and classified, identified and "labeled" (131), she undergoes precisely the procedures she undergoes every day, only her masters have become the Unicorn and the Caterpillar and Humpty Dumpty, instead of the schoolmaster and her parents and the clergyman.

In fact, the usefullness of the *Alice* books for my purposes is their parodic exaggeration of the scenes and events we will see time and again in the realistic novel. When the mock-turtle's self-(un)naming, "Once . . . I was a real Turtle" (74), mocks Alice's "I—I hardly know [who I am], Sir, just at present—at least I know who I *was*" (35), it mocks at the same time the kind of tragic dissociation of name and person we see in *Clarissa* when the heroine declares, "My name is—I don't know what my name is!" and, "my name was Clarissa Harlowe."[31] Alice's "I'm not myself" echoes the tragic cry repeated everywhere in Richardson's novel and crystallizes an inquiry that the novelistic tradition takes up always in the same formulation: what does it mean to be equal to oneself and one's name? And when, in the *Alice* books, the child is alternately called "a thing" and "Nothing," and when "Nobody" (170) is reified by becoming the name of a person, I recall the way in which Mrs. Glendinning in *Pierre* stigmatizes the bastard child Isabel by calling her a "thing"; or the bastard child Esther's self-naming in *Bleak House* names her as no one ("I was no one"); or Esther's father actually literalizes such a name by taking for himself the pseudonym "Nemo," or "No one." And when, in the *Alice* books, Humpty Dumpty wants to convert the name "Alice" into meaning, just as his name signifies his shape (or just as "M. Hatter" is a hatter and "W. Rabbit" is a white rabbit), I recall the move to translate the proper name or the family name into a common noun (with a slanderous signification) in *Clarissa* and *Tess*. And finally, when, in the *Alice* books, the animals turn the science of classification on the child, I recall that such a system of naming is in fact turned on human beings, and especially on the child and the woman, in the novel from *Clarissa* to *Lolita*.

In Part One of this book I present three exemplary naming plots. It would be possible to see a large number of novels as structured through these three plots. In Part Two, however, I have a different goal in mind: to study the central role of naming within the discourse by which a family constitutes itself, and thereby to understand family naming plots in relationship to the entire enterprise of fiction. In other words, in Part Two I attempt to suggest not simply that fiction organizes itself around naming plots, but that fiction is itself an act of naming that revises the way in which naming functions within the family. For this reason, each of the chapters in Part Two falls into two sections: the first formulates the subject of naming for the family, while the second formulates fiction as a revision of the family's system of naming. Only in the case of *Tess of the d'Urbervilles* does this strategy break down; the profound tragedy of *Tess* will not allow the recuperation of naming under the sponsorship of fiction. Thus the silencing of Hardy's own novel writing in the 1890s may signal a deep suspicion about the procedures and the benefits of fiction generally. *Tess*'s position in the novelistic tradition makes one further goal possible in Part Two: a reflection backward on the circumstances that make the daughter the best illustration of the problems of naming. In Part Three, I discuss at some length Enlightenment traditions of naming, and explore the ways in which *Lolita* can help us see the novelistic uses to which such traditions may be put. In *Lolita* and in two of the texts to which it directly alludes (*Fanny Hill* and *A la recherche du temps perdu*), I find clarified what I take to be the most potent threat that systems of naming pose to the novelistic tradition: the complete valorization of the master name undermines the narrative act by which a life story is told. The valorization of the master name simplifies the complications and variabilities of a life story by reducing a person to a meaning; to bestow a name is the means by which one becomes the author of the text of another. Nabokov shows this by making the violation of the child (especially the daughter) a moment in the larger violation that unnames and renames, and by making *Lolita* a late moment in a tradition of novels that shows (in *Clarissa*, say, and *Tess*) the way in which the (family) rape of the daughter cooperates with a profoundly insidious and inescapable system of (family) naming. Through parodic exaggeration *Lolita* brings to a new pitch the novel's exploration of the question the Red Queen asks Alice: "What do you suppose is the use of a child without any meaning?" The novelistic tradition exposes the presumptive and utterly devastating implications of such a question by ruthlessly identifying those acts of naming that appropriate a person, especially those acts of naming that define the use of a child.

PART ONE

THE NAMING PLOTS
OF FICTION

The honour of a maid is her name, and no legacy is so rich as
honesty.

SHAKESPEARE, *All's Well That Ends Well*

A man's name is not like a cloak that merely hangs around him, that
may be loosened and tightened at will; it is a perfectly fitting gar-
ment. It grows over him like his very skin; one cannot scrape and
scratch at it without injuring the man himself.

GOETHE, *Dichtung und Wahrheit*

1

Clarissa,
or the Name Lost

In *Clarissa* the philosophic desire "to call everything by its proper name" (3.85) is domesticated and made the common thread of everyday life.[1] Characters are brought into relationship with each other—as friends, as enemies, as family members, as lovers—insofar as they meet, takes sides, and clash on the battleground of names. *Clarissa* presents a culture in search of itself through the corroboration of the names of value, or what Hume was to call (some few years after the publication of *Clarissa*) the shared language of morals, whereby a community constitutes itself in publicly recognizing the meanings of certain key names.[2] But in *Clarissa* the characters take their cue from Locke's famous dictum of the previous century: each person seems at liberty to mean by any name only what he or she chooses.[3] For example, while Clarissa tells Anna Howe by way of attacking Lovelace, "love, that deserves the name, seeks the satisfaction of the beloved object more than its own" (1.325), Lovelace complains to Belford about Clarissa, "Love, that deserves the name, never was under the dominion of *prudence*, or of any *reasoning* power" (3.175). The text of *Clarissa* is everywhere embedded with such definitions of love, friendship, virtue, and so on.

But the disagreement over names takes on an even more troubling dimension. In the midst of the continuing debate over the meanings of particular names, the underthought of *Clarissa* asks if names have any value at all. Names are alternately—almost schizophrenically—valued and devalued, filled with significance and emptied of it. We hear of the "empty name" (4.183, 4.226) and of the distinction or quality that is "*merely* nominal" (1.451) or "a *mere* name" (3.169); at the same time, the question that asks if a thing "deserves the name" (as we saw above) or is "worthy of the name" (1.76, 1.91) approaches asking if something is "worthy of that sacred name" (4.146), as if the name were a transcendent signifier next to which all things fall short. In the context of such extremes, *Clarissa* asks with urgency, how are human beings named, with empty names or sacred names? Are names for persons of a different order from names for things? We find in *Clarissa* a delicately drawn curve of names that slopes toward the naming of personhood, moving from the names of things, to the names of moral qualities (such as "virtue" or "principle"), to the names of those relations based on such qualities (such as "friendship" or "love"), to the names of kindred and the names of gender, until we reach the proper name itself—in this case, Clarissa. Such a curve might seem to approach exactitude, the least ambiguous name of all, the proper name. But I will argue that the inquiry into names in *Clarissa* reaches its most problematic point of signification with the proper name itself.

In *Clarissa* the language of English empiricism—of "trial" (1.2, 1.335, 2.318) and "test" (1.79, 1.98, 1.201), of "postulata" (3.145), "demonstration" (2.104), "evidence" (4.182), and "proof" (2.185, 4.465)—is the measure of all things, and of all people. The family turns this terminology on Clarissa, in an examination where even the terminology of science is tried, a clue that the central test in *Clarissa* is a nominal proof, a proof of name; the mother threatens Clarissa, "You have never been put to a test till now, that deserved to be called a test" (1.98). The central question the test asks is whether or not Clarissa is "*worthy of the name of daughter*" (1.91). The father, for example, instructs the mother to bring to him "your daughter in your hand, if worthy of the name" (1.76). In this way *Clarissa* shows us that in those families where the facts of kinship are known, familial titles are nonetheless charged with equivocal and shifting significance—in short, that Clarissa, though no orphan, needs to win the name "daughter." The father makes this clear by insisting that Clarissa must pass the test, must prove she is worthy of the name "daughter," "or be none of our child" (1.96)—an apparently naive tautology whose meaning is as complicated as it is malign. The father begins with the name, and requires that the child adjust to it, fulfill its moral requirements, with the fact of blood ignored and even overruled. He threatens to take the name away as a mark of his own power and her disgrace, and he eventually makes good his threat.

Clarissa, with family intact at the beginning, reverses what is one of the most characteristic plots of fiction: the course of the novel describes not the orphan's or bastard's discovery of family and name, but the orphaning and unnaming of the child. Clarissa becomes a "lost creature" (1.119), a "helpless orphan" (4.95). Both Lovelace and Cousin Morden offer "to be a father, uncle, brother . . . all in one" (1.480, 4.283), but Clarissa comes closest to taking Anna's advice: "you must be father, mother, uncle to yourself" (2.294). In a world where the literal names of kinship are questioned, what other family does one have? What, in fact, do the names of kinship mean? In the light of such questions Lovelace's taunting joke turns serious and suggests how even the most literal names are undermined in *Clarissa*: "But here's her mistake; nor will she be cured of it—she takes the man she calls her father . . .; she takes the men she calls her uncles; the fellow she calls her brother; and the poor contemptible she calls her sister; to *be* her father, to *be* her uncles, her brother, her sister" (1.148). In *Clarissa* no name is secure. *Clarissa* shows us, first, the orphan with a family and, second, the nameless child about whose name there is, from the simplest point of view, no doubt. In other words, *Clarissa* puts the orphan inside the family, the nameless child inside the child whose name is incontestable. In this way the story of the nameless orphan becomes the seminal text of fiction, even in novels in which the child knows both her name and her parents.

That the plot of *Clarissa* functions through a manipulation of names, a powerful and eventually tragic dissociation between name and person, is made especially clear in what is perhaps the most eccentric feature of the text's discourse, an unleashing of the name's conventional syntactical function so that it overloads and dominates the grammar and meaning of the text. Names assume the role of verbs and thereby literally seem to take over the central action of the novel, to constitute *Clarissa*'s plot: people are "Mr. *Solmes'd*" (1.32), "*Belforded*" (3.110), "*Antony'd* into" (2.3), and "*Harlowed off*" (2.3). Seeing how Clarissa's family functions, Anna Howe writes about her own mother, "She had not best *Harlowe* me at this rate" (2.6). In a similar vein one realizes that the source of the family dispute is founded in what Clarissa christens as the new "language of the family" (1.58) in which her siblings attempt to undermine her position as "daughter" and "sister." For example, Arabella addresses her, "Sister that was!—For I know not what name you are *permitted* or *choose* to go by" (2.170). In *Clarissa* the Harlowes turn familial titles into verbs that tell the story of familial displacement: "to *out-uncle*" and "*out-grandfather*" (1.58), to "*grandfather-up*" (1.222). James's retaliation against Clarissa's out-grandfathering him is to out-father Clarissa.

Clarissa's tragic dilemma within this family arrangement can be stated simply: to be worthy of the name daughter means to be fundamentally nameless, because it means changing her name at the will of the family. In *Clarissa* the paternal injunction is so simple it borders on the brutal: the father writes to the daughter, "Nor shall you hear from me any more till you have changed your name to my liking" (1.211). The apparently capricious command means, of course, that Clarissa must marry Mr. Solmes as part of the father's shrewd strategy "to build up the name" (1.58) of the family. The daughter's name is to be exchanged for Solmes's money; that is, the father "sell[s] his child's virtue" (1.352), the same transaction we will find at the heart of the naming plot in *Tess of the d'Urbervilles*. The father's injunction does not have behind it the idealist's valorization of the name, or the philosopher's examination of the moral dimension of names; it seems to be mere parental bullying in the service of good business. And yet the function of the name has deeper significance, both for the father and for Clarissa. After all, the father's direct requirement (that Clarissa marry Solmes) is significantly subsumed in the telling rhetoric of the power of naming (that Clarissa change her name according to his liking.) And Clarissa's response to the father's plan catalogues a series of horrors whose final limit is the sacrifice of her name: "To be given up to a strange man; to be ingrafted into a strange family; to give up her very name, as a mark of her becoming his absolute and dependent property" (1.153). Clarissa's sole power to resist her father resides in the fact that he needs her signature on the Solmes treaty: "How shall I be able to refuse to my father the writing of my name?" (1.439). In a similar situation, Tom Tulliver in *The Mill on the Floss* proves his filial identity (as we will see) by writing his name at his father's command. But Clarissa refuses the writing of her name, and thereby relinquishes her title as "daughter."

Lovelace takes over with relish the family's terminology of the trial, and makes it the foundation of his entire rhetorical stance: "To the test then—and I will bring this charming creature to the *strictest* test." He is the philosopher–scientist in charge of testing what "Clarissa" is. Lovelace's trial of Clarissa proceeds as a series of questions that forms "a strict discussion of this subject." But on inspection the questions turn out to be specious, only the empty shell of inquiry. Typically, his questions teeter on the brink of prejudice, when they pull back for the sake (or the show) of scientific objectivity. "Is not, may not, her virtue be founded rather in *pride* than in *principle*? Whose daughter is she? And is she not a *daughter*?" (2.35). In such an example, the genuine question is placed inside the purely rhetorical question. Lovelace looks like the scientist who sets up a series of experiments to prove what he thinks he already knows. The characteristic form of Lovelace's mock inquiry replaces one name with another—"principle" with "pride," for example—and thereby rewrites the equation of Clarissa's identity: "Clarissa" equals "pride" (not "principle"), or "Clarissa" equals "daughter." In asserting Clarissa as "daughter," Lovelace takes her to be what her family doubts, and converts the title so lofty in the father's eyes to the mark of her dishonor; namely, as a daughter she is the mere stuff of which humans (not to mention Harlowes) are made.

For the center of Lovelace's inquiry into the nature of Clarissa is formulated through the antithesis angel/woman. Like the natural scientist, Lovelace seeks directly "to class" (2.400) Clarissa, and he uses her moral attributes (virtue or pride or principle) to discover the species to which she belongs. He must make an

> "effort . . . to know if she be really an angel or woman" (2.140); "Surely, Belford, this is an angel. And yet, had she not been known to be a female, they would not from *babyhood* have dressed her as such" (2.375); "[She is] something *more* than woman, an *angel*, in some things; but a *baby* in others" (2.187); "should not my beloved, for her own sake, descend by *degrees* from *goddess-hood* into *humanity*" (2.477).

The thread of inquiry moves back and forth within the limits of a system, in which "angel" and "woman" function as the key opposition, with terms like "goddess" being an extension of "angel," and "daughter" and "female" and "baby" extensions of "woman." But such an order, for all its systematic pretensions, cannot hide how loaded the terms are, and the impartial scientific inquiry into the nature of Clarissa founders in prejudice, mockery, and desire: "Is then the divine Clarissa capable of *loving* a man whom she ought *not* to love? And is she capable of *affectation*? And is her virtue founded in *pride*? And, if the answer to these questions be affirmative, must she not then be a *woman*?" (2.38). In Lovelace's hands, investigation is a means to satire, objectivity a mask for desire. Lovelace intends to explode the community's valuation of Clarissa and to make her his own. He correctly judges that these two goals are in fact one.

Lovelace's analysis of Clarissa makes classification an act of possession, confirming the empiricist's axiom, "Knowledge is power." The clearest sign of such power will come when Lovelace is revealed as the natural scientist whose entire investigation awaits one moment, when his own name is given to the newly discovered species. Even leaving Lovelace's peculiar prejudices aside, *Clarissa* calls into question the concept of classifying, especially as it is directed at human beings. Locke, of course, had illustrated the way in which the names we give to things are artificial, arbitrary, and, above all, subjective and private—and he did not have a scheming lover in mind. Lovelace's philosophical position, which we will recognize in succeeding novels, assumes that a crucial name, or master word, will unlock Clarissa's identity. The name he seeks is empowered to do this insofar as it ceases to be a proper name and becomes a common noun. In other words, the crucial name Lovelace seeks is the one that will position Clarissa in a grid within which her common meaning can be read. In short, Lovelace's classificatory system, like all such systems, disallows the individual. What challenges such systems is the individual, the exceptional, the eccentric, and for this reason proper names have no place in classification. And this is why the proper name, even when it is allowed to exist and identify Clarissa, is significantly altered. Clarissa often ceases to be Clarissa Harlowe, and instead becomes "a Clarissa" (2.162, 2.515, 3.199, 4.439, 4.533). This is to attack the proper name not by replacing it with a common noun ("woman," say), but by generalizing it into a category. Some of the other characters suffer the same conversion in this world where the proper name is always on the verge of representing a common property or general meaning, but no one to the extent of Clarissa. "But is not this girl a CLARISSA?" (3.100). The simple question, like all of Lovelace's questions, is insidious. Typically, it equates one name with another name, but, more significantly, it buries the modesty of personal identity in the capitalized and generalized name, so that the proper name becomes a class name.

Lovelace's classifying system has the further effect of disallowing Clarissa's humanity. Even when in the service of his hyperbolic rhetoric of love, which questions whether Clarissa is "angel" or "woman," Lovelace's classifications appear to exalt Clarissa while they nonetheless conveniently allow him to call into question her humanity. We in fact begin to realize that the name "woman" represents a highly questionable class that is immediately overwritten in one of two ways, each of which distinguishes "woman" from "human": "as a neat and clean woman must be an angel of a creature, so a sluttish one is the impurest animal in nature" (4.381). Woman is never herself, neither a distinct gender nor the common human species, but either angel or animal. The name "woman" specifies no one, just as "man" specifies everyone. But even leaving aside the class to which Lovelace assigns Clarissa, his entire project robs her of her humanity by reducing her to a sign in a system. Locking her inside the airtight logic of a verbal system, Lovelace pits "Sinclair" against "Clarissa." Who—what—is "Mrs. Sinclair" but a verbal construct created to test another such construct? Isn't she—it—simply the negation of another sign, "Clarissa"? *Clarissa* is a record of fiction's puzzlement over human beings turned into signs. When Clarissa declares, "I am but a *cypher*, to give *him* significance" (2.264), she has realized the power of the classifier or interpreter to make meaning by bleeding dry human identity. She anticipates an entire novelistic tradition in which the child who is conceived as a hieroglyphic meaning depends for her value on some (perhaps unknown) master interpreter.

I have shown how both the family and Lovelace attempt to undermine Clarissa's proper name by making her take a place in a system of classification that is the key to an entire moral, cultural, or quasi-scientific order: will she be classed "daughter," "angel," "woman," or what? I wish now to explore how the attempts at assigning Clarissa a surname expose the way in which the father's injunction that Clarissa change her name to "Solmes" becomes elaborately extended in Lovelace's attempt to rename Clarissa with the name "Lovelace." Such an identity between father and lover is significant insofar as it ironizes the distinction between kindred and nonkindred by which the family names itself. We are made to see the way in which nonkindred, or the "alien" (1.268), or, to push the terminology to its conventional limit, the "enemy to the family" (1.63), is not outside the family, but inside, an idea I will explore in detail in succeeding chapters. The naming plot of *Clarissa* accomplishes this by collapsing the family plot and the love plot. While the Harlowes and Lovelace are genuine antagonists, the naming plot of the novel reveals the father (or the daughter's protector) and the enemy-lover (or the daughter's violator) to be the same man, the man who desires to change Clarissa's name. In such a way the naming plot sometimes functions to subvert, or at least qualify, the text's more overt plot. We will see a similar case in *The Scarlet Letter*, when the naming plot reveals the cuckolded husband and the lover, ostensible antagonists, to be the same man, the man who wants Hester to keep his name secret.

The lover makes clear that he plays the role of the father when he describes himself to Belford in one of the most telling self-namings in the novel: "Knowest thou not that I am a great name-father?" (2.267). His boastful self-denomination follows upon his making "Captain Mennel" out of "young Newcomb" in order to fool Clarissa: "And I have changed his name by virture of my own single authority" (2.267). Lovelace consistently imagines for himself a series of conventional male roles, each of which allows him to rename Clarissa. Like the father whose paternal authority is represented by his power to name the child, Lovelace is also like the parson—in fact, like Parson Tringham, who initiates the plot of *Tess* by the act of naming: "No parson ever gave more *real* names, than I have given *fictitious* ones. And to very good purpose: many a sweet dear has answered me a letter for the sake of owning a name which her godmother never gave her" (3.61). The power of the lover is to make the woman own the "love-names" (3.61) he bestows upon her; of the husband, to make her take his own name. Hence Lovelace's desire: "I can think of nothing, of nobody, but the divine Clarissa Harlowe. *Harlowe!* How that hated word sticks in my throat—but I will give her for it the name of love" (1.147). Lovelace plays the roles of father, parson, lover, and husband to empower himself, but his role as rake promises him the most power. I mean here that Lovelace's most elaborate plot attempts to make Clarissa go by the name of Lovelace when she is still Clarissa Harlowe—in other words, to name her with his own name, but to keep the legal right to that name entirely within his own power. Hence, immediately upon abducting Clarissa he devises his central strategy: "Well then, here are—let me see—how many persons are there who, after Monday night, will be able to swear that she has gone by my name, answered by my name, had no other view in leaving her friends, but to go by my name?" (2.219). Clarissa runs away with him to retain her own name, but Lovelace rewrites her motive. The plot becomes deeper, darker, worse than the rake's triumph over virtue, when the power to name seems to have as its goal no less than the entire eradication of a human being: "there is no such lady in the world as Miss Clarissa Harlowe; . . . she is neither more nor less than Mrs. Lovelace" (2.215). But sooner or later the illusory name change no longer satisfies him, so that in the end what Lovelace wants and cannot get is what the father wanted and could not get: "If she will sign but *Cl. H.*" (3.298)—that is, place her name on the document that will allow him to change her name legally. In this light the failure of the love plot at the end coincides with the failure of the family plot at the beginning. Lovelace sums up the entirety of his relationship with Clarissa, including her death, through the failure of his plot to rename her. While Clarissa is dying, Lovelace writes, "Curse upon that name!—and curse upon myself for not changing it" (4.439). The last pathetic desire remains unfulfilled: "she shall die a Lovelace" (4.69).

Lovelace is unable to obtain Clarissa's name legitimately, but he does obtain it by subscribing it with his own hand. Because the name is for Lovelace the center of a ravishment even deeper than the sexual— "CLARISSA LOVELACE let me call her. . . . Her very name, with mine joined to it, ravishes my soul" (4.525)—he still seeks to possess the name well after he takes the body. He manages to insinuate himself into the private correspondence between Clarissa and Anne Howe by intercepting one of Anna's letters to Clarissa. First, by placing this intercepted letter inside his own to Belford, and by placing marks in the margins next to all those phrases of Anna's that deserve his vengeance, he literalizes the way in which he possesses, masters, marks, and thereby defaces what he calls the "female dialect" (3.68) or "women's language" (3.471). Like the "woman-eater" (2.496) he imagines, he contains this woman's language, assimilates it, engorges it, just as he swallows up the genuine question inside the rhetorical, and the proper name inside the common. Second, by cautiously leaving the seals entire, he is able to mimic this letter from Anna to Clarissa. By crucial omissions and additions of his own he copies Anna's words to use to his own advantage and sends the forgery to Clarissa as if it were Anna Howe's own. He impersonates Anna, steals the words meant for Clarissa, and subtly changes their meaning. Finally, he invents a letter from Clarissa to Anna. He writes in Clarissa's stead, he mimics her hand, he invents her words for her, and he signs her name—what the family and he have sought all along. All his impersonations reach their apex in this impersonation of "Clarissa Harlowe." He allows the name Clarissa Harlowe only when he himself subscribes it, when it is attached to his words, when it ceases to be her own. While Lovelace's power seems greatest here, he comes dangerously close to what he has feared all along—namely, that Clarissa "half-assimilates" him (2.400). The moment of power through a name disguise ironically becomes the moment of vulnerability and self-alienation. The symbolic annihilation of Clarissa Harlowe is at the same time a version of self-annihilation, a confusion of identities in which neither Clarissa nor Lovelace survives, a pyrrhic victory in which only the *name* of Clarissa survives.

It is time to acknowledge that Clarissa herself enters the naming plot, neither by simply refusing her signature on the contract with Solmes nor by declaring solemnly, "I never will be Lovelace" (3.211). While she successfully resists the names Solmes and Lovelace, she does not simply remain "Clarissa Harlowe" through the course of the novel. Like so many of the daughters we will study, Clarissa bears a string of names. But unlike Pearl, or Esther, or Tess, or Lolita, Clarissa assumes such names herself. Clarissa's dilemma can be stated in the following way: to keep her name, she must give it up provisionally, periodically—but at least she, and not the family or Lovelace, assigns the new names. Clarissa Harlowe is Harriot Lucas, Miss Laetitia Beaumont, Rachel Clark, Mrs. Dorothy Salcomb, and Mrs. Mary Atkins. These pseudonyms predict the denouement of the naming plot: Clarissa will not be named by the family or Lovelace, nor will she simply keep her own name. The other strategy Clarissa uses to protect her name—withholding it—is equally portentous: "[I] only subscribe myself, without so much as a name" (4.4). The naming plot eventually will reach a climax that describes a different kind of namelessness, not one in which Clarissa hopes to harbor and protect her real name, but one in which she no longer knows her name: "My name is—I don't know what my name is!" (3.206); "my name *was* Clarissa Harlowe: but it is now *Wretchedness!*" (3.427).

At this point the naming plot looks as if it describes a series of failures: the family fails to name Clarissa "Solmes"; Lovelace fails to name Clarissa "Lovelace"; and Clarissa fails to remain "Clarissa Harlowe." But this last failure is equivocal. The namelessness that results from the radical disorientation Clarissa suffers at the hands of the family and Lovelace is a grotesque and violent version of the equivocalness of names she learns from Anna Howe. I am suggesting that inside the dark hollow of Clarissa's tragedy—her loss of family, her rape, her loss of name—lies her own awareness of the way in which "Clarissa Harlowe" is a fiction. And while the family and Lovelace cause the rape of her identity, her dire nameless-ness, Anna Howe is the cause of a benign violation: the name questioned and qualified. We have here a special kind of dialectical movement that typically informs the naming plots of fiction: if the family plot seems to exist as an intransigent and inescapable pattern (especially insofar as it is repeated in the love plot), Anna and Clarissa's relationship enters the text as a significant revision of such a plot.

Anna Howe's correspondence with Clarissa sets for the heroine "a trial of *you* to *yourself*" (1.335), and thereby gives us the plot that runs parallel to the family's and Lovelace's trials of Clarissa: Clarissa's self-examination. The friend (as opposed to the family member and the lover) significantly places the trial within Clarissa, not entirely outside her, not directed by a master. The moral spirit of Puritan self-examination checks and redirects the empirical study of Clarissa that is performed by the philosopher–scientist. But such a trial does not take place solely within Clarissa. After each letter from Anna, Clarissa is sent back to herself for a deeper self-investigation; but while Clarissa remains in charge of her own meaning, the friend helps to bring this meaning to the surface. Clarissa learns that her own investigation of "self-significance" (1.247) paradoxically occurs only through another. Anna teaches Clarissa to see at a critical distance that "desire of appearing . . . the person I ought to be" (1.191), Clarissa Harlowe. Anna Howe serves as the critic of Clarissa Harlowe's texts, charging Clarissa with being reserved and evasive, and stopping her when she gives "new words for common things" (1.188). Anna's pen assumes the function of the good physician's "lancet": "What patient shall be afraid of a probe in so delicate a hand?" (1.345). Clarissa is "thankful for the wounds given by a true friend" (1.345), reminding us of the "wound" (4.10) she receives from her family and Lovelace. She writes to Anna: "Yours is intended to instruct; and though it bites, it pleases me at the same time; no fear of a wound's rankling or festering by so delicate a point as you carry; not invenomed by personality, not intending to expose, or ridicule, or exasperate." The wound or cut that Anna produces in the until now inviolable self named Clarissa Harlowe is the analogue, with a difference, to Lovelace's rape—so that Anna's probing letters make her into the preferred lover in terms that remind us of the male's more brutal equipment: "I may *feel* your edge, fine as it is. I may be pained: you would lose your end if I were not: but after the first sensibility . . . I will love you the better, and my amended heart shall be all yours" (1.345). Anna Howe wounds the text of Clarissa's heart—"I wrote my heart" (1.190), Clarissa tells her—to amend it. Lovelace, on the other hand, wounds it to mark it, deface it, change its essence. Lovelace, Clarissa's mimic self, steals the signature that subscribes her letters. Anna Howe, Clarissa's "other self" (1.281), understands and articulates what "Clarissa Harlowe" only half guesses. In this way we sometimes find Clarissa most nakedly represented in those letters subscribed Anna Howe, just as the name Howe is a suggestive blunting or distillation of the name Harlowe.

The epistolary form of the novel helps to undermine the idea of the simple and autonomous self, an idea by which Clarissa typically represents herself. Whether we choose to focus on Anna Howe or Lovelace as the reader of her texts, Clarissa Harlowe always has an interpreter. The single letter, given under hand and seal with concluding signature, is a naive representation of the self self-enveloped—an unassailable summation, in monologue form, of one's being. *Clarissa* dramatizes the way in which the letter enters the world to be opened up to the reader's interpretation. The family and Lovelace misuse this circuit, break it down, violate it, in order to master the self. We see letters refused, forged, smuggled, ripped to pieces. While the family and Lovelace try to master Clarissa's significance, Anna and Clarissa's correspondence is a model of what might be called the intertextual self—the self signified, interpreted, amended, and perpetually resignified in the space that exists between the letter writer and the letter reader. This intertextual self is similar to what I will call the adulterous self in *The Scarlet Letter*; it is a self formulated through an attack on the proper name as we conventionally conceive it, or on the strict division between "I" and "s/he" (or, in the epistolary novel, "I" and "you"). Fiction revises what I will be calling the naive equation of self-identity, the self equal to itself, equal to its proper name or to a simple, single, static "I." Such a revision, insofar as it exists as a central theme in fiction, is often experienced by the characters as a tragic self-division. In *Clarissa* this division is by no means limited to the heroine herself: "I am no longer what I was" (Clarissa, 3.205); "I am not myself! I never shall be!" (Anna Howe, 4.402); "I am still, I am still most miserably absent from myself! Shall never, never more be what I was!" (Lovelace, 4.439).

The significance of such an experience is twofold: first, it problematizes the entire question of human naming; second, it informs at the deepest level the conventions and techniques that constitute a fictional text (in this case, the epistolary novel). I am suggesting that the issue of human naming develops its deepest significance precisely at that point when philosophical tautology no longer is true—in other words, when we move from statements such as "a man's a man" (1.162) (we have seen how a woman is *not* a woman) or "Truth is truth" (2.132) to statements such as "I am not myself." If science seeks to make name and thing equal, and the name equal to itself (where tautology is a linguistic version of mathematical equation), fiction finds that people are named most authentically at the point of rupture in such equations. The epistolary form of *Clarissa* underscores such a rupture, first, through foregrounding that circuit of correspondence whereby Clarissa receives an interpretation of herself not equal to the representation she thinks she has written and, second, through undermining the substantiality of the proper name by presenting the shifting personal pronoun as a model for naming.

The epistolary form of *Clarissa* quite naturally demonstrates the relativity of such personal pronouns as "I" and "you," the ways in which they shift, until their value is fixed tentatively at the end of each letter through the signature. In this way the personal pronoun and the proper name define the opposite extremes of naming. But Clarissa and Anna do not simply leave the fluctuation of personal pronouns to the natural course of correspondence; the two women deliberately radicalize such shifts, and then choose such shifts to name themselves. At first these demonstrations may look like mere rhetorical flourish, what Lovelace would call examples of the female dialect: Anna tells Clarissa, "your concerns are my concerns, . . . your honour is my honour" (1.3). But as we proceed and begin to understand how the correspondence between the two is contracted on the basis of an exchange of selves, the terminology becomes a profound version of naming: "Suppose yourself to be *me*, and me to be *you*" (2.174)—in fact, "you are me" (1.43). Such exchanges formulate a self grounded outside itself, in another—in another so fundamental to me that I call it my other self, myself. The self named pronominally is the self named provisionally, between selves. And perhaps it is the author of the epistolary novel who best experiences the provisional and fictional quality of such naming, as we see in the case of Richardson's explanation that the very form of fiction depends on an authorial "I" that is perpetually disembodied and reembodied, fictionalized: "It is not fair to say—I, identically I, am anywhere, while I keep within the character."⁴ In any case, Anna is the friend to whom Clarissa brings the broken "I" (a layered "I" that contains within it another "I"), the self split almost beyond healing, violated by Lovelace: "Once more have I escaped—but, alas! *I*, my *best self*, have *not* escaped! Oh, your poor Clarissa Harlowe! . . . But no more of my self! . . . *YOU* shall be my subject . . . and let me . . . revere my beloved Anna Howe, and in *her* reflect upon what her Clarissa Harlowe once was!" (3.321). I become you, or I no longer exist except as you—Clarissa's tragic version of the voluntary exchange of selves ("you are me") that existed in happier times.

In addition to the shifting personal pronoun, *Clarissa* imagines one other alternative to the proper name and to those class names (such as "daughter" and "woman") that are used to fix Clarissa's identity, possess her being, take charge of her meaning. In doing so, *Clarissa* moves toward a middle term, one that offers an alternative to the strict division between family and enemy. First, we must realize that the family uses such a division to fix its own boundaries, and thereby to threaten the disobedient family member with ostracism—a threat that is carried out in Clarissa's case. Often in the novel, Clarissa reacts to such a threat by seeking to reconfirm her status as a member of the family: she writes to James and Arabella, "in order to be thought *less an alien* and *nearer of kin to you both*, than either of you have of late seemed to suppose me" (1.268). But Anna recommends that Clarissa allow the familial bond to loosen, for in her view Clarissa is not a Harlowe at all: "You are not one of them" (1.283). What Anna ultimately does is to propose "friend" as a significant alternative to the division between kindred and enemy, and even to the terminology of the lover. The friend is especially well suited to take the place of both kindred and lover because the term has both meanings well into the eighteenth century, and Anna is covertly suggesting herself as a successful substitute for both the family member and the lover. The friend in *Clarissa* consistently defines her own status by instructing Clarissa to question the terminology of kindred: "He [James] is not *my* brother. Can you say he is *yours*? So, for your life, if you are just, you can't be angry with me: for would you side with a *false brother* against a *true friend*? A brother may *not* be a friend: but a friend will be *always* a brother" (1.248). By the end of the novel, Clarissa accepts Anna's revisionary naming: "You would not call them my friends—I cannot call them relations" (4.102). Here, at the end of her story, Clarissa is following Anna's earlier lead to unname the family:

"But for your relations (*friends* no more will I call them, unworthy as they are even of the *other* name!)" (1.131). Just as Clarissa has no status for the family, she now relinquishes them by disallowing them their conventional name. Anna Howe, then, bestows a crucial name on Clarissa, and her subtle and scrupulous distinctions as a letter reader invite Clarissa to understand the fineness of the name "friend." For example, when Clarissa repeats what her cousin has told her, Anna replies with a rebuke to the terms: "he declares . . . you shall not be imposed on either by friend or foe—By *relation* or foe, should he not have said?—for a friend will not impose upon a friend" (4.267).

In *Clarissa* the friend is "my other self" (1.281), "my better pilot" (1.346), my "echo" (2.104) and "shadow" (2.234), and "my better half" (4.404). These are the names that Clarissa and Anna give to each other, the names that allow them whatever success they achieve in living beyond the patriarchal family and the lover. In fact, it is not too much to say that Anna as friend allows a complete superseding of the male, so that the male lover, for Clarissa and Anna, becomes a supernumerary. If Lovelace's strategy is to appropriate the female, to be the keeper of the master language, and even to imagine himself "like Tiresias [who] can tell what they [women] think, and what they drive at, as well as themselves" (2.55), Anna and Clarissa's reaction is to bypass the male, to love without him. I am thinking of the series of acts that shut out the male, or translate him into the female, such as Clarissa's refusal to have anyone not of her own sex touch her corpse, or "the naming of the subject of the discourse" as "she," not "he," so that the text from Job that Clarissa has delivered at her funeral exchanges "the words *her* and *she*, for *him* and *he*" (4.427).

Such pronominal transpositions displace the male from the center of language; in the context of the plot of *Clarissa*, they unname him. Lovelace is the particular man who suffers an unnaming that, from several angles, points to his unmanning. He has feared all along that Clarissa will "unman" (2.526) him, and has sought to keep the gender equations fixed and clear: the failure of the love plot would mean "she would be *more* than woman, . . . or I *less* than man" (2.42). But in this sexually threatening tale in which such mythological figures as Tiresias and a "*man-woman*" (2.118) transgress what is taken to be the natural order of classification, the simple equation "a man's a man" is exploded in an unexpected way. Lovelace keeps his right to his gender name, but loses his title to his humanity: "*man* he cannot be called" (4.24); "if thou art a *man*" (2.254), Belford chides him. Lovelace's last wish is that Clarissa will bear him a child, but the love plot's final twist makes us see that Lovelace is "the last of thy name" (2.160), and that her failure to bear a child is a way of unnaming Lovelace and the entire Lovelace family. I take her failure to have a child almost as an act of will, a refusal of "the old patriarchal system, to go on contributing to get sons and daughters" (3.316). After all, of whom but Lovelace does Clarissa write in her wandering theological meditations, "he shall have no name in the streets. . . . He shall have neither son nor nephew among his people" (4.437)? In this light Hickman, the lover against whom Anna has protested all along, seems brought in after Clarissa's death to serve a function, to participate in bringing back Clarissa in the most elementary way. Anna gives birth to a child she names Clarissa, the child born more of her love for Clarissa than of her love for Hickman. The child that Clarissa does not have (thereby cutting short the name Lovelace) becomes the child that Anna has (thereby perpetuating the name Clarissa). Such events subvert the roles of the man and the lover while honoring the roles of the woman and the friend.

Anna carries such subversions further by attacking the authority of names when she storms into the funeral asking, "why, Mr. Morden, was she sent *hither*? Why not to *me*? She has no father, no mother, no relations; no not *one*! They had all renounced her. I was her sympathizing friend—and had not I the best right to my dear creature's remains? And must names, without nature, be preferred to such a love as mine?" (4.402-3). Such a question is not simply an attack on the power and authority of names, but on their literalness, for as Anna reminds us, "She [Clarissa] honoured me with the title of *the sister of her heart*" (4.510).

I take such a symbolic renaming as the signal by which the text reflects back upon the failures of what one might call the literal name, the name that seeks to fix identity. First, *Clarissa* shows how the philosophic desire to call everything by its correct name is exploited in the master language of the patriarchal family and of the lover, a language that deindividualizes and dehumanizes through a system of naming in which the person disappears under the cover of the name. Second, *Clarissa* shows how the proper name, with its view of the crystallized and static self, names less authentically than personal pronouns, with their shifting meanings and their ability to name between names, between selves. Third, *Clarissa* shows how the symbolic names we bestow and honour—especially when our "literal" names are disallowed ("daughter") or denigrated ("woman")—give us the meaning we call human. Clarissa herself pushes such an idea to the limit when she calls Anna "Sweet and ever-amiable friend—companion—sister—lover!" (4.340). The friend is kindred and lover both—names in this case we perhaps mistakenly discredit by calling only metaphoric, but which fiction, in its undermining of the literal, valorizes.

The plot of *Clarissa*, which begins by presenting the daughter in danger of being "sacrificed in marriage" (1.40), turns to a grander tragedy: Clarissa's sacrifice to the name—not simply to the name Clarissa Harlowe and all it means in the community's eyes, but to the name "virtue." Clarissa rewards Lovelace and the entire population that watches her— "Every eye is upon you with the expectation of an example" (1.3)—with the same revelation: "There must be something more than a *name* in virtue!" (3.261). This is the final proof of names, one that the culture requires of her as much as she requires it of herself. While Lovelace forces her to give up her body to prove the name "woman," Clarissa chooses to give up her body in death to prove the name "virtue," to inscribe that name over the (woman's) body (just as the Puritan community inscribes the same body with the name "Adultery," as we will see in chapter 4). The tragedy of *Clarissa* is contained within this paradox: in having proved that virtue is no mere name, Clarissa dies in the service of names; nonetheless, in the end Clarissa thinks of herself as having lost her name.

2

Oliver Twist,
or the Name Found

The philosophic desire in *Clarissa* "to call everything by its proper name" is deratiocinated in *Oliver Twist*, where the same desire explodes from the murderer Sikes—"Speak out, and call things by their right names" (122)[1]—and becomes a furious injunction, actually a deadly threat, directed at his fellow criminal, Fagin. Sikes persists in making Fagin keep to the proper name—"None of your mistering . . .; you always mean mischief when you come that. You know my name: out with it!" (77)—precisely because the criminal world at large depends on a highly encoded and duplicitous language to which Sikes himself does not want to fall victim. Unlike *Clarissa*, then, *Oliver Twist* takes us not to the names at the moral center of society, but to an elaborate system of code names—castor, crib, fogle, Jack Ketch, prad, sort, wiper—and to the watchwords and secret signals that preserve a criminal underground. And yet it is precisely by plunging the child into the midst of such a world that *Oliver Twist* becomes a moral fable, as Dickens makes clear in his Preface, when he admits that he sought "among what companions I could try him best" (lxii). *Clarissa* and *Oliver Twist* make extraordinarily clear the way in which certain novels are designed as the moral trial of the child. As if Oliver were the original *tabula rasa*, the battle to possess him—for this is the central contest in *Oliver Twist*—proceeds as a struggle to indoctrinate him, to fill the pure blank space that the child is. Fagin, for example, knows that "once fill his mind with the idea that he has been a thief; and he's ours! Ours for his life!" (126), while Mr. Brownlow similarly sets about "filling the mind of his adopted child with stores of knowledge" (367–68). Like the starved corpses of parish children of whom we hear that the surgeon "always opened the body and found nothing inside" (4), the child in *Oliver Twist* seems to begin as an elemental blank, a pure nothingness—if not to be filled with costly food, then to be filled with names. In this way, both *Clarissa* and *Oliver Twist* reveal the way in which certain cultural values are tested through testing the child and the names the child will uphold—in *Clarissa*'s case, "virtue," and in *Oliver Twist*'s case, "innocence" (the actual sobriquet by which he is dubbed, almost allegorizing the novel into pure fable). In *Clarissa* the child seeks to preserve herself at the same time that she preserves, from Lovelace's assault of false names and meanings, the names that center an entire culture. The novel, however, describes a tragic exchange in which only the sacrifice of Clarissa herself will uphold such names. In *Oliver Twist* the child preserves himself from the criminal plot that uses the name to defame, bury, and thereby annihilate. In this way the child becomes the key term in a fablelike tale in which good is preserved from evil. Between these two plots we detect the difference of gender: the daughter dies for such names as virtue and vice, while the son survives to uphold the difference between them, and to become the inheritor and the guardian of the family name.

Oliver Twist's opening sentences are dominated by a rather nervous attention to the idea of the name, ironically christening the newborn child blandly as an "item of mortality whose name is prefixed to the head of this chapter," explaining the doubt surrounding "whether the child would survive to bear any name at all." The name Oliver Twist, and the weight of pages that lie under it, are offered to the reader as a rather simple assurance that Oliver will live, and have a history. But even here we find adumbrated what will become a subtle association between bearing a name and living and dying, with the name functioning as an extremely concentrated synecdoche for an entire life story. But the most overt indication of the theme of naming at the beginning of *Oliver Twist* occurs as the text's first narrative act, when the narrator self-consciously refrains from the kind of naming that is persistently performed as a violation against Oliver: the narrator declares about the town in which the hero is born, "I will assign no fictitious name." This prepares us for a significant reversal, when it is made to look as if the author himself does not invent the name of the title character. Like most heroes in fiction, Oliver has an invented name, but Dickens makes Bumble, and not himself, responsible for this. When asked, "How came he to have any name at all?" Bumble answers, "I inwented it"—"We name our foundlings in alphabetical order" (7). The child produced by chance is named by chance; his name is found in the arbitrary order of language. Such an act, from which the narrator steadfastly holds back, lies at the opposite extreme of the theory of names that believes the name naturally expresses the true essence of the object or person named.

The social system that names the child acknowledges openly that "Oliver Twist" is a pure fiction by cancelling this name in a highly charged class name. In short, the fact that Oliver is an orphan, no less a bastard, means that "Oliver Twist" is no proper name at all. Such a system classifies the child in order to fix his place in the order of things; it dehumanizes him through a generic name that is a stigma. The trial whereby the human child is reified in order to be assigned a place begins with a characteristic double question: Mr. Grimwig asks Brownlow, "Who is he? What is he?" (88). It is the same slurring double question asked rhetorically of Nancy—"Do you know who you are, and what you are?" (103)—and asked of Pearl in *The Scarlet Letter* and of Tess in *Tess of the d'Urbervilles*. The second question undermines the first by disqualifying the person's humanity in a kind of shameful materiality, in a generic class (such as "bastard" or "whore") that runs counter to the kind of individual status that we commonly see as the ground of humanness. After all, with no living mother, born of the flesh of a corpse, Oliver is delivered by a makeshift mother named "Mrs. Thingmummy." The ontological status of the orphan, born of the dead mother or mummy, is that of a mere thing. How can such a thing bear a proper name?

At first, then, to "call things by their right names" in *Oliver Twist* takes the form of denying the orphan his humanity, and then of educating the child by informing him of that generic classification to which he belongs. We see such a procedure when Oliver comes to trial to be apprenticed (or, to use a truer name, sold):

> "Boy," said the gentleman in the high chair, "listen to me. You know you're an orphan, I suppose?"
> "What's that, sir?" inquired poor Oliver.
> "The boy *is* a fool—I thought he was," said the gentleman. . . . (9)

Oliver's first vocabulary lesson masters him by giving him a name for himself whose meaning he does not understand. "Boy," "orphan," and "fool"—are these synonyms?—are the names by which the "gentleman" assigns the child's position. Moreover, Dickens shows us that the title "orphan" is part of a carefully articulated though esoteric system of classification whose boundaries are as rigid as they are fine:

> Noah was a charity-boy, but not a workhouse orphan. No chance-child was he, for he could trace his genealogy all the way back to his parents, who

lived hard by; his mother being a washerwoman, and his father a drunken soldier: discharged with a wooden leg, and a diurnal pension of twopence-halfpenny and an unstateable fraction. The shop-boys in the neighbourhood had long been in the habit of branding Noah, in the public streets, with the ignominious epithets of "leathers," "charity," and the like; and Noah had borne them without reply. But, now that fortune had cast in his way a nameless orphan, at whom even the meanest could point the finger of scorn, he retorted on him with interest (28).

The shop-boys brand the charity-boy, and the charity-boy brands Oliver "Work-us." The brand as name, an idea I will take up in more detail regarding *The Scarlet Letter*, suggests the name written in the flesh as a mark of shame. *Oliver Twist* is an attack on the name as stigma, as "ignominious epithet." Oliver fights Noah, we recall, because "He called my mother names" (41), and when Monks calls Oliver a "bastard child," Brownlow replies, "The term you use . . . is a reproach to those who long since passed beyond the feeble censure of the world. It reflects disgrace on no one living, except you who use it" (350). The history of fiction charts an attack on the name as stigma, especially on those generic names that cancel the individual in a socially or politically charged class, and the child is frequently the carrier of such names: "woman" in *Clarissa* (and in the tradition of fiction generally, ending with "nymphet" in *Lolita*), "bastard" and "orphan" in *Oliver Twist*, "savage" in Cooper's novels, "children and niggers" (paired together on a telling signboard) in *Huckleberry Finn*, "idiot" in *The Secret Agent* and *The Sound and the Fury*— one could even add "monster" in *Frankenstein*. But *Oliver Twist* does something more: the attack on the name as stigma turns into an extraordinary valorizing of the name, so that the name becomes, first, a form of merciful recognition, then a form of exalted honoring, and finally a mystical borderland between life and death.

The name is valorized in *Oliver Twist* in the simplest way: it literally carries a monetary value. The social system that classifies Oliver as a nameless orphan values him accordingly, and makes quite literal what I earlier called the issue of possessing the child. Oliver Twist "To Let"— "five pounds would be paid to anybody who would take possession of him" (19)—puts at the center of the novel a theme that lies at the heart of Dickens's plots and forms the backbone of an entire tradition of fiction, from Richardson through James and Twain to Nabokov: the child bought and sold, or at least assigned a monetary value (the most conventional version of which pictures the child as inheritor). I am especially interested in how the child's monetary value is signified in his or her name. We will see that in *Tess of the d'Urbervilles*, for example, the father offers to sell the title of the d'Urberville name through (selling) his daughter, and in *The Scarlet Letter* the name directly signifies the child's value, albeit symbolically—"she named the infant 'Pearl,' as being of great price,—purchased with all she had,—her mother's only treasure!"[2] In both cases the child is meant to save the parent, either monetarily or spiritually, and in both cases the child seems to discharge a debt. In *Oliver Twist*, at least from the most obvious angle, the dead parent saves the child: Oliver is the rightful inheritor of his father's money. Oliver Twist, then, is worth much more than the five-pound value the beadle places on him (or even the five-guinea reward Mr. Brownlow later offers for his recovery), but this value depends entirely on knowing his true name. To Fagin, he is worth hundreds of pounds, because Monks will pay such an amount if Fagin successfully corrupts Oliver. Monks is willing to do so precisely because his own fortune depends on it: the father's will stipulates that Oliver will inherit the money on condition that "in his minority he should never have stained his name" (351). In *Oliver Twist* it is not sufficient to be the simple bearer of the name. Only the successful preservation of the name from scandal has as its direct reward the inheritance of the father's money.

But far more is at stake in the naming plot of *Oliver Twist*. One could argue that the plot which makes the name the key middle term between bastard and inheritance is merely the superficial overlay of the conventional fable that Dickens inherited from his eighteenth-century precursors, most notably Fielding and Smollett. The deeper meanings of the name in *Oliver Twist* begin to emerge when we inquire into the motives behind Mr. Brownlow's search for Oliver's name and the consequences of the discovery of Oliver's name beyond its monetary value. At this point it should be clear at least that *Oliver Twist* shares with *Clarissa* a plot in which two adversary camps seek the power to name the child. Monks (assisted by Fagin and the criminals) seeks to reveal that Oliver is the child with a stain upon his name, while in the counterplot Mr. Brownlow (assisted by the Maylies) attempts to reveal Oliver's proper name.

I have already explained the name branded into the flesh as a sign of the outcast's shame, but I now wish to explain that the marked body may function in another way, as a sign of familial identity, or in other words as a legitimizing name.[3] From this angle the plot of the criminals who seek to assign Oliver a name that sticks, and stains, is undermined by the plot of his friends who seek to reveal the name that Oliver has from birth. Oliver's mother does not name him, but at the moment of her death she places on him a mark of identification: "She imprinted her cold white lips passionately on its forehead; passed her hands over its face; gazed wildly round; shuddered; fell back—and died" (2). One could say that, at the literal level of story, the pursuit after the locket engraved with the name (which the mother means to be kept for Oliver, as proof of his familial identity) is simply an externalized quest, in the world of things, for the symbolic engraving on the child himself. Fagin remarks about Oliver, "His mug is a fortun' to him" (141), meaning simply that Oliver's innocent looks are the best equipment a criminal can possess, but we eventually realize that Oliver's face is in fact one of the strongest clues that wins him his family inheritance. This idea of the imprinted brow as a sign of identification looks forward to Hester's description of Pearl to Dimmesdale in *The Scarlet Letter*—"I know whose brow she has!"—and the child's attempt to wipe off the kiss the minister secretly "impressed" there.[4] The antithesis of the marked brow that makes one a pariah (as Hawthorne reminds us in his allusion to Cain) is the brow marked by family resemblance. On the brow of the bastard the mark may have both meanings, as it does in Pearl's case.

These examples of the marked brow from *Oliver Twist* and *The Scarlet Letter* are a highly symbolic way of putting a commonplace—namely, that in Oliver's countenance, for example, we can discover the features of his mother. But by so insistently dramatizing this through the idea of a bodily writing,[5] fiction suggests that the body actually bears the name as the ultimate mark of identification.[6] The most blatant version of this idea occurs in *Through the Looking-Glass*, with Humpty Dumpty looking "as if his name were written all over his face."[7] The name written on the face, of course, represents what Humpty Dumpty argues (via Cratylus) in his philosophic debate with Alice: a name expresses the essential being of the thing named. What I am calling the family plot undermines the traditional notion of the *tabula rasa* by showing the child as marked from the beginning; in such a plot, to trace the child's genealogy is to read it, in the marks that make his face an unofficial but entirely natural document. In seventeenth- and early eighteenth-century language philosophy, the terms *mark* and *name* are used almost interchangeably,[8] and in the tradition of fiction I am describing the marked face tells one's name— after all, the marks on one's face reveal who one's parents are. We will see many examples of this in the following pages, but I wish to give an especially relevant one from *Tess of the d'Urbervilles*. Tess's first reaction to Alec is to miss in him "an aged and dignified face, the sublimation of all the d'Urberville lineaments, furrowed with incarnate memories representing in hieroglyphic the centuries of her family's and England's history."[9] Hardy suggests here that if Tess had relied on her reading of the face she would have known from the start that Alec was not kin, not the true bearer of the family name. Such examples are a transference to human beings of what we typically take to be a system of signatures on things in the world of nature. But in the family plot such marks or names actually humanize; the child entirely unmarked, with no identification, is classed as the nameless orphan and thereby "badged and ticketed" (3) as a mere thing. The child bearing the family mark, however, is eventually named and thereby connected to his family—in other words, made human. In *Oliver Twist* the divergence between the fictitious name Oliver Twist and the imprinted forehead—or what it stands for, the child as the "living copy" (72) of the dead mother—measures the duration of the plot. When the true name and the mark on the face become fully legible and correctly read, when they become once more equal, the plot is resolved.

With Oliver as a "living copy" of his dead mother, we come to the idea that charges *Oliver Twist* with so much of its power: the raising of the dead, the dead coming alive through the living. In *Oliver Twist* the excitement of fast pursuits and narrow escapes, of living perpetually just this side of death, is counterbalanced by numerous narrative asides and extended meditations on the dead. Such passages of mourning, at once lyrical and discursive, are always retrospective, and seem to retard the otherwise urgent pace of the tale. But they are in fact a symptom of its deepest motive: *Oliver Twist* is a powerful cry to bring back the dead. Mr. Brownlow's first meeting with Oliver, for example, sends the old man into a long and melancholy meditation because the child's face calls up "faces over which a dusky curtain had hung for many years," "faces that the grave had changed and closed upon, but which the mind, superior to its power, still dressed in their old fashions and beauty: calling back the lustre of the eyes, the brightness of the smile, the bearing of the soul through its mask of clay: and whispering of beauty beyond the tomb, changed but to be heightened" (61–62). In this context I will be able to show that if Oliver's value for Monks is literal, material, his value for Mr. Brownlow is symbolic, spiritual, a value fueled by the extraordinary personal loss Dickens suffered when his beloved sister-in-law Mary died during the writing of *Oliver Twist*.[10]

Dickens clarifies the way in which the child is valued in *Oliver Twist* through Mr. Brownlow's contrary reactions to the two sons, Oliver and Monks. At the end of the novel Mr. Brownlow takes as his son the child in whose face he can trace the features of his dead beloved (the girl who died on their wedding day, and who, incidentally, turns out to be Oliver's aunt), and the child in whose face as well "he traced . . . new traits of his early friend" (368). While Brownlow adopts the child who perfectly reproduces the familial features, he spurns the child Monks in whom those features are defaced: "you, who from your cradle were gall and bitterness to your own father's heart, and in whom all evil passions, vice, and profligacy, festered, till they found a vent in a hideous disease which has made your face an index even to your mind" (336). I have been viewing face and name as correlates: the unblemished face is the surest sign of the unstained name in this fable (not until *Bleak House*, with Esther's scarred but innocent face, does Dickens complicate this pattern). From this it follows that Brownlow adopts the child who preserves the name from infamy, and spurns the child who defames it and changes it. When Brownlow reveals Monks's true name as "Edward Leeford" and says that he "blush[es] for your unworthiness who bear the name," his deep and mysterious regard for the name utterly confounds Monks:

> "What has the name to do with it?" asked the other, after contemplating, half in silence, and half in dogged wonder, the agitation of his companion. "What is the name to me?"
> "Nothing," replied Mr. Brownlow, "nothing to you. But it was *hers*, and even at this distance of time brings back to me, an old man, the glow and thrill which I once felt, only to hear it repeated by a stranger. I am very glad you have changed it—very—very." (332)

In *Oliver Twist* face and name function to make manifest the distant, the otherworldly, and in this light I recall their function in the Bible. In the Old Testament, the immateriality of the divine is signified by a God who will neither unveil his face nor speak his name; in the New Testament, the Son makes the Father manifest by being the face we see, by bringing the name among us.[11] The family plot domesticates such a typology in the child who brings alive, in face and name, the dead parent.

The function of bringing back the parent from the dead situates the child, at least symbolically, on the brink of death. No other novel I know, except perhaps *Huckleberry Finn* and Dickens's next novel, *The Old Curiosity Shop*, exploits more completely the association between death and the child. One could say that *Oliver Twist* begins with what appears to be the unpassable gulf between "the rigid face of the corpse and the calm sleep of the child" (310), and shows us how the child can make the crossing possible. At first the association between death and the child seems mere Gothic machinery, with Oliver sleeping among the coffins, or social commentary, with the foundling an "item of mortality" (1) unlikely to survive. But the theme has a dogged persistence—Oliver "looked like death" (128), "Oliver, more dead than alive" (144), Oliver "Alive or dead" no one knows (161)—and seems to structure the entire tale. The child who almost does not survive his first moments nearly dies after each encounter with the criminals before being brought back to life by his friends, first by Mr. Brownlow and next by the Maylies. In this light the description in *Oliver Twist* of the newborn infant "rather unequally poised between this world and the next" (1) registers his ontological status for the remainder of his life: Oliver is the child whose life depends on the dead. Quite simply, that is what it means to be an orphan: Oliver's mother dies in giving him birth. The denouement of *Oliver Twist* seems the payment of a debt, whereby the child successfully brings the mother alive again. In this way the successful and repeated regeneration of the child has as its ulterior motive the successful and ultimate regeneration of the mother. The tale that seems to have as its end the child's winning of his inheritance, then, has an additional goal of equal significance: the rejuvenation of the dead parent. Another way of putting this is to say that Oliver is not simply the hero of a rags-to-riches fable, but also the child in the role of instrument, a figure we will meet time and again. Just as Pearl in *The Scarlet Letter* is said to be the instrument whereby her mother will be brought to heaven, Oliver is the instrument whereby his mother will be brought back to earth. What *Tess* contemplates with horror, being one flesh with the dead, so that the young girl is haunted and finally brought down by the dead yet potent ancestral body, *Oliver Twist* makes into a naive fable of regeneration: "The eyes, the head, the mouth; every feature was the same. The expression was, for the instant, so precisely alike, that the minutest line seemed copied with a startling accuracy" (72). *Oliver Twist* presents the tradition's most patent example of personal regeneration through the child: Oliver is the body reincarnate of his dead mother, the mother whose tomb holds no body.

In Sikes's murder of Nancy, Dickens shows us how the murderer plays counterfoil to the child. Sikes literalizes, in reverse, the symbolic function of the child: he makes the living dead. Nancy plays the role of the mother in relation to Sikes, "nursing and caring for you, as if you had been a child" (258); but while the child Oliver, the instrument of regeneration, copies the face precisely in every line, Sikes murders to deface. Sikes beat his pistol "upon the upturned face that almost touched his own. She staggered and fell: nearly blinded with the blood that rained down from a deep gash in her forehead" (322). The murder directly contradicts those acts of recognition and love—whether maternal, sisterly, or even nuptial—that we see elsewhere, when Oliver's mother imprints the child's forehead with a kiss; or when Rose's "tears fell upon his [Oliver's] forehead . . . as . . . marks of pity" (191); or when Henry Maylie "imprint[s] one kiss on her [Rose's] beautiful forehead" (235). The murderer marks to deface, ultimately eradicating what we have seen is the mark that names, and he thereby makes the victim unidentifiable, so that those who discover her body do not even known her gender: "'Man or woman, pray, sir?' 'A woman,' replied the gentleman. 'It is supposed—'" (326). If the denouement of *Oliver Twist* makes legible the mark that names the child, articulating his place in the human community by restoring to him his family history, the murder of Nancy can be viewed as the climactic moment in the subsidiary or subversive plot in which Dickens describes her death as an erasure of the mother, the woman, the child—the roles, symbolic and literal, that mark her as human.

Before the murder, Dickens's study of the women who consort with the criminals carefully shows us their symbolic death as an erasure: "and women: some with the last lingering tinge of their early freshness, almost fading as you looked: others with every mark and stamp of their sex utterly beaten out, and presenting one loathsome blank of profligacy and crime" (166). The murder, then, is the climax to a life that beats out of such women the name, the mark, the sign—what Rose Maylie, for example, has "stamped upon her noble head" (187). The blank is not the *tabula rasa*, but rather a complete darkness, an obscurity of error and crime that prevents the sign of any humanity from showing through; we remember that Fagin tries "instilling into his [Oliver's] soul the poison which he hoped would blacken it, and change its hue for ever" (120). But Nancy is a crucial figure in *Oliver Twist* precisely because "there was something of the woman's original nature left in her still," even though she sometimes mistakenly feels "too proud to betray a feeble gleam of the womanly feeling which she thought a weakness, but which alone connected her with that humanity, of which her wasting life had obliterated so many, many traces when a very child" (270). While the major thrust of the novel saves from obliteration the traces that link the child to his parents and to goodness, in the passage just quoted the narrator mourns such an obliteration as it describes the loss of the child in Nancy. As the reverse image of Oliver, Nancy is the child corrupted, dehumanized, deadened, wiped out. In such a way the plot of the fallen Nancy, like that of the dead child Dick, is the tragic undercurrent of *Oliver Twist*, a warning that the happy fable is not every child's story. In fact, in a novel built upon life-and-death exchanges, with characters bought and sold, we can say that Nancy is ransomed to give Oliver life. Showing Oliver the marks on her body, she tells him, " I have borne all this for you" (132). Such marks, like the final gash on the forehead, do not hide the woman, but finally make her the martyred victim in whose suffering and death another—the child—lives. In dying to give him life, Nancy is the symbolic double of Oliver's mother. But, one might ask, is the novel's happy ending paid for by too great a price?

The dead Nancy becomes for Sikes an ironic version of what the dead mother is for the child. Sikes's earlier jibe at Nancy, "You look like a corpse come to life again" (266), is now literalized in the murderer's maddened imagination. In a grotesque variation on the central motive of the novel, the dead Nancy is brought back to life, tagging Sikes everywhere and eventually bringing him down; this is the inheritance the murderer wins. Like the orphan seeking to trace his genealogy in order to find the dead parent who shadows his life, Sikes "could trace its shadow . . . ; it followed . . . like a corpse endowed with the mere machinery of life" (327). As Sikes lies on the road, the inescapable phantom of Nancy stands at his head, "a living grave-stone, with its epitaph in blood" (327). Nancy is turned into a blood-red gravestone that publishes the murderer's foul crime, an indictment before which he stands not only convicted but condemned to death; it is his own gravestone that he lies before. If Sikes's crime is to beat out of Nancy the human mark or stamp, his punishment is to see her loss of name transformed into his own epitaph. In short, the blankness of Nancy is written up with the murderer's own name—on his gravestone, no less. And the murderer's name is allowed only on the gravestone, for unlike the child who wins a name, Sikes is the murderer who loses a name. The man whose life is lost in the crimes he commits earns a symbolic anonymity, his history encapsulated in a series of unheroic epithets ("the robber," "the housebreaker," "the murderer") until he is no longer named at all. After the murder, upon asking his fellow criminals, "Don't you know me?" he is told that he is a "monster" (343). In the end Sikes becomes simply "'He' (none of them called the murderer by his old name)" (341), an ironic reflection on Sikes's earlier injunction, "You know my name: out with it!" An inversion of the divine power, "He" is not the ineffable God who gives life, not the "Maker" (323) to whom Nancy breathes one final prayer for mercy, but the murderer who takes it away.

The avenging ghost of Nancy, what the murderer wins, is matched at the end of the novel by the benign shadow of Agnes, the innocent child's most valuable inheritance. The shadow of the mother can be found in one particular place, hovering over a memorial to her name before which the child reverently stands. The engraved name at the end becomes the mystical center empowered to call back the dead mother, as the narrator's curiously personal wish borders on belief: "But, if the spirits of the Dead ever come back to earth, to visit spots hallowed by the love—the love beyond the grave—of those whom they knew in life, I believe that the shade of Agnes sometimes hovers round that solemn nook." The happy fable culminates in the mother's name unearthed and reclaimed, memorialized and honored. While the blankness of Nancy is turned into a blood-red epitaph to haunt the imagination, the unknown and nameless mother becomes "a white marble tablet" on which, in the last paragraph of the novel, the name "Agnes!" is seen engraved. The engraved locket, the sign of lawless passion, is cancelled in the engraved tablet that restores the law which the child obeys: honor the name of thy mother.

The name saves the mother from the obscurity of death; it remains to be shown that the name saves her as well from the oblivion of shame. *Oliver Twist* delineates such a theme by making us realize what it means not simply to find a name, but to be found through a name. With misogynistic fervor, Monks describes those women who are untrustworthy to keep any secret except "the loss of their own good name" (250), but who will go to any length to do that, even "hid[ing] their shame, rot 'em, in the grave" (246). The female especially falls victim to the stigmatized name, as Dickens makes clear in the case of Rose, with "a blight upon my name," "a stain upon my name" (233–34). Like the stain that Monks tries to fix on Oliver's name, this stain is no more than the slanderous product of Monks's mother, but until this is known Mrs. Maylie reminds her son of the consequences of marrying such a woman. On her deathbed Agnes understands her greatest danger: her name may be kept from her son because of her errors, or he may refuse to recognize and name her. She understands that the erring are cast out by a prohibition against the name, as in *Clarissa*, when the father "can hardly bear your name" and "wishes you had never been born" (2.160); or in *Oliver Twist*, when Mr. Brownlow thinks himself betrayed by Oliver and declares, "Never let me hear the boy's name again" (113); or in *The Sound and the Fury*, when the mother forbids the name of her daughter Caddy in the Compson household. Such examples show a parental figure banishing the child through the power of the name, but in *The Sound and the Fury* the idea has another side: Caddy, a young and erring mother like Agnes, has her name denied to her own child. The denouement of *Oliver Twist* fulfills the mother's wish: "the day might come when it [her child] would not feel so much disgraced to hear its poor young mother named" (156). Oliver names his mother in a striking reversal of the roles of parent and child. He names her insofar as he allows her name to be spoken, recognizes her in that name, and loves her through it.

The name lost and the name found—such are the endpoints of the murderer's and the child's stories in *Oliver Twist* and, more generally, of the naming plots of fiction, which I am representing here by *Clarissa* and *Oliver Twist*. In *Oliver Twist* the erasure of the criminal's name counterpoints the publication of the mother's name. These two naming acts encapsulate the two largest movements of the narrative—one toward silence, secrecy, a hidden and unreadable language; the other toward discourse, disclosure, a manifest and legible language. The naming of the mother at the end is a highly concentrated version of the entire drive toward discourse itself—what Dickens meant in his Preface when he said, against those who would have silenced this tale of criminals, "it needed to be told." In short, the name in *Oliver Twist* is the sign so highly concentrated that it holds an entire story—an entire life—within its bounds. When I called the deepest motive of *Oliver Twist* the raising of the dead, I had in mind that this text defines the dead as the silent, the unknown, the nameless. In one of those extended asides in which the narrator seems to be a man who finds his own personal mourning in the tale's, the narrator wonders, "if we heard but one instant, in imagination, the deep testimony of dead men's voices" (193). *Oliver Twist* is precisely such an imaginative instant mysteriously delayed and suspended but realized at the end. What the narrator wishes here, the tale accomplishes, through the discovery of the story of Leeford and Agnes, or Oliver's family history. To put this another way, the unravelling of Oliver's story fulfills the wish of the mother, whose portrait looks at Oliver "as if it was alive, and wanted to speak to me, but couldn't" (71). The entire narrative which seeks to give the dead a voice by naming them counters the criminal act that silences, obliterates, unnames. We recall that Monks throws to the bottom of the sea the locket that contains the name, and that his mother burns the father's will. The criminal desires to cut short a significant utterance; his maxim, which the plot of *Oliver Twist* seeks to overturn, requires that "dead men never bring awkward stories to light" (52). The constant threat in the novel is to "throttle" (171), to "strangle" (167), to "choke" (260), to "stifle" (193), to "stop his mouth" (82), to "cut her throat" (267): "Wolves tear your throats!" (179). The threat turns on the criminals themselves, when both Sikes and Fagin hang. What haunts the criminal is the fear that "there are those who will lie dead for twelve thousand years to come, for twelve million for anything you or I know, who will tell strange tales at last!" (252). Oliver, the child positioned between life and death, excites precisely this fear in Monks: "He'd start up from a marble coffin, to come in my way!" (217). And this is just what I am arguing that Oliver does, by raising his father and mother from the quiet of the grave and giving them body and voice, face and name.

3

Pierre, or the American Myth of the Name Transcended

The desire to call everything by its proper name becomes a practical caution in *Pierre or The Ambiguities,* a warning that not only shapes the plot but gauges the ironic tone of the narrator from the beginning: "But the magnificence of names must not mislead us as to the humility of things" (9).[1] The caution has its origin in the democratic spirit, for *Pierre* at first turns the distinction between names and things into a political barometer used to measure the success of the American experiment in democracy. At the outset of *Pierre,* in one of the many extended narrative digressions that frequently displace the family plot of this novel, the narrator decides to "compare pedigrees with England" (9), and thereby takes the opportunity to characterize England as a culture that safeguards and even magnifies certain family names while neglecting the individual men and women who bear those names. In England the magnificence of the name tells us little of its humble bearer; in fact, it often deliberately hides such information, especially since the peerage in England is often manufactured by the state, and created and restored perpetually by the art of lawyers, so that "if Richmond, and St. Albans, and Grafton, and Portland, and Buccleugh, be names almost old as England herself, the present Dukes of those names stop in their own genuine pedigrees at Charles II; and there find no very fine fountain" (9). In short, the name is powerful where the man is inconsequential: "Perishable as stubble, and fungous as the fungi, those grafted families successively live and die on the eternal soil of a name. In England this day, twenty-five hundred peerages are extinct; but the names survive. So that the empty air of a name is more endurable than a man, or than dynasties of men" (10). Is America a democratic experiment devised to enable a man to win his freedom from the powerful name? Is America not only a geographical locale of certain political freedoms, but an ontological realm where the idea of "man" comes into being and survives the threat of mighty names? These are the questions that the preamble of *Pierre* suggests; the Pierre Glendinning family becomes the medium through which such questions are filtered and embodied.[2]

Pierre is not bent on perpetrating an American myth. While the narrator posits the democratic distinction between names and things, he shows us with bitter irony that in the heart of America "an eastern patriarchalness sways" (11). In this way *Pierre* disabuses us of the myth of America. "The monarchical world very generally imagines, that in demagoguical America the sacred Past hath no fixed statues erected to it" (8), but *Pierre* describes the Glendinning family as a monarchy in miniature, with Mrs. Glendinning—playfully called "Dowager Duchess Glendinning" (14) and "Your Majesty" (103)—as the successful transporter to America of a system of "fealty," "allegiance," and "homage" (15). Moreover, the family builds its memorial to the sacred Past in a metaphoric marble statue which allows the son to worship the dead father: "There had long stood a shrine in the fresh-foliaged heart of Pierre, up to which he ascended by many tableted steps of remembrance" (68). The tableted steps direct the reverent child to worship the law of the father. In fact, the child himself is no more than a living memorial of the dead parent. The son takes "the perfect marble form of his departed father" (68) and brings it alive in his own body (a version of which we have just seen in *Oliver Twist*), and loses himself as completely in the name of the father as he does in the body. In Pierre's "inheriting brow" (73) we recognize the brow of the father; but Pierre's claim to be the perfect duplicate of the marble father rests finally on his name, "for Pierre was not only his father's only child, but his namesake" (73), the child "whom thy own father named Pierre!" (66), the child who is in fact the fourth bearer of the name. In such ways the naming plot in English and American fiction is the same: it casts the child in the role of the preserver of the family body and the family name, both in *Oliver Twist* and in *Pierre*. In fact, at this point *Pierre* is the more conservative text. In its legitimization of the name "bastard" and its bestowal of honor on the name of the adulterous mother, the rags-to-riches framework of *Oliver Twist* is a democratic text. In *Pierre* we ironically enter the Old World through the monarchy of the American family.

The ostensibly virgin soil of America, where we expect things to shine naked and clear, seems no more than an extension of the Old World. In both worlds, it is in the "eternal soil of a name" that the individual roots himself, flourishes for his hour, and then is buried. The soil of America is denatured, etherealized, made the pure empyrean on which we read the inscription of the Platonic idea "Pierre Glendinning." For the Glendinnings are "that family [which] always keeps the title and the name a-going; yes, even to the christian name,—Pierre" (153). But whatever we may think of the existence of "such mighty lordships in the heart of a republic, and however we may wonder at their surviving, like Indian mounds, the Revolutionary flood; yet survive and exist they do, and are now owned by their present proprietors, by as good nominal title as any peasant owns his father's old hat, or any duke his great-uncle's old coronet" (11). *Pierre* is a Revolutionary flood in print, its object to bring down the mighty lordship of Glendinning, a world based upon nominal title.

The assault on nominal titles is executed abruptly in Isabel's letter and her subsequent narrative—an extended lesson, for Pierre, in namelessness. With a letter announcing at the outset an unknown name, the illegitimate half-sister of Pierre cuts short the idyll that pictures Pierre as the new Adam: "The name at the end of this letter will be wholly strange to thee" (63). Isabel enters *Pierre* not simply as the figure we will see so often, the nameless orphan—"no father, no mother, no sister, no brother, no living thing in the fair form of humanity . . . holds me dear" (64)—but as the quintessential form next to which all other nameless orphans seem mere copies. She is the most disinherited, the most dispossessed; she is the dark angel who is an instructress, a kind of deathly muse (like Keats's Moneta) who teaches the lessons that lie beyond names. She seems at once a satiric attack, through exaggeration, of a well-known convention, and a poignant crystallization of a type that Melville deepens and personalizes; but then in *Pierre* irony masks the most personal revelations, and satire is built over the deepest wellsprings of passion. One is tempted to say—indeed Melville seems tempted to say—that Isabel enters the text of *Pierre* to bring into it the pure world of things, from which the varnish of names has been stripped. Pierre certainly sees her function this way, passionately dedicating himself to truth following his receipt of her letter: "From all idols, I tear all veils; henceforth I will see the hidden things" (66). And it is true that Isabel overwhelms him with a "nameless fascination of the face" (51) and "its nameless beauty" (49), with a "nameless presentiment" (61) and a "nameless sadness" (37) and "nameless forebodings" (62)—in short, with "things I have no name for" (37). But it is characteristic of *Pierre*'s ambiguities that, while the nameless and illegitimate orphan lifts the veil—or name—from things, her story is a nightmare of what it is to live without names. Isabel's story purifies the world of names at the same time that it shocks us with how entirely impoverished is the child who possesses no names.[3]

Isabel's life story, ruptured at all points by namelessness, presents a model of the riddled text, with "an unraveled plot" and "no proper endings" (141)—the kind of text *Pierre* aspires to be. The plot of the illegitimate and nameless daughter overtakes the plot of the legitimate and hereditarily named son. The critique of the idea of the name in Isabel's story finally undermines the logic of those plots that are resolvable in the end through the name (as in *Oliver Twist*). Perhaps the simplest way of putting such differences is to say that the two stories in *Pierre* are alternate family texts. While Pierre's story begins with a long and well-known family history that predates the child's entrance into this world, Isabel's story begins with a hiatus, with no proper beginning. Isabel's story begins with a contradiction of human origins that, as in the case of Pearl in *The Scarlet Letter*, calls into question the human nature of the child, and what we mean by the term *human*: "I seem not of woman born" (114). Isabel is the child entirely ignorant of the function and even the fact of parents. For this reason Isabel's story replaces the human birth process and the succeeding stages of a young child's development with what looks like a nightmarish fantasy in which the child is moved through a series of cold, dark, womblike houses. What Isabel remembers most about the first house is its failure to name, its barrenness of words: "No name; no scrawled or written things; no book, was in the house; no one memorial speaking of its former occupants. It was dumb as death" (115). Namelessness is for Isabel the absence of any human sign.

Isabel is more than the traceless orphan whose utterly dark origin calls into question her humanity; she is the child so deprived of human contact that she is uncertain about how to name what is human. "No living human soul came to the house," except a nameless man and woman whom Isabel hardly recognizes as human: "To me the man and the woman were just like the cat; none of them would speak to me" (116). Because no one will speak to her, Isabel is deprived of the names for things, and deprived of recognition, of knowing herself as human by being reflected in other human beings. Isabel is the entirely eccentric, the opposite of Pierre Glendinning, the perfect duplicate. The second house she inhabits, an "unnameable large house" (138) or madhouse, is the place not simply where others refuse to speak to her, but where they have lost that ability, imprisoned in the silence of madness—a danger that threatens Isabel throughout the novel: "most of them [the inhabitants] were dumb, and could not, or would not speak, or had forgotten how to speak" (120).

Isabel thinks herself saved when, in the third house of her story, she lives with a family and acquires her first names: "human," "mother," and "father." With the child's three symbolic houses, Melville reminds us of the romantic proclivity for parables of the soul's development—Keats's Mansion of Many Apartments, say, or its precursor, Wordsworth's three stages of development in "Tintern Abbey." Isabel does not, however, begin her education like Wordsworth's blessed infant babe who takes in the universe at its mother's breast, but as the spectator of such a babe: "how I envied it, lying in its happy mother's breast, and drawing life and gladness, and all its perpetual smilingness from that white and smiling breast" (122). By watching the fortunate child, Isabel discovers at a distance what it is to be human: "This beautiful infant first brought me to my own mind, as it were; first made me sensible that I was something different from stones, trees, cats; first undid in me the fancy that all people were as stones, trees, cats; first filled me with the sweet idea of humanness" (122). Through the crucial name "human" Isabel learns the lesson of differentiation that at the same time makes her part of a community: "That thing is not human, but I am human" (122). Isabel's decision that she is human has less the effect of convincing us of this fact than of making us question what we actually mean by "human," what border—of language, of names, of self-consciousness, of duplication and identification, of family history—the child must cross before winning the name "human." I recall Mrs. Glendinning's response to Isabel: "My own only son married to an unknown—thing!" (193).

Isabel is a study in what it means to acquire names before we acquire the things themselves. When Isabel tells Pierre, "speech being sometimes before the thought; so, often, my own tongue teaches me new things" (123), we recognize the way in which the possession of names may precede the comprehension of the things named. Isabel's story tragically exaggerates this gulf because, unlike most children, she is the orphan who by definition lacks the objects to which the names apply. While the typical young child mistakenly makes "Mother" a proper name by which all people should call his or her own mother, Isabel makes the mistake in the opposite direction: "I called the woman mother, and so did the other girls; yet the woman often kissed them, but seldom me" (123). Similarly, Isabel fails to understand that the name "Father" by which she calls Glendinning—in this case, her parent in fact—designates a special relation: "Then he whispered a word into my ear; 'Father,' was the word he whispered; the same word by which the young girls called the farmer.

Then I knew it was the word of kindness and of kisses. I kissed the gentleman" (124); "I did not then join in my mind with the word father, all those peculiar associations which the term ordinarily inspires in children. The word father only seemed a word of general love and endearment to me—little or nothing more; it did not seem to involve any claim of any sort, one way or the other" (145). Like the monster in *Frankenstein*, who learns words by spying from the outside on the family he wishes to call his own, Isabel seems on the ouside of such simple names as "Mother" and "Father." Even her use of "human" does not differentiate her from the world of things: "I thanked the bright human summer, and the joyful human sun in the sky" (123). Rather than demystifying the world of names so that things and people stand naked and clear—a philosophic idealism that the ambiguities of *Pierre* will not allow—Isabel's story shows the world confounded in namelessness, and then named too late, named from the outside, named eccentrically. Isabel's misapplication of names makes an ironic but poignant commentary on the text's initial caution about names: for Isabel, such humble names as "Mother," "Father," and "human" announce the mighty things she neither has nor comprehends.

The plot of revolution in *Pierre* begins with a rebuke to the tradition in which the child perpetuates the father by carrying his face and name into the future. Pierre reacts to the knowledge of Isabel by "obeying an irresistible nameless impulse": he reverses the portrait of his adulterous father on the wall and stares at the "defaced" (87) back. Pierre even performs a symbolic parricide on the already dead father by burning his portrait and refusing "to rescue the imploring face" (199). It is an erasure of the father that, in a novel like *Oliver Twist*, we associate with the evil disfigured son Monks, and not with the son who is the living copy. Pierre's prayer to be cured of the illusion of paternal value takes the form of a wish to be defaced himself: "deface in me the detested and distorted images of all . . . convenient lies and duty-subterfuges" (107). Merely upon receiving Isabel's letter, the face he sees in the mirror has "the outline of Pierre, but now strangely filled with features transformed, and unfamiliar to him" (62). Pierre finally reverses the convention by which the child is cast out: in *Pierre* the son "banish[es]" (197) the father, declaring, "I will no more have a father" (87). Hence Isabel's letter begins "Pierre's great life-revolution" (225); it "revolutionize[s] all the circumstances of his life" (92); it causes "the interregnum of all hereditary beliefs" (87). Pierre's life-revolution fulfills the narrator's earlier prediction that the hero's youthful pride in his family's patriarchal system would wane—in short, that we would have an American plot: "believe me you will pronounce Pierre a thorough-going Democrat in time; perhaps a little too Radical altogether to your fancy" (13). Casting out his father, Pierre nonetheless describes himself as the abandoned one: "Henceforth, cast-out Pierre hath no paternity, and no past" (199). Pierre's strategy here is to become a Democrat by making himself over into Isabel, making their stories the same, turning himself into the nameless orphan—in short, by giving up everything to which the name Pierre Glendinning entitles him, becoming (in the words of his mother) "he who was once Pierre Glendinning" (185).

Pierre disinherits himself for another reason. He realizes that, along with his father's name and face, and wealth and land, he inherits his father's sin. The New World, as *Pierre* imagines it, is not free from the Old Law; perhaps this is the tragic consequence of transplanting the patriarchal system to America. The letter of the law declares that the sin of the father is, in the family plot in America as well as in England, the law of heredity: "the infamous consequences of sin shall be hereditary" (100). One could read the tradition of the novel as a commentary on the Old Testament text, "the sins of the father shall be visited upon the children" (100), directly alluded to in such novels as *Tom Jones*, *Bleak House*, *Oliver Twist*, *Tess of the d'Urbervilles*, *Daniel Deronda*, *The Ordeal of Richard Feverel*, and *Absalom, Absalom!* The response to the biblical text seems to shift rather predictably with history. In *The Castle of Otranto* the allusion appears at the beginning of the text as the unambiguous moral of the tale, while by the time we reach the Victorian period it comes under attack in a rather straightforward argument for social reform in Wilkie Collins's novel tellingly entitled *No Name*. But Gothic fiction actually turns out to be the crucial bridge between the novels of Fielding and Smollett, where the bastard wins his birthright as the comic solution to the plot, and nineteenth- and early twentieth-century fiction, where the Gothic family curse is reinvented and modernized through tragic conceptions of heredity, repetition, and retributive justice, in such novelists as Dickens, Hawthorne, Melville, Hardy, Conrad, and Faulkner.

The novel typically imagines the sins of the fathers visited upon the children in the form of a bodily inscription. In chapter 2 on *Oliver Twist* I took up the figure of the marked brow and the way in which it functions equivocally as the mark of familial identity that, at the same time, can represent the mark of infamy. Mordecai's remark to his sister Mirah in *Daniel Deronda* makes this clear: "That such a man is our father is a brand on our flesh."[4] I now wish to extend such an idea by examining how the child's body is seen as recording a crucial moment in the text of the family history. In the darkest version of this idea, the sins of the father inscribe the child's memory, or heart, or soul, or face—an idea that we meet time and again in the novelistic tradition, especially in the figure of the marked son or daughter. In *Pierre* Isabel uncovers a crucial but hidden chapter in the authentic family text, inscribed but nearly effaced on Pierre's own memory: "if, in after-life, Fate puts the chemic key of the cipher into his [the child's] hands; then how swiftly and how wonderfully, he reads all the obscurest and most obliterate inscriptions he finds in his memory; yea, and rummages himself all over, for still hidden writings to read" (70). In such a view the child's body carries a complex linguistic sign that is charged with the potential significance of unlocking a larger linguistic puzzle—the authentic, complete edition of the family text. The question becomes, will the child eventually be able to read the marks that write up the complete text of the family history? Will Pierre be able to read the inscriptions on his memory, and will Esther in *Bleak House* and Razumov in *Under Western Eyes* be able to read the marks and traces on their faces?[5] Such inscriptions punish the child for the sins of the father by marking the child's body with the letter of the law. In this way the child becomes equal to an enigmatic linguistic sign that can either complete the family text or make the central hiatus in it; hence, the "entirely strange" name of Isabel, once understood, may eventually revise the Glendinning genealogy, just as the unreadable "hieroglyphic" Pearl in *The Scarlet Letter* may some day be deciphered and made part of a readable family history. In all these cases, the child's body carries the sign of the father's sin, just as the entire body of the bastard child always functions as the visible sign of the parents' crime.

The inscription on Pierre's memory eventually forces on him the role of reader, a role that every crucial moment of his life requires of him, whether reading human identity ("Read me through and through," Lucy enjoins him [40]); or the letter that reveals the deep familial bond (Isabel's "Read, Pierre, though by reading thou may'st entangle thyself" [63]); or the letter that asks him to fake the familial bond (Lucy's letter of "cousinship"); or the enigmatic (but all too deeply understood) Plinlimmon pamphlet; or the letter from Glen Stanly and Frederic Tartan (which provokes the final deaths). The message remains the same: Pierre's ultimate lesson must be in learning how to read: "hitherto I have but piled up words; bought books, and bought some small experiences, and builded me in libraries; now I sit down and read" (91). Keeping in mind this view of Pierre as reader—especially as the reader of the inscription on his memory that records the sin of the father—we recall that the family plot of *Pierre* begins in chapter 2, with the young hero

reading the (inauthentic) text of his family, contemplating a single emen-
dation: "So perfect to Pierre had long seemed the illuminated scroll of his
life thus far, that only one hiatus was discoverable by him in that sweetly-
writ manuscript. A sister had been omitted from the text" (7). The irony
is almost heavy-handed when the sister arrives on the scene, not as the
completion of the incomplete text, but as its alternate, its counterstate-
ment, its negation—as the bastard nameless half-sister, the hiatus not
emended but personified. The entire denouement of the novel depends on
Pierre's reaction to the dark inscription of his father's sin, to the obscure
text printed within himself that negates the perfectly illuminated scroll.

If the first ambiguity of *Pierre* shows how mighty lordships, based on
nominal title, hold sway in America as they do in England, and if the
second ambiguity shows how namelessness, in Isabel's story, works not
to clarify things but to confound and madden the child as the deepest sign
of her abandonment, then the third ambiguity of *Pierre* shows how
Pierre's revolution is a disastrous regression, so that his embracing of
namelessness becomes a covert form, first, of protecting the father's name
and, second, of disallowing the child's name. Both of these acts function
to blot out the dark inscription on his memory. While Pierre decides to
protect Isabel, to make good her claim as sister, he is motivated at least as
powerfully by a prior—and reactionary—claim: he must protect "the
good name of the purest of husbands and parents" (170). While Pierre
furiously attempts to eradicate the face and name of his father from his
own memory, he refuses to allow his mother and the community to know
his father's crime. In this way he attempts to hold the sacred past of the
father "inviolate," "intact," "untouched" (177–78)—terms which, he
naively fails to recognize, reflect on the father's illegal engendering of the
bastard Isabel. The safeguarding of his father's name leads directly to
Pierre's second mistake: he calls Isabel his "wife" and not his "sister." He
sees no other way of protecting both his father and his sister, so he
produces Isabel to his mother, to Lucy, and to the world generally, as his
wife. He does not realize that in so doing he repeats his father's crime; he
refuses Isabel her natural familial title. The father failed to acknowledge
her publicly as "daughter," and now Pierre fails to acknowledge her
publicly as "sister." In this way the revolutionary plot of *Pierre*, like the
love plot in *Clarissa*, becomes an ironic duplication of the primary—and
inescapable—family plot.

One could read the entire plot of *Pierre* through a similar series of
name changes, once one realizes that Pierre is in the habit of arranging
his life through bestowing fictitious names on the women in it. In this
way Pierre uses, albeit in an unconventional way, the patriarchal system

he inherits. First, he calls his mother "sister" in the novel's idyllic prelude where the mother is at once the "dearest mother" (48) (not to mention "Dowager Duchess Glendinning") and a consoling substitute for the sister he lacks. Second, he calls his sister "wife" in the novel's prolonged second movement, where Pierre's self-dedication to truth is undermined in such a "fictitious alliance" (175). The narrator carefully reminds us that this change in names is a tragic variation on the earlier: "the latent germ of Pierre's proposed extraordinary mode of executing his proposed extraordinary resolve—namely, the nominal conversion of a sister into a wife—might have been found in the previous conversational conversion of a mother into a sister. . . . in sport he learnt the terms of woe" (177). For Pierre people become no more than shifting names in a text, signs in an equation: "like an algebraist, for the real Lucy he, in his scheming thoughts, had substituted but a sign—some empty x—and in the ultimate solution of the problem, that empty x still figured; not the real Lucy" (181). The ultimate irony of this name-changing plot initiates *Pierre*'s third and concluding movement by showing us how Lucy finds her way back into the tale, at Pierre's side. She seems to have unconsciously divined Pierre's strategies, for she proposes to him that she live with him and his "wife" as his "cousin." Pierre accepts her proposal, and Isabel now exchanges roles with Lucy as the plot's primary dupe: not only is she denied her natural familial title, but she is also denied the information that Lucy is Pierre's ex-fiancée, not his cousin. Only Pierre knows who is hidden behind each false name.

In *Pierre* the hero declares that the goal behind such name changes is to rewrite the family text in order to redeem it. He vows to Isabel, "I stand the sweet penance in my father's stead, thou, in thy mother's. By our earthly acts we shall redeemingly bless both their eternal lots; we will love the pure and perfect love of angel to an angel" (154). But Melville undermines such a view by questioning the pure and single motive of his hero, showing us self-interest in Pierre's self-renunciation, as when the narrator speculates on what Pierre's reaction would have been "if accosted in some squalid lane, a humped, and crippled, hideous girl" (107) had claimed him as her brother. It is such ambiguous motives that make us see Pierre's motivation to fictionalize—to call his sister "wife," for example—not simply as an attempt to redeem a past crime, but also to serve his own desire. This ambiguity makes *Pierre* a dark and self-perplexing mockery of the work that Melville so praised, the work of the friend from whom Melville had grown bitterly estranged by the time of *Pierre*, for it is precisely in *The Scarlet Letter* (as we will see in chapter 4) that Hawthorne makes the delicate distinction between hiding a past crime (with the motive of self-preservation) and redeeming a past crime (with the motive of self-renunciation) through a plot in which the central acts are the altering and withholding of names. Certainly *Pierre* takes over its central topoi from *The Scarlet Letter*: the token, the brand, the blood writing and the flesh writing, the familial or ancestral curse, the adulterous parent, and, not least of all, the attempt to right a wrong done to a woman by a father or an ancestor. It is almost as if *Pierre* is a satire (though a deeply veiled and self-tormenting one) on Hawthorne's project in *The Scarlet Letter*.

Pierre's reaction to the true family history, then, is to fictionalize it, and in this way *Pierre* gives us a privileged moment inside fiction whereby we can witness the fictional act and measure its consequences. *Pierre* allows us to see the fictional act of renaming at two levels. Because Melville gave to the central characters in *Pierre* thinly disguised versions of the names of his own family members,[6] the hero of the novel represents, inside the novel, the fictional plot to change the name that proceeds as well at the authorial level. And I am suggesting that Melville exposes the fictional impulse that seeks to change the family text. In *Pierre*, such an impulse has as its unconscious (or unnamed) goal the bowdlerization of the family text, where true family names are prohibited and where the name of the sinful father remains protected while the sinless child suffers unrecognized. When we study Pierre's acts of renaming in this light we see that *Pierre* reveals the ways in which an author self-consciously contemplates the act of fiction: do I expose myself in fiction, or conceal myself; do I articulate my family history and thereby redeem it, or do I erase it, bury it in ambiguities and false names, in order to forget it, wipe it out? These are questions to which we will return in the course of this study.

Pierre's fictionalized plot suggests that his goal, at its farthest limit, is the redemption of a family history through a kind of eradication. But Pierre's plot of false names flies in the face of what we have learned from Isabel's story, even though he ostensibly places his life at her service. Isabel, who seems to be the muse who sings the song of divine nameless-ness, is the abandoned child who seeks the name that will give her an earthly family and her humanity; after all, she writes to Pierre to claim him as her brother. Isabel seeks to decipher "the talismanic word" (147), to spell out the "abbreviated name" (148), to uncover "the secret name" (149), and in this way she mimics the traditional plot of the bastard which seeks resolution in a name. But Pierre works in fact to achieve the hidden name, the secret name—and he makes it "sister." His philosophical aspirations for the namelessness of truth sink, in the family plot, to an unconventional version of the conventional prohibition of the bastard's true name and the protection of the patriarchal name. Moreover, while Isabel seeks the talismanic name in order to become human, to have a human family, and to share its name(s), Pierre seeks just the opposite. Pierre's way of erasing the father's sin and thereby making the family slate clean is to do away with history altogether, to have no memory and no past. This means no longer being mortal. Upon disinheriting his father and mother, "Pierre felt that deep in him lurked a divine unidentifiableness, that owned no earthly kith or kin" (89). "Thus, in the Enthusiast to Duty, the heaven-begotten Christ is born; and will not own a mortal parent" (106). He similarly converts Isabel's father and mother, the hardwon knowledge of whom is the potential solution to the mystery of Isabel, into abstract phenomena, making Isabel (at least in his own eyes) more than human: "She had impressed him as the glorious child of Pride and Grief, in whose countenance were traceable the divine lineaments of both her parents" (173). Pierre's goal is to become "superhuman, angelical" (309), and Isabel tells him, "Were all men like to thee, then there were no men at all,—mankind extinct in seraphim!" (156). *Pierre* begins by imagining the special province of the American plot as that which allows "man" to come into being; *Pierre* ends by showing us how the revolutionary desire to erase the family text cancels Pierre's humanity in unreal angelhood.

Moreover, rather than being an example of that divine being in whom mankind becomes extinct, Pierre is an example of that human being in whom the family becomes extinct: "his own hand had extinguished his house in slaughtering the only unoutlawed human being by the name of Glendinning" (360). Pierre turns out to be the opposite of Oliver Twist, the child who is the living copy of the parent. If Pierre begins as the symbolic carrier of the ancestral body, "his body only the embalming cerements of his buried dead within" (94), in the end he can declare with literalness, "I leave corpses wherever I go!" (206)—especially family corpses. Oliver Twist and Pierre Glendinning show us the two extremes of power that reside in the child: the regeneration of the family or its extinction. As "the only surnamed male Glendinning extant" (7), Pierre reminds us of the way in which family plots are drawn to the sole surviving carrier of the family name—Jack Durbeyfield in *Tess of the d'Urbervilles*, or Lovelace in *Clarissa*, or Roderick Usher in Poe's "The Fall of the House of Usher," or Maury Bascomb in *The Sound and the Fury*. Pierre's failure to replot the family text, to rewrite the genealogy, ends it. The child, not in charge of his own birth, bewailing the day he or she was born (Clarissa and Tess are notable examples), takes charge of his or her own death; it is the final power the child has. It is the way out of what is variously conceived as the fatality of heredity, family reduplication, or the family curse (from Hawthorne and Melville through Hardy to Faulkner). It is the child's cry against engendering, against being born. We hear it in Tess's suicidal sacrifice of herself and in her murder of the (albeit false) bearer of the family name; in Clarissa's elaborate management of her own death or quasi-suicide, after she courts death as the final displacement of Lovelace and the ultimate refusal to bear him a child; in Father Time's murders and suicide in *Jude*; in the plot that has one male child castrated, the second take his own life, and the third swear off women in *The Sound and the Fury*; in Pierre's murders and suicide. Pierre takes poison from the sister who, in the plot's final exchange of family roles, becomes the mother (we have already seen the mother as sister): "Girl! wife or sister, saint or fiend! . . . in thy breasts, life for infants lodgeth not, but death-milk for thee and me!" (360). Pierre takes charge of his existence by being the double of the mother, who imagines the following malediction for her son: "Oh viper! had I thee now in me, I would be a suicide and a murderer with one blow!" (194).

This freedom from the family, in death, appears to be Pierre's final desire. It is apparently the only freedom from names. In *Pierre* the world is obsessively, ridiculously inscribed, inscribed to the point of madness, especially with the name. One finds the name everywhere, as a half-teasing inscription that one can hardly decipher and can never escape. It appears as the hammered but half-obliterated initials ⸀ ⸄ a rock, or it invidiously seeks one out, invisibly buried in the heart of a handkerchief or secreted in the belly of a guitar. One's entire anatomy seems no more than a scripted text—there is the "poor book of Isabel" (156), and the fleshless Lucy shrinks up in death "like a scroll" (360)—so that not only the memory (as we have seen) but the soul (62, 69, 304), the mind (62), the heart are all invited to reveal their inscriptions: "could'st thou take out my heart, and look at it in thy hand, then thou woulds't find it all over written" (158). But worst of all, such inscriptions typically taunt us from the inside. From one's innards, one hears the cry to read and make public the text, even if it means turning oneself inside out: "Tear thyself open, and read there the confounding story of thy blind dotishness!" (171). There is not even the hope of localizing the name so that one can remove it, cut it out of oneself: "were it like this dress, I would tear my name off from me, and burn it till it shriveled to a crisp!" (193). The fact is, "From the spell of that name . . . [one] never afterward escaped" (342). In such examples *Pierre* provides us with a grotesque version of the way in which the self lives and dies in the eternally corrosive soil of a name.

As an American novel, *Pierre* imagines reaching some higher wisdom by climbing out of the naming plot altogether. It is, in my model of three paradigmatic naming plots, a description neither of the name lost nor of the name found, but a genuinely revolutionary search after namelessness, where what I have been calling fiction's attack on the names that philosophers bestow becomes an attempt at transcending philosophy and names once and for all: "from that divine thing without a name, those impostor philosophers pretend somehow to have got an answer" (208). But I have tried to show how the attempt at divine namelessness in *Pierre* founders precisely in the characters' mortality, especially in the family plot that makes each of us sons and daughters.

There remains one final way of attempting to escape names in *Pierre*: to forge out of the multiplicity and arbitrariness of names a conception of ambiguity that will be equal to namelessness itself. In other words, the second half of the title of the novel, *The Ambiguities*, takes as its goal a namelessness founded in the interchangeability of names, and for this reason the term *ambiguity* appears in the text coupled with "namelessness," as in the phrase "ever-nameless, and ambiguous" (196), or as the basis of that narrative act of silence that claims its right to nameless ambiguity: "Some nameless struggles of the soul can not be painted, and some woes will not be told. Let the ambiguous procession of events reveal their own ambiguousness" (181). But this is hardly a solution; in fact, it seems in its own way peculiarly philosophic, a stance outside of life, comfortable only for the spectator, the quasi-philosophic narrator who can keep the ambiguities turning as the hero descends from one circle of hell to another in the plot of *Pierre*. Such a view does succeed in destroying the old order at least from one angle. What holds the world together, in *Clarissa* as well as in *Oliver Twist*, is the unambiguous distinction between names, between virtue and vice or good and evil. The child, in both cases, is the test case whereby the difference between such names is proved. Clarissa dies for such names, and Oliver survives to uphold the difference between them. When we see how Pierre dissolves in names—in "Virtue" that is "Vice" (274), in "Life" that is "Death" (124), in a philosophic round robin in which every name is "Another name for the other name" (274)—we realize that the ambiguity which poses as a pure namelessness is no more than a deadly language game, or what's worse, a hopeless nihilism, which is precisely what I think Melville intends by a "democratic" plot in *Pierre*.

PART TWO

FICTION AND FAMILY DISCOURSE

Come, in fairness,
tell me the name you bore in that far country;
how were you known to family, and neighbors?
No man is nameless—no man, good or bad,
but gets a name in his first infancy,
none being born, unless a mother bears him!

HOMER, *The Odyssey*

The child has got no name yet, though he will be two months old on Thursday next. . . . I don't know who he's like. . . . I think a child should be allowed to take his father's or mother's name at will on coming of age.

JAMES JOYCE, Letter to Stanislaus Joyce

He was my son;
But I do wash his name out of my blood . . .

SHAKESPEARE, *All's Well That Ends Well*

4

The Scarlet Letter

At one level the plot of *The Scarlet Letter* reinvents what we have seen as the Platonic search for the name: the entire narrative depends on whatever hinders or hastens the fulfillment of the Puritan injunction, "Speak out the name" (iii, 54), or, as its purport is more accurately defined, "speak out the guilty name" (iii, 53).[1] At such a level the text is shaped by the Puritan law, which requires the ur-name, the master name; it is the criminal's name, the name of the lawless father. But the narrative project in *The Scarlet Letter* revises the goal of Puritan law, and even at the close of the novel the name of Hester Prynne's fellow transgressor is not spoken in the way in which the Puritans require, as the single guilty name. While the text derives much of its intensity of focus from the community's interest in this hidden name, *The Scarlet Letter* shows us a family that is tragically splintered because all four of its members are unnamed or misnamed. It is in this way that *The Scarlet Letter* enlarges the mystery of the single guilty name into the issue of naming within the family generally.

Hawthorne and his characters imagine naming as an act of potency: "Speak; and give your child a father!" (iii, 54). After all, to recognize publicly one's kindred is the moral concomitant to engendering, defining the family not merely biologically but morally. But the ban of silence lies on everyone in *The Scarlet Letter*. The act of naming is baffled everywhere in the text, suppressed from without and repressed from within. This paralyzing silence originates with the four family members, in such acts as Hester's refusal to name Pearl's father, Dimmesdale's refusal to name himself as Hester's fellow transgressor, Chillingworth's command that Hester not speak his name, and Hester's refusal to explain to Pearl the name whose abbreviation the mother wears on her bosom. Speech, like the act of engendering itself, is under lock and key, so that in *The Scarlet Letter* the silence that withholds the name becomes empowered to obscure, to erase, to violate, and to orphan. The text's origin, therefore, lies less in the crime of sexual transgression than in the crime of silence.

In the first part of this chapter I will examine the silence that prevents those acts that name the members of the family. In the second part I will take up the speech act that breaks this silence: Dimmesdale's confession. I find in the minister's confession a rhetorical strategy that represents the entire fictional enterprise of *The Scarlet Letter*. It is a method of naming that eschews the law's insistence on the single guilty name, the literal name. The first consequence of such a discovery is a revision of our understanding of the terms by which we name ourselves and others. The second consequence is a revision of our understanding of the ends of fiction. In its exploration of the question of naming, fiction develops a critique of literalism, and thereby finds in its own fictionality an antidote to the letter—and the name—that killeth. In fact, the entire project of fiction can be seen as a complicated series of revisionary acts of naming.

"The guilty name"

The ban of silence in *The Scarlet Letter* appropriately begins when all four family members are brought together for the first time. The first act that the reader sees Chillingworth perform is an act that silences another: the physician raises his finger and lays it on his lips, gesturing Hester not to reveal his identity. This gesture of silence precedes, only by moments, Hester's crucial act in the same chapter: "Madame Hester absolutely refuseth to speak" (iii, 49). Hester's silence is, of course, meant to protect Dimmesdale, but Hawthorne begins at this point to show us a strange complicity between the two men. At first Dimmesdale seems to be Chillingworth's opposite because the minister appears to be asking Hester to reveal his identity, to name him as her fellow criminal. But Dimmesdale's speech is equal to Chillingworth's silence. He calls on Hester to speak, but he delights in her silence: "Wondrous strength and generosity of a woman's heart! She will not speak!" (iii, 54). Hester's silence, then, hides the identities of both men or, what amounts to the same thing in this text, their familial relationship to her and her child. At the same time this silence begins a new bond: silence obfuscates the differences between husband and lover. The two are one in their single desire to have the woman remain silent.

Hawthorne places the events I have just described side by side in the chapter shrewdly entitled "The Recognition." Hawthorne has in mind here the Aristotelian idea of *anagnorisis*, or "the change from ignorance to knowledge of a bond of love or hate."[2] In *The Scarlet Letter* the obfuscated and persistently delayed recognition of enemy and kindred—another way, for both Hawthorne and Aristotle, of putting the dichotomy between "hatred and love" (xxiv, 193)—is the source of the prolonged suffering of each of the family members. "The Recognition," standing as an introduction to the family as a group, is an ironic title; no recognitions are made public, and even those that occur are unrealized in the deepest sense. When Dimmesdale requests that Hester speak the name of Pearl's father, for example, the power of his voice almost gives him away to his child, "for it [the baby] directed its hither-to vacant gaze towards Mr. Dimmesdale, and held up its little arms" (iii, 53). But the blood bond is not publicly recognized. It is instead painfully pictured in the child's helpless gesture toward her hidden father. The child unable to speak is at the mercy of adult hypocrisy, false words, and false names. In fact, the chapter closes with a silencing of the child that, with Hester's silence over Dimmesdale and Chillingworth, brings all four family members under the same tragic cover of silence: "The infant . . . pierced the air with its wailings and screams; she [Hester] strove to hush it, mechanically, but seemed scarcely to sympathize with its trouble."

"The Recognition" ends with mother and child once again disappearing behind the "iron-clamped portal" (iii, 54) of the Puritan jail, but now we understand how the self is incarcerated within the walls of its own silence. The text deliberately connects silence and symbolic imprisonment, explaining how Chillingworth possesses "the lock and key of her [Hester's] silence" (ix, 87–88). Hester is imprisoned in this way in "The Interview" (the chapter following "The Recognition"), where the power of speech is subverted, to be used in the service of silence. Chillingworth replaces the blood bond with the "secret bond" not to speak—Hester's slavish bondage, her "oath" (iv, 59) to silence. The prison of silence is equal to his repetition of the suffocating command, "Breathe not" (iv, 59). The silence Hester keeps in order to protect her lover merges with the silence that prevents him from discovering the identity of his worst enemy. If speech is the medium for recognizing the difference between kindred and enemy, silence dissolves the difference between the real father and the evil father-surrogate or "enemy" (xiii, 116). The family drama of *The Scarlet Letter* is played out between the subverted recognitions I have just described and the recognition scene that occurs between child and father at the end. But, as I will show, with a child consistently hushed and educated in the family language by her mother and the Puritan authorities, and with a father who, even when he speaks the truth, transforms it into falsehood, the denouement of the tale is delayed.[3]

The crying infant hushed mechanically by its mother becomes the child learning to speak, but in this apparent progression we learn how the methods of silence are merely refined. When Mr. Wilson asks Pearl who she is, he seems to be rephrasing, without the sharp edge of command, his earlier call to Hester to speak. But we soon see that the apparently open question is a disguised command to answer by the book. The question of the child's identity is persistently reshaped by an inevitable corollary. Mr. Wilson first asks Pearl, "who art thou?" and then, "Canst thou tell me, my child, who made thee?" (viii, 81, 83). It is essentially the same question asked of Hester, but now Mr. Wilson wants a different answer—not the earthly father, but the Heavenly Father. In this way Mr. Wilson inadvertently contributes to Hester's hiding of the father. The child is viewed as the product of a mysterious and contradictory process in which her maker is either spiritual or biological or—worse—indiscriminately both. In Pearl's case, both answers are incomprehensible; both fathers are absent, invisible, bodiless.

Pearl's refusal to name "the Heavenly Father" as her maker is, stated baldly, a refusal to name Him, the unnameable source of her being, that "Creator of all Flesh" (viii, 85) who is fleshless himself. The Heavenly Father here seems at once an idealized and ironic double of the earthly father who neglects to name Pearl, and who, after engendering her, disappears from the flesh. She might as well invent her identity, since she seems an invention, a fanciful unreality: "the child finally announced that she had not been made at all, but had been plucked by her mother off the bush of wild roses, that grew by the prison-door" (viii, 83). The fatherless and lawless child appropriately provides her own genealogy according to no law we can understand, as if she were a freak of nature, either plucked from a rose bush or engendered by one parent alone: "I am mother's child" (viii, 81).

Pearl's mother questions the child's origin by repeating the pattern of Mr. Wilson's questions: "Tell me, then, what thou art, and who sent thee hither" (vi, 74). The mother's puzzlement over who made the child— Pearl's own identity is consistently displaced in the search for another's— reaches its farthest point when Hester questions even the immediate and visible bond that is the child's only certain knowledge: "Child, what art thou? . . . Art thou my child, in very truth?" (vi, 73). Hester actually disowns Pearl "half playfully" in what must be a bad joke: "Thou art not my child!" (vi, 73). Both father and mother, then, deny Pearl her source. For these reasons the name the mother bestows, the child's other source of certain identity, becomes the locus of abuse and displacement, and a way of disqualifying Pearl's human nature, for even Pearl's mother "could not help questioning whether Pearl was a human child" (vi, 69). Pearl is identified through a series of "ill name[s]" (xxii, 174) that place in quarantine the child who is so avoided she must be considered contagious: she is a "demon offspring" (xxiv, 184), an "imp of evil" (vi, 70), an "airy sprite" (vi, 69), and a "little elf" (vi, 69). We will momentarily see that what Pearl suffers—not being allowed a human name because of her mysterious origin—Chillingworth wills for himself (without realizing the consequences) when he chooses "to withdraw his name from the roll of mankind" (ix, 88). Finally, unnamed by her father and ill named by the community, the child is renamed by Mr. Wilson. He objects to the child's answer to his question, "who art thou?" by arguing with her name. Judging by appearances she should be named "Ruby" or "Coral" or "Red Rose"—more names that deny her a human engendering. Such are the liberties taken with an unnamed bastard; Mr. Wilson knows better than the child who made her and the child's own proper name. Pearl's life is specified far outside herself, and her name seems an ironic tease. Mr. Wilson calls her "my child" (has *he* made her?), but she appears to belong to no one. As a bastard, she is a counterfeit pearl, disowned by father and mother alike.

The questions that both Mr. Wilson and Hester direct at Pearl, and the ironic corrections of the child's name, are part of an educative system that confounds the issue of personal identity. The social authorities, as I have already implied, "analyze . . . the child's nature" to find the perpetrator of the crime she represents, and "put the child to due and stated examination" (viii, 86) solely to prove and insure their own beliefs. In such ways the child's life is posited outside itself, and questioned from the outside by a catechism whose questions are hypocritical at worst, rhetorical at best. The child–puppet must give another's answers: Pearl's "one baby-voice served a multitude of imaginary personages" (vi, 71). Pearl's attempt to ask her own questions is limited by a system that allows only two kinds of questions: those that have a priori answers (like "the Heavenly Father") and those that should not be asked at all: "There are many things in this world that a child must not ask about." Nevertheless, Pearl appears in the text, time and again, as an almost disembodied string of questions that have been prohibited: "[S]he put these searching questions, once, and again, and still a third time. . . . What does the letter mean?—and why dost thou wear it?—and why does the minister keep his hand over his heart?" (xv, 130). Such questions are part of the child's native understanding that it is her prerogative to ask, and that the mother (not the child) should explain the scarlet letter: "It is thou that must tell me! . . . Tell me, mother! . . . Do thou tell me!" (vi, 74). When Hester answers that she wears the scarlet letter "for the sake of its gold thread," the narrator marks one of those turning points in the text where the ostensible crime (the sexual transgression) shrinks beside a more profound one: "In all the seven bygone years, Hester Prynne had never before been false to the symbol on her bosom. . . . [S]ome new evil had crept into her heart, or some old one had never been expelled" (xv, 130).

The lie about the letter is so serious because it breaks the sacred bond through which the mother teaches the child the alphabet that articulates her identity and her place in the human community. Hester is, in the educative system I am describing, the teacher of the mother tongue, as Pearl herself acknowledges: "It is the great letter A. Thou hast taught it me in the hornbook" (xv, 128). Hester's refusal to inform the child of the letter's special significance makes the child fail her examination in the simplest of categories, the ABCs of who she is. Hester's final answer to Pearl's questions is a command to be silent, which equals shutting the child away—"Hold thy tongue . . . else I shall shut thee into the dark closet!" (xv, 131)—by returing her to the dark unknown from which she came, denying her here and now, refusing her any existence at all. Not allowed her own questions, kept from the meaning of the letter A, Pearl is reduced either to a perverse silence (self-hushed with a vengeance) or to an incomprehensible language unable to bear or articulate the burden of her rage: "a perversity . . . closed her lips, or impelled her to speak words amiss . . . putting her fingers in her mouth" (vii, 83); "If spoken to, she would not speak again," or would rush forth "with shrill, incoherent exclamations that made her mother tremble, because they had so much the sound of a witch's anathemas in some unknown tongue" (vi, 71).

The child's relentless but unsatisfied questions and the mother's taunting questions and answers about the letter tease Pearl to the quick because, as Hawthorne insists, the child is in fact "the scarlet letter endowed with life!" (vii, 76). Pearl is a baffling linguistic figure come alive: "She had been offered to the world, these seven years past, as the living hieroglyphic, in which was revealed the secret they so darkly sought to hide,—all written in this symbol,—all plainly manifest,—had there been a prophet or magician skilled to read the character of flame!"

(xix, 148). The letter shows Pearl as a contradiction, a language whose meaning is at once self-apparent and mystifyingly in need of being read by another. With Pearl as the letter, Hawthorne chooses to show us the most painful way in which the self depends upon another—namely, through the child who carries her own meaning conceived as another's. Pearl is divided from the meaning she is equal to, whether staring at the mirroring brook, experiencing herself as another (as if her identity resides in a mysteriously impalpable image outside herself), or trying to understand her life conceived as a linguistic equation whose first term (the letter A) she is unable to read. The child's identity is conceived as another's; that is, as a letter she is a clue to the full reading of another's identity. *A* is an abbreviation for *adultery*, even for *Arthur*, while the first two letters of *adultery* are the initials of the father. Pearl, as the first initial of some hidden word or name, is an abbreviated form of her father, just as the face she sees in the mirroring brook (as Dimmesdale fears) traces her father's features and is thereby capable of revealing him as Hester's fellow transgressor. Finally, Pearl is a living hieroglyphic or abbreviation because she is made out of her parents' linguistic half-truths and deceptions. To deny the facts of Pearl's biological making, to deny that she is their own child, is to transform her into a disembodied linguistic conundrum, as Hester's experience shows: "the mother felt like one who has evoked a spirit, but, by some irregularity in the process of conjuration, has failed to win the master-word that should control this new and incomprehensible intelligence" (vi, 70). Hester sees herself as a wizard–scientist who fails to understand the monster–spirit she has conjured, but she (like the father) has in her own keeping the master word that will make Pearl human.

The letter as an unreadable abbreviation of a human life is the most appropriate sign of Pearl's half-life because a letter or a child is, in isolation, a sign divorced from meaning, in need of definition through others. A letter and a child are trapped in a past each is ignorant of, a history of meanings that in turn delimit individual meaning. Each depends upon an authorizing context which, in Pearl's case, is hidden. For this reason Pearl, like a symbolic letter, becomes a battleground of meaning—among parents, society, and heaven. Pearl has only a representative meaning: she is "meant, above all else, to keep the mother's soul alive." In fact, Pearl is a prize to be won, a bargain between two beings outside herself, a middle term, even a test case. Her daughter is supposed to remind Hester that "if she bring the child to heaven, the child also will bring its parent thither!" (viii, 85). But, for the mother, Pearl is as well a constant reminder of her sin and shame, just as for the father who fears he will be traced in his child's features Pearl is the only visible clue that links him to his crime. Because the child, like the scarlet letter, is the public sign of their most private acts, the parents try to obscure its meaning by hushing it, or simply refusing it, denying that it is their own. Such acts become criminal when we realize how meaning becomes human, how the child is the letter endowed with life.

When we are told, "in this one child there were many children" (vi, 68), we see that the statement means two things: first, that Pearl is divided from herself, splintered, and, second, that the child, the character at the center of the text, is a multiple reflection of all the characters in *The Scarlet Letter*. The child, reduced to a mere fleshless symbol of herself (like the image of Pearl in the brook, or the ghostly disembodiments that Dimmesdale and Hester undergo), is a helpless creature in another's control, denied meaning by others (mastered by another's master words and silences), living in fear of the incomprehensibility of another. At the same time, the process of conjuration, like that of engendering, shows us that the creator's magic backfires. The control we think we exert over another often produces a new, incomprehensible, and uncontrollable intelligence. Hence Pearl is a "deadly symbol" (xix, 151), the letter that killeth. Pearl's mere gaze at the letter on her mother's breast, for example, is "like the stroke of sudden death" (vi, 73). In the person of the child the letter becomes a vengeful literalism that strikes through guise and deceit. For the child, despite all the methods of parental and societal control exerted on her, represents an alien other to be feared, and one who—though we may deny it—we in fact produce ourselves.

To move from Pearl's fate to Dimmesdale's is to see how one depends on the other. The child owns him as much as he owns her. The father cannot be himself until he acknowledges his child. Dimmesdale's identity, too, rests on a linguistic deadlock that makes for the durance, and duration, of the tale. On the one hand, neither Pearl's nor Chillingworth's guesses, nor Hester's betrayal of his name, will solve the riddle of the father's identity. The father must speak for himself. On the other hand, Dimmesdale's life fluctuates between two linguistic poles—between asking another to speak for him and speaking for another—that makes solving the riddle impossible. I take this characteristic of Dimmesdale's speech to be the central symptom of a "disorder in his utterance" (xx, 156) which Chillingworth, for all his probing of the minister's illness, fails to recognize. By asking another to speak for him and thereby name him, Dimmesdale childishly places his identity outside himself, at the mercy of another. Hester, of course, protects him, and refuses his plea to name him as her fellow transgressor, but even she eventually tries to rename him (the way Mr. Wilson tries to change Pearl to Ruby). She does not realize that to "give up this name of Arthur Dimmesdale, and make thyself another . . . thou canst wear" (xvii, 142), would be to make the minister more lost to himself, and one step closer to another "wearer" (ix, 87) of false names, Roger Chillingworth. When not asking another to name him, Dimmesdale himself speaks for another. Speaking for Hester—she later commands him, "Speak thou for me!" (viii, 84)—is like speaking for his flock generally, or for his God. In this way Dimmesdale becomes a selfless medium, his own voice in another's body or someone else's voice in his body. Such transgressions, meant to hide his crime, only repeat it. As "the mouth-piece of Heaven's messages" (xi, 105), he is like the puppet–child, a linguistic tool given up to represent another's meaning. In fact, just as Pearl is equal to the scarlet letter, Dimmesdale is equal to his voice, to his utterance. While Dimmesdale rightly wonders "that Heaven should see fit to transmit the grand and solemn music of its oracles through so foul an organ-pipe as he" (xx, 160), Hawthorne makes the equation clear. It is not simply mouth, throat, or tongue that Heaven takes over as its conduit, but the whole man, "he." And yet the minister's function as a medium is a useful hiding place that obviates his speaking for himself, being his own person. The father actually courts obfuscation and misrepresentation, and turns those acts that endanger the child— being unnamed or misread or silenced—to his own purposes. His utter-ances are part of a system of counterspeech where even the truth becomes a hiding place, a deception: "The minister well knew—subtle, but re-morseful hypocrite that he was!—the light in which his vague confession would be viewed. . . . He had spoken the very truth, and transformed it into the veriest falsehood" (xi, 106). To speak double, to intend the opposite of what one's words say, repeats the strategy behind his request that Hester reveal his identity.

Such speech acts, like his passion, "hurrieth him out of himself" (x, 101), and thereby show his complete confusion over self and other. The minister eventually moves to the opposite extreme, and by speaking only to himself he literalizes—and unwittingly parodies—the idea of speaking for himself. He imagines speeches (in "The Minister's Vigil" and "The Minister in a Maze") that are in fact never spoken. The self makes itself an audience and attempts recognition without the aid of another. These speeches, spoken only on the inside, completely dispense with other people and divide the self in two; that is, they make Dimmesdale "another" in yet another way. They are a narcissistic self-communication, a misconstrued lesson learned from Dimmesdale's sexual transgression, a false antidote to intercourse with another. Speech, like the self it grounds, has become mere hallucination, mere fantasy. The father works himself like a puppet.

The equivocal status of Dimmesdale's identity—the way he seems both to court obfuscation and yet to suffer from the very acts of speech that make him over into another—is most sharply expressed when he poses for the entire community the "riddle" (ii, 49) of Oedipal identity. In the marketplace Dimmesdale, like Oedipus, calls for the solution of the crime he himself has committed. Knowing that he is the man everyone (himself included) seeks, he is at once a criminal and a hypocrite, a knowing Oedipus. Nonetheless his knowledge of his own identity turns out to be, in substantial ways, incomplete; he, like the child, depends on another. Dimmesdale does not realize that the physician is cast, in this compli-cated family drama, in the role of the minister's father, with the old man's feigned "paternal and reverential love for the young pastor" (ix, 93) an ironic echo of the true father's refusal to come forth and love Pearl. Dimmesdale's accusation of Chillingworth, the father-substitute—"You speak in riddles" (x, 100)—names the crime he himself commits. What Pearl suffers—the painful riddle of the father's identity—is now turned on him. He has a "nameless horror" (xii, 114) of the father-substitute whose namelessness becomes the source of a deadly riddle; "he could not recognize his enemy" (x, 96) in a drama where he withholds recognition from his own flesh-and-blood kin.[4]

Neither Dimmesdale nor Chillingworth realizes that the self disguised, the self that prevents another from recognizing it, is the self lost through the very process of self-defense. Dimmesdale's double failure—to recog-nize Pearl and to recognize Chillingworth—is part of a single confusion: the deliberate failure to recognize one's kindred merges with the involun-tary failure to discover one's enemy. When Chillingworth catches in the mirror a grotesquely evil image of himself "which he could not recognize" (xiv, 124), he doubly represents Dimmesdale; neither man can recognize the leech, neither man can recognize himself (as the enemy). The attack against the simple and easily identifiable enemy becomes the attack against the family member, and ultimately self-attack. The question about the enemy—Dimmesdale asks about Chillingworth, "Who is he? Who is he?" (xii, 114)—merges with the question asked about oneself—Chillingworth asks about Dimmesdale, "Who is he?" (iv, 58). It is the same question asked about the child, the same question one asks about oneself, and for this reason it is first asked in the autobiographical sketch as the question Hawthorne's forefathers ask about him—"What is he?" (12)—and therefore as the motivating force of Hawthorne's entire project.

The father's refusal to recognize his real child leads to his production of a mock child, to his engendering the enemy in and by himself. In this light Pearl (the child) and Chillingworth (the enemy) play a similar role. Both seek to expose Dimmesdale's secret; both ask him leading questions; both frighten him. But who is Chillingworth anyway, and why do his questions often coincide with Pearl's? The man "Chillingworth" comes into being only because of Dimmesdale and Hester's passion; he is as much their child as the unclaimed Pearl. In fact, as the leech, he is the man completely and grotesquely "dependent for the food of his affections and spiritual life upon another" (xxiv, 183), a child dependent on Dimmesdale for the pound of flesh he exacts. Or, to put it another way, the "devil" (xiv, 122) Chillingworth is an example of the guilty offspring produced by men who "propagate a hellish breed within them[selves]" (x, 98). The question asked Pearl, "who made thee?" Chillingworth asks about himself, mystified by the new demonic identity he sees in the mirror: "Who made me so?" (xiv, 125). But while the text persuasively shows how the self is dependent on another, Chillingworth functions as a limit to this idea; he is responsible for himself (even as he allows himself to become completely dependent on Dimmesdale). One could argue that the two men reciprocally produce each other; like Dimmesdale's guilt, Chillingworth's revenge produces the enemy. The real child Pearl is lost among the shadow children produced in these mock engenderings. But then Pearl learns to play the same game: she engenders her own dummy "offspring," "puppets" who are nameless and passive victims held in the child–parent's power. The child repeats the way in which she is displaced—through mock engendering and through viewing her offspring as "enemies" (vi, 71–72).

The family member frames and limits one's life, but in what sense he assumes the publicly recognized, or even literal, relationship of kindred is another matter; he is a sign, like "A," with too many significations. Family titles, one could argue, are linguistic shifters,[5] like the pronoun "he" that alternately represents Dimmesdale, Chillingworth, and Hawthorne himself; they relativize the single proper name (which, in this text, is already a ghostly sign, if not a downright lie). The names "parent" and "child," for example, shift both literally (the text carefully shows us both Hester and Dimmesdale as children by showing us their parents) and symbolically (with Chillingworth as the product of Hester and Dimmesdale's passion, or of Dimmesdale's guilt; with Hester as Dimmesdale's mother, when he walks with "the wavering effort of an infant, with its mother's arms in view" [xxiii, 177]; with Pearl as the parent of her play offspring, or an "authority" over Hester and Dimmesdale [xix, 149]).

The family's acts of silence unwittingly bring such meanings to the surface and reveal that the deepest family discourse—not the one the world finds acceptable—casts the family member in every role, including that of enemy. The letter of the law tries to control such meanings, to fix such names as "father" and "husband" and "child," but the scarlet letter, as it exhausts the single meaning the law attaches to it, exhausts such controls generally. It is the badge every family member wears.

The sexual act lies outside the narrative not because of some peculiar Puritanical censor at work in Hawthorne, but because the family itself redefines engenderment. Hawthorne shows the family as the creator of its own system of suppression, torture, and violation. This is the deepest meaning of engenderment in *The Scarlet Letter*—the violation and death the family makes for itself. In *The Scarlet Letter*, the family sees fall before its own eyes the mythology that divides enemy from kindred, other from self, in a mythology that every family makes itself. In this light the search after the identity of Pearl's father, after his proper name and the child's, is foiled not simply because of the particular acts of secrecy and deception performed by particular family members, but because it is the nature of families, and the self they define, to undermine such literal, fixed, or single names. For such reasons the text postpones through its entirety answering the literal questions the community asks. Who is the father, or, for that matter, who the child? What is the crime, and who the criminal? Who is *he*?

On the border in fiction

The foregoing discussion of silence and speech, and of parent and child, is open to the charge of being incomplete. I have neglected Dimmesdale's confession, the speech that names the child's father. Moreover, I have neglected to say that the acts of silence (and counterspeech) that make up the action of the tale are anticipated and framed by the author's own analogous acts. In the first sentence of the text Hawthorne is "taken possession of," against his natural instincts and perhaps better judgment, by an autobiographical urge to speak. At the beginning of "The Custom-House" he hesitates and cautions himself in a stop-and-start-again style almost paralyzed by interrupting dashes (six occur in the first two sentences alone) and limiting conjunctions ("but" and "though" and "however") that reroute the direction of his desire: to speak or not to speak. What finally allows him to write this autobiographical preface is the carefully rehearsed set of checks and balances that becomes its subtext—namely, cautions about speaking, while speaking. The strictures are clear:

the "decorous" (7) and "modest" (37) style of a man who does not want to become "the intrusive author" (6); a writer who is ever ready to "plead guilty" (14) to his mistakes, to avoid "violating either the reader's rights or his own" (7). Hawthorne lays down "the law of literary propriety" (24) that makes speaking "pardonable" (7). To be silent, to hide your name and history from the text of your writing, is to repeat the father's criminal acts of silence, concealment, and abandonment. To speak, to probe and expose another, to unveil oneself in public, is to repeat the speech act that violates—that is, to be at once another's and your own enemy. My excuse for postponing both the father's confession and the author's halting autobiographical prelude stems from my effort to underscore a significant structural device of the text: the confession at the end (postponed by the narrative itself) turns us back to the prefatory essay, where we find Hawthorne's desire to "confess the truth" (34) and the complex desires and laws that possess the author himself in the contest between speech and silence. Dimmesdale is given another double, Hawthorne himself, and the author seems to know already from the start the lesson the reader will learn, namely that both silence and speech can be criminal acts. But this knowledge hardly saves him from their dangers.

When we take a careful look at Dimmesdale's confession and Hawthorne's autobiographical sketch, we begin to see how both, apparently the most sincere acts in the text, might better be termed fictions. The minister's confession holds the key here. Dimmesdale is so much at the center of this text because he exaggerates, to the point of madness, a universal ambivalence: he at once dreads discovery and longs for it. Confession, rather than solving this painful contradiction, underscores it. But Dimmesdale's fictionalized confession protects him at the same time that it lets him speak the truth and name himself.

In *The Scarlet Letter*, confession occurs paradoxically through a process of apparent self-alienation and fiction. During his public confession, Dimmesdale (like a novelist) speaks of himself in the third person: "But there stood one in the midst of you, at whose brand of sin and infamy ye have not shuddered! . . . It was on him! . . . But he hid it cunningly from men, and walked among you. . . . Now, at the death-hour, he stands up before you! He bids you look at Hester's scarlet letter! He tells you, that, with all its mysterious horror, it is but the shadow of what he bears on his own breast, and that even this, his own red stigma, is no more than the type of what has seared his inmost heart" (xxiii, 180). Who is the secret man the minister names? The minister's truest moment, when he is most himself, is a moment of self-alienation, of ghostly autobiography and confession; it shows the self in a mirror, as "he." Appropriately, the man the minister names (or does not name) as "he" answers the question that has echoed through the text: "What is he?" (12) (the forefathers ask about Hawthorne); "Who is he?" (iv, 58) (Chillingworth asks about Dimmesdale); "Then, what was he?" (xi, 105) (the narrator asks about Dimmesdale); "Who is he? Who is he?" (xii, 114) (Dimmesdale asks about Chillingworth). "He" is the man who walks always beside you, unrecognized. Dimmesdale finally becomes the "exemplary man" (xx, 153) in an unexpected way—not through his virtue, but through his power of representation. A man dramatizes himself, to himself and others, as another; he makes himself visible, to himself and others, in a reflection, or a representation that is fictional; he/"he" tells the truth.

The fiction of Dimmesdale's confession, as I understand it, is defined in opposition to *The Scarlet Letter*'s view of writing in general. Writing is a form of literalization that puts the blame simply and mercilessly on another. The text's powerful example here is the way in which the Puritans use writing to label Hester. Fiction, on the other hand, is a more generous and complicated form of what Hawthorne in another context sees as "the propensity of human nature to tell the very worst of itself, when embodied in the person of another" (xiii, 118)—in other words, to confess as "he," like Dimmesdale or like a novelist. There is a discrimination here that will become clearer as my argument proceeds, but let me immediately try to clarify my terms, admitting that while writing and fiction are close doubles, the slightest discrimination makes all the difference—between branding and casting out a single victim, and accusing an unspecified person who walks among you; between depersonalization as attack (writing's criminal is the Adulteress, the dehumanized Hester), and impersonalization as merciful defense (fiction's criminal is an unnamed "he"). Writing violates, with a sharp-edged instrument; fiction deflects and defends, with a language that shows that pain and guilt are common to all. These are the two ways in which the two criminals of adultery are named in the text: one is named by another at the beginning of the text, while one is named as another by himself at the end of the text. The first is an object of scorn set apart from all others; the second is "he" conceived as the invisible self that we all share but fail to recognize.

In writing (as in the simplified discourse families use) you accuse another in place of yourself; the confusion over self and other is naively solved by labelling the other a criminal. But Hawthorne shows that this kind of writing is itself a crime. Reduced to a "text" (v, 65), "giving up her individuality, she [Hester] would become the general symbol at which the preacher and moralist might point, and in which they might vivify and embody their images of woman's frailty and sinful passion" (v, 60).

Text and symbol vivify and embody, but at great cost; they mortify and feed off Hester in a further example of the text's view of the parasite or leech. Writing as embodiment takes over the body to make it a symbolic representation, "the body . . . of sin" (v, 61). As writers, the Puritans are "iron men" (xvii, 142) who use the equipment of their apparent antitype, "the Black Man." The "iron pen" (xvi, 133) violates and thereby engenders the body of sin (repeating the crime it punishes); Hester's cry is that she has been "too deeply branded" (iii, 54), just as Hawthorne himself complains of the "deep print" (xxiv, 182) in his brain which he cannot erase, the product of self-mortification that follows upon his recognition of his ancestors' crime. In the same movement the iron pen imprisons the body of sin it has made and labels it for all to see. It makes violation and shame public, and this is the most scandalous side of writing. Puritan society, in its search after visible truths in signs, types, and tokens, consistently errs on the side of literalism. The Puritans, in a theological confusion of the Pauline distinction between letter and spirit, transfer the letter of the law from the tables of stone to the fleshy tables of the heart.[6] In this way their writing makes Hester's heart into a dead stone, a "tomblike heart" (xv, 130). The letter is her epitaph, and Hester as a living text or sermon is a dead woman awaiting burial: "Thus she will be a living sermon against sin, until the ignominious letter be engraved upon her tombstone" (iii, 50). The letter on her heart is a proleptic sign that from the beginning seeks fulfillment in the story's final writing, the letter written on the gravestone. The letter is the sign of the "ministration of death, written and engraved in stone" (II Cor. 3:7). Fiction becomes defined against this system of writing—in fact, in order to elude the kind of writing that is part of that "penal machine" in which the gripe "forbid[s] the culprit to hide his face for shame" (ii, 45). Fiction discovers that "neutral territory"—Hawthorne's term for the border "where the Actual and Imaginary may meet" (31)—where it is safe to confess, where you neither label yourself nor are labelled by another. In fiction you speak the truth in the third person.

The scarlet letter itself helps clarify the difference between writing and fiction precisely insofar as it resists the (literal) function the Puritans assign it. In this way it becomes the key to writing's failure when writing tries to fix meaning. The letter's meaning is knotted, intertwined, a complete mesh not to be unravelled. This is why Hawthorne tells us that its art cannot be reproduced or analyzed, "even by the process of picking out the threads" (27). The scarlet letter turns against its Puritan authors by revealing the judges' failure at "disentangling . . . [the] mesh of good and evil" (ii, 51); it comprehends the complexity of human action by representing characters who "continually did one thing or another, which intertwined, in the same inextricable knot" (xi, 108). The "margin" or "edge" or "verge" where Dimmesdale and Chillingworth (xiii, 120; xx, 158) and even Hawthorne the writer (31) live, and where Pearl plays (xiv, 121), is a knotted or entangled world, an *adulterated* world where all things are alloyed. The alchemical search to "distil" (v, 65), to separate out the "residuum" (32), to have the soul "dissolved, and flow forth in a . . . transparent stream" (ix, 92), is foiled in a world in which things are "intermingled" (ii, 46), "thoroughly interfused" (ii, 41), in an "admixture of . . . ingredients" (17). For this reason Pearl (or the letter she is) reminds us of a "necessity that always impelled this child to alloy whatever comfort she might chance to give with a throb of anguish" (xix, 151). "A" stands for such *adultery*—for the knot, the margin, the alloy. It suggests a complex moral world that resists a Manichaean unravelling of good and evil, a simple alchemical distillation of value. Adultery, in this light, is at once an act that lies outside the law of Puritan society and a meaning that explodes the limits of writing.

With this definition before us, the adulterous self is the self shared with another—not necessarily through sexual trespass, but through a marginality that stems from the beginning. "A" stands for *adultery* at the beginning, for the impossibility of finding an unadulterated origin. The text's adulterations are interpolations between epochs, made most patent in the formal movement between the contemporary events of the Custom-House and Puritan New England. The self is an adulterated compound because it exists "across the gulf of time" (12), "across the verge of time" (xiii, 117): "The victim was for ever on the rack" (xi, 103), stretched between times. This is another way of saying that the self is familial, that it contains the genealogical trace or blood guilt of its ancestry. The man Chillingworth is "[m]isshapen from birth" and seeks the "veil" that will disguise his "physical deformity" (iv, 57); the physician's disguise here becomes the object of our mercy. Even Dimmesdale's crime of passion can be referred, at least in part, to someone or something before him: he "inherited a strong animal nature from his father or his mother" (x, 95). The family member, then, is not only the person found on the border of another in his present family relations; he is also the person who is a "residuum" (32) or "diluted repetition" (xxi, 164) or "vestige" (xvii, 141) of the ancestors who went before him. This is what it means to be a daughter or a son, all one's life. The mark on Dimmesdale's breast is the scarlet letter with a particular or literal meaning: Dimmesdale is the man who committed adultery, even as the law defines it. But the mark on his breast is also the universal mark of all men born of woman—"the natal spot" (12).

The idea of the adulterous self—the self that is mixed with another, from the beginning—explains Hawthorne's skepticism about autobiographical speech. Then why preface the tale with an autobiographical sketch? Because, as the analogue to the minister's confession in the third person, the autobiographical sketch fictionalizes the first person. "The Custom-House" exists, at the head of the text, to warn us from the beginning that it does not want to speak the entire truth about the self, nor could it even if it wanted to. It exists to subvert itself, to fictionalize itself deliberately before its own eyes and the reader's. In this light we begin to realize that both sections of this text are alloys. Can we distinguish between the truth of autobiography and the fiction of the tale by saying which event—Hawthorne's discovery of Pue's papers or the death of Governor Winthrop—belongs to which half of the text? The autobiographical sketch is a series of clues and red herrings left at the scene of the crime. Its most blatant lie—Hawthorne's explanation that he is not the author but an editor who has accidently found the story of the scarlet letter—is a repetition of Dimmesdale's criminal concealment, a casting off of the child, a withholding of the father's name. But such a lie reveals a truth that we discover is the heart of the tale as well. First, the lie understands how the self needs to be defended against writing's tendency to literalize, against its own urge to label itself and to assert itself as a subject, against the egotism of thinking itself a first cause. The lie shows that what we call the subject, or in this case the author, is a fiction, as Hawthorne suggests elsewhere: "A person to be writing a tale, and to find that it shapes itself against his intentions; that the characters act otherwise than he thought; that unforeseen events occur, and a catastrophe which he strives in vain to avert. It might shadow forth his own fate—he having made himself one of the personages."[7] The autobiographical sketch makes the author a character (just as the tale does). The man who finds and edits Pue's papers is a fictitious character who nevertheless reveals the truth about "the author" Hawthorne. The autobiographical preface rests on the following paradox: it tells the truth through an oblique and fictionalized attack on the idea of the subject, through an understanding that the self (even when a father or an author)[8] is at least in part the product of another's making. Hawthorne's reminder that "both truth and error" (xix, 149) can coexist in a single impression becomes a warning that the opposites the text contemplates—kindred and enemy, love and hatred, good and evil—and their literary coordinates—autobiography and fiction, author and character—are so many different ways of repeating the same mythical search for purity, the same naive unravelling of self and other. Read in this way, "The Custom-House" bestows upon "I" and "he" the function of doubles, where no one is prior or original; we can use either to hide ourselves, to confess the truth about ourselves.

The fiction in Dimmesdale's confession and in Hawthorne's autobiography is not solely a practical psychological defense. It is also a moral critique of the categorical opposites I have just listed. Fiction understands that the most radical name we bestow upon the self, the name that logically follows from "the author" and "the subject," is "the criminal." The idea of the criminal stems from the false differences the self ascribes to another, the way the self writes him off; we mark him clearly so that we can safely stay away from him. But he is, as my string of associations suggests (the author, the autobiographical subject), the other side of oneself. Based on a darker and more threatening view of the self as a first cause, the term *criminal* shows how the idea of the subject backfires: it can be used against oneself. By showing the family as a tangle of crimes where kindred and enemy often change places, Hawthorne shows how criminal and victim are one, with each member of the family on both sides of the border of crime. In this light the way we typically define the self merges with the discourse of the family: the reified self is the subject–author–criminal–father. The deepest refutation of the idea of the father as first cause shows that what the family (not just the father) *makes* is "mutual victims" (xxiv, 183). Fictionalized autobiography is a formal structure based on the same truth; it shows the author as the editor, and even as a character in his own work, just as it shows the man Hawthorne has behind him a stern "progenitor" (11) and other ancestors. The father is always a child first. This is another way of putting the more philosophical view of the self as an adulterated compound from the beginning, as the object of someone else's making.

The single crime is invisible and unknown, then, not because it is hidden by the criminal (what the Puritans think), but because it is a lie, a false hypothesis. Elsewhere Hawthorne contemplated a kind of fiction that would forgo characters (as the separate entities, or subjects, we usually take them to be) to people the text with conjunctions, "To personify If—But—And—Though &c."[9] But *The Scarlet Letter*'s description of the self as a conjunction of selves already enacts this idea, without capitulating to a moral relativism that relieves us of all responsibility, and all humanity. I recognize I am subject to what has gone before me, to my history, as a means not of excusing myself and escaping my acts, but of participating in the larger world of shame and guilt that I share with another: "I, the present writer, as their representative, hereby take shame upon myself for their sakes" (11). I exist insofar as I am a representative of another at another time; I exist in the place of mercy, between times, on the border of myself and another, in fiction. Mercy, the indwelling form of fiction, rewrites the subject as universal representability, as the exemplary man. And I am he.[10]

That mercy is in fact the form of fiction (and not simply its subject or its effect) is especially well dramatized at certain moments when the narrative comes to a brief halt, in a significant meeting of "author" and "character" (terms that are now as loaded as "self" and "other"). In each case Hawthorne's reticence is a sign of the author's hesitation to judge, to publish another's guilt or shame.[11] There is Hawthorne's hesitation to report that the first object of Pearl's consciousness is the scarlet letter— "shall we say it?" (vi, 72); and his blush at recording (in a recognition of the power of words and their potential criminality) Dimmesdale's scandalous impulse to teach the children wicked words; and his refusal to describe the central revelation of the scarlet letter—"But it were irreverent to describe that revelation" (xxiii, 180); and his modesty about speaking what Hester cannot reveal to herself, namely an undiminished love for Dimmesdale—"It might be, too,—doubtless it was so, although she hid the secret from herself, . . . —it might be," where he shifts back and forth between certainty and doubt, for Hester's sake (v, 61); and even his eschewing to spell out *adultery* anywhere in the text, to fix and publish its meaning; and generally his hesitation to reveal feelings and events "which we have faintly hinted at, but forborne to picture forth" (xi ,107)—in this instance, the minister's midnight vigil, where Hawthorne seems almost to have the vision of the minister's pain forced out of himself: "nay, why should we not speak it?" (xii, 139). Hawthorne seems under a double obligation (to defend his characters and to inform his reader) that is difficult to reconcile: "[to] hesitate to reveal" and "to hold nothing back from the reader" (xx, 153). Silence again and again seems the proper mode of response, even while the story dramatizes a criminal silence—the refusal to name oneself, to recognize one's family, to confess. "It is scarcely decorous, however, to speak all, even when we speak impersonally" (7). It is a crime to speak and not to speak—a riddle that only fiction can begin to solve because, like no other writing, it has as its goal to reveal and to conceal. The foregoing moments of narrative self-consciousness suggest the conjunction of selves that characterizes fiction: where the author hesitates or refuses to write about his characters, I feel I know him best, and see his sympathies most clearly—he gives himself away. In his mercy for his characters he is most himself. It makes mercy no less generous to admit that its teacher can be self-consciousness, and perhaps even narcissism. The pain of speaking autobiographically in "The Custom-House" leads to moral delicacy in the tale. Both author and reader see themselves in the mirror of character, of another, and at the point of painful exposure shrink, and proceed only in the knowledge that in fiction they are defended by seeing themselves in another, by sharing themselves with another, and that in fiction public exposure occurs during the private act of reading. Fiction converts hypocrisy into mercy; what I earlier called the minister's speaking for and as another is what the author does in fiction, and what the reader does in reading, as an expression of mercy for himself and another. In this way fiction erases the Puritan interdict, "transgress not beyond the limits of Heaven's mercy!" (iii, 54), by taking the terrifying border on which characters live in fear of displacement, in desperate confusion over self and other, and refashioning it into a neutral territory. Trespass is converted into sufferance and mercy, the conjunction of selves where we meet.

The minister's voice reaches the same merciful pitch as the author's, when it merges with another's voice because its source is the same: "the same cry of pain" (xxii, 173). When all else deserts one, pain remains, the surest sign that one has a self: "The only truth, that continued to give Mr. Dimmesdale a real existence on this earth, was the anguish in his inmost soul" (xi, 107). Pain substantiates the man not by differentiating him from another, but by allowing him to see himself in others. In this way Dimmesdale discovers the genuine power of speech and identity: "The burden . . . of crime or anguish . . . kept him down, on a level with the lowest. . . . But this very burden it was, that gave him sympathies so intimate with the sinful brotherhood of mankind; so that his heart vibrated in unison with theirs, and received their pain into itself, and sent its own throb of pain through a thousand hearts, in gushes of sad, persuasive eloquence" (xi, 104). Pain gives Dimmesdale a real existence on earth because it makes him human, part of the brotherhood of mankind. Without this human pain, a man "becomes a shadow, or, indeed, ceases to exist" (xi, 107). Pain rewrites one's genealogy. By insistently pressing how Hester bears her almost unbearable pain—"It was almost intolerable to be borne" (ii, 46); "She had borne . . ." (iii, 54)—Hawthorne describes her pain as a new birth: "Her sin, her ignominy, were the roots which she had struck into the soil. It was as if a new birth, with stronger assimilations than the first, had converted the forest-land . . . into Hester Prynne's wild and dreary, but life-long home" (v, 61). The new self, like the "new man" (xxi, 163) Dimmesdale becomes, is born through a crisis in pain that discovers the common heart: "The complaint of a human heart, sorrow-laden, perchance guilty, telling its secret, whether of guilt or sorrow, to the great heart of mankind" (xxii, 173). What will unlock the secret heart is the call to "be once more human" (xiv, 125), spoken in a "human language" (xii, 114), the language that the tale has sought from the beginning.

The humanizing power of pain, its ability to replace one's literal family with "the human family" (15), is the end toward which the tale travels. The discovery of the literal father's identity flows into a larger current of revelation. But to see how the tale's last scene humanizes both father and child, we must first acknowledge that the broken heart can be used as a false sign of humanity, and made an empty symbol: "Not seldom, she [Pearl] would laugh anew, and louder than before, like a thing incapable and unintelligent of human sorrow. Or—but this more rarely happened—she would be convulsed with a rage of grief, and sob out her love for her mother, in broken words, and seem intent on proving that she had a heart, by breaking it" (vi, 70). Pearl instinctively knows that sorrow has the capacity to transform her from "a thing," to make her "human." But Hawthorne knows that to be in love with sorrow—a morbid danger both he and his characters court—is merely to find the darker side of narcissism. Pearl requires "a grief that should deeply touch her, and thus humanize . . . her" (xvi, 133). Her lack of grief shuts her out even from the brook's melancholy sorrow: " 'If thou hadst a sorrow of thine own, the brook might tell thee of it,' answered her mother, 'even as it is telling me of mine!' " (xvi, 135). Of course, Hester's chiding is unfair; Hester and Dimmesdale rob Pearl of her humanity by not allowing her the grief that is her greatest inheritance. Pearl is cut off from all humanity, then, not simply because she is an unlawful child, but because she has neither sorrow nor sympathy. Pearl becomes human only when she understands her father's words at the end, and sees him "in the crisis of acutest pain" (xxiii, 180). The wild infant is prophesied a woman not simply when she learns who her father is, but when she shares his pain. "The great scene of grief, in which the wild infant bore a part, had developed all her sympathies; and as her tears fell upon her father's cheek, they were the pledge that she would grow up amid human joy and sorrow, nor for ever do battle with the world, but be a woman in it" (xxiii, 181). Neither discovering she has a father nor having the father's name is sufficient to make the child human. Pearl becomes herself when her heart is broken for another. The part she bears in the scene of grief bears her anew. What the child learns from her father is how to realize her own pain through another's. Father and child meet on that common ground where each can say: I now can put myself aside for another, instead of living in terror of being put aside by another.

The kiss Pearl bestows upon Dimmesdale in this last scene unlocks a double mystery. Earlier in the forest Pearl refused the minister a kiss as "talisman" (xix, 152) because it was a repetition of the secret passion that begot her. But at the end, in the public marketplace, "Pearl kissed his lips. A spell was broken" (xxiii, 181). Father and child bring each other alive and make readable the ghostly and unintelligible text the other has been. Hawthorne imagines this breaking of a linguistic spell, in another context, for the writer himself: "Here I have made a great blot . . . , a portrait of myself in the mirror of that inkspot. When it reaches thee, it will be nothing but a dull black spot; but now, when I bend over it, there I see myself, as at the bottom of a pool. Thou must not kiss the blot, for the sake of the image it now reflects; though if thou shouldst, it will be a talisman to call me hither again."[12] The pool in which Pearl sees herself reflected becomes, for Hawthorne's own self-reflection, a pool of ink. The spot of ink, the inviolable circle of self, is transgressed only when the reader, in a fictional trespass, offers the talismanic kiss to the text and reawakens it. The talismanic kiss is offered to the shame we seek to hide (Pearl kisses the scarlet letter in the forest when she refuses the minister's kiss) as the sign of a reader who sympathetically can read the heart almost hidden by *The Scarlet Letter.*

Fiction's most significant accomplishment is not, then, the thoroughness with which it defends the self, but its ability to keep the self alive and human while defended. This means keeping pain sharp but bounded. The secret power of fiction is pain, publicly expressed and shared, but deflected and bounded in the ways I have shown. Hawthorne describes Hester's decision to bear her pain in order to purify herself as "half a truth, and half a self-delusion" (v, 62); he hesitantly records (in what I have called his reticent style) her love for Dimmesdale as another source of her decision to remain in the spot of her public ignominy. We think of fiction as such a half-truth, half-delusion, but the sustained cry of pain in this text leaves almost no room for its farthest fantasy, one that the reader along with the writer hides close beside the secret place of pain— namely, to be "wise . . . not through dusky grief, but the ethereal medium of joy" (xxiv, 185–86).

5

Bleak House

As the painful embodiment of a series of injunctions to speak—I recall Pearl's cries, "Tell me! Tell me! . . . It is thou that must tell me!" (vi, 74)—the child in both *The Scarlet Letter* and *Bleak House* is held in bondage to a secret about her own identity. Like Pearl, Esther brings alive, and shows at its most human, the plea for discourse: "Oh, dear godmother, tell me, pray do tell me" (iii, 19).[1] Both children meet the silence that disallows them their lives, the silence that is equal to wishing them unborn: "It would have been far better, little Esther, that you had had no birthday; that you had never been born!" "Ask me no more, child!"

> Oh, do pray tell me something of her [mama]. Do now, at last, dear godmother, if you please! What did I do to her? How did I lose her? Why am I so different from other children, and why is it my fault, dear godmother? No, no, no, don't go away. O, speak to me! (iii, 19)

Like Pearl, Esther is the bastard child, caught in a family plot compounded of silence, misnaming, and namelessness. Like Pearl, she is the palpable—and marked—sign of her parents' crime at the same time that she is unable to read the text of who she is. There is this difference: Esther eventually becomes the writer of her own text. The bastard child shares with the omniscient narrator the responsibility for authoring the text in *Bleak House*.

In this way Esther turns the prohibition against speech into the lengthy narrative in which she writes her own life story. Pearl is the child who finds her freedom at the very end of the text; her womanhood is only a prediction, after which she disappears to resurface briefly as no more than a series of surmises. Esther, on the other hand, writes her own text from that point in time at which she becomes a woman. The writing of her story is itself evidence of the fact that she no longer suffers the bondage of the unnamed and unknowing child. Her womanhood is confirmed in the power of the discourse that she finally commands. In writing, Esther becomes the author of the family plot. She supersedes her parents' desire for silence, their disguise of false names, and in this way she writes the text that they try to erase. She takes the linguistic conundrum that she embodies and transforms it into a readable and reliable text, an achievement that in *The Scarlet Letter* is reserved for the omniscient narrator alone.

As a writer, Esther revises the kind of writing that is most prevalent in *Bleak House*: the writing of the law. As in *The Scarlet Letter*, the law in *Bleak House* functions as a model for a kind of literalism, or what Jarndyce calls the "dead letter" (viii, 88). In the first part of this chapter I will take up the ways in which writing (especially under the aegis of the law) is responsible for the "kindred mystery" (x, 123) of *Bleak House*— the family hidden behind a series of false names. Perhaps even more demonstrably than *The Scarlet Letter*, *Bleak House* presents itself at one level as a plot that seeks to discover the correct name, the kindred name. In the second part of this chapter I will discuss the way in which Esther's lengthy narrative supersedes this search after the key name. In representing so vividly the consequences of the dead letter of the law, *Bleak House* defines its status as fiction by freeing itself from the circumscribed search after the literal family member and the proper name. The discovery of a goal that lies beyond the literal—especially in another kind of naming— belongs to Esther, the ultimate writer of the family text in *Bleak House*.

"Kindred mystery"

Even the title is duplicitous, signalling from the outset that this is a novel whose mysteries depend on naming. When the Lord Chancellor remarks that Bleak House is "a dreary name," Mr. Kenge counters, "But not a dreary place" (iii, 31). This divergence between name and place creates a kind of nostalgia in the novel for that time when words did simply name the objects they represented—"when [for example] Turnstile really was a turnstile" (x, 119). If Bleak House, at least at present, is a pleasant place with a bleak name, it is no wonder (in this topsy-turvy world of names) that there is "a rather ill-favoured and ill-savoured neighbourhood, though one of its rising grounds bears the name of Mount Pleasant" (xxi, 257). Names seem to function not as reliable signposts, but as ironic commentaries on the present text of the place, or even as deliberate masks. Places present themselves through the imposture of names. Even the omniscient narrator puzzles over the name "Tom-all-Alone's" as if he were not himself the maker of names: "Whether 'Tom' is the popular representative of the original plaintiff or defendant in Jarndyce and Jarndyce, or whether Tom lived here when the suit had laid the street waste, all alone, until other settlers came to join him, or whether the traditional title is a comprehensive name for a retreat cut off from honest company and put out of the pale of hope, perhaps nobody knows" (xvi, 198). Was there once a human "Tom" behind the place "Tom," and was he the original bestower of the name, or is such a "Tom" a mere fiction? As signposts, place names seem enigmas that hide rather than disclose the nature and history of the place, and hide especially their own human origins, the originating act of naming. At their worst, place names seem false directions to the traveller who, apparently defrauded, fails to recognize in the destination what the name has suggested to him: go to Bleak House, go to Turnstile, go to Mount Pleasant, even go to Lincoln Inn Fields, and you will discover a world whose mysteries immediately lie in its names. Dickens's embroidery of this last name subtly finds in it an ironic truth, revealing how in the middle of London these are in fact fields, where "the sheep are all made into parchment" (xlii, 514), a brilliant suggestion that takes us to the heart of the novel's understanding of how both places and people are sacrificed, like Hester in *The Scarlet Letter*, to the sign each bears.

If place names function enigmatically in *Bleak House*, we quickly find relief in the realm of the human: the names of people function transparently. I am, of course, referring here to one of the most well-known features of any text by Dickens: the author names his characters by a leading characteristic, as in the cases of Woodcourt, Flite, Krook, and Smallweed.[2] But the central family plot of *Bleak House*, Esther Summerson's story, flows athwart this typical flood of appropriate names, and makes us reconsider this characteristic of Dickens's style: Esther is "friendless, nameless, and unknown" (xvii, 213), and, like her father (alias Nemo, and called Nimrod by Mrs. Snagsby) or her mother (ironically named Honoria), she shows us how the dissociation between name and place is echoed more gravely in the dissociation between name and person. In this context I will begin by investigating *Bleak House* as a novel of misnomers, a mystery story in search of the "proper name" (x,

117), where names—even the novel's own name—seem like "the impromptu name" (xx, 255) Jobling takes, an alias meant to throw us off
the scent.

In investigating personal names in *Bleak House*, one discovers almost
immediately that the apparent division I have just set forth—between
transparently named characters and characters unnamed and misnamed—is misleading. Esther is the test case here. Precisely insofar as
"Esther Summerson" fulfills both categories at once, we realize that the
issue of personal names is more complicated than my initial hypothesis
suggests. While Esther is "friendless, nameless, and unknown," and while
a significant part of the text is given over to the discovery of her unknown
history, she bears one of the text's most patently transparent names, one
whose meaning the text goes so far as to foist on us: "They said there
could be no East wind where Somebody was; they said that wherever
Dame Durden went, there was *sun*shine and *summer* air" (xxx, 378;
emphasis added).[3] Such a name disallows Esther a history, her own
personal history, and instead substitutes a descriptive name that designates her function in the world she presently inhabits. While the minor
characters can bear being swallowed up by their names, with little or no
identity apart from that sounded in the name, Esther's role as heroine in
Bleak House disqualifies such a name for her; in other words, insofar as
the uncovering of her personal history plays a major role in the narrative
unravelling of *Bleak House*, her merely symbolic impromptu name is
insufficient. For this reason all the symbolic names in the world, no
matter how accurately they point to characteristics in Esther, seem finally
to make more apparent that her proper name is unknown: "This was the
beginning of my being called Old Woman, and Little Old Woman, and
Cobweb, and Mrs. Shipton, and Mother Hubbard, and Dame Durden,
and so many names of that sort, that my own name soon became quite
lost among them" (viii, 90). Such names, like the name Summerson,
suggest the way in which Esther's individual identity is sacrificed to her
instrumentality, her common usefulness, just as in *The Scarlet Letter*
Pearl takes her name from the function she represents in the complicated
patterns of punishment, retribution, and reward in her mother's life.

"Summerson" makes us see the way in which being "overnamed"
(where one's name is a symbolic signpost weighted with meaning) can
function as a version of being "undernamed" (where one's true name is
unknown and masked). Such an example makes us ask, where do name
and person meet in balance, without one overwhelming the other? Can
human identity be revealed, or at least signified, in a name? I wish to take
up these questions by looking in detail at "The Law-Writer," a chapter

that explores the problem of naming through an elaborate series of names to which I will now turn—first "Guster," then "Allegory" and "Rumour," and then "Snagsby" and "Peffer," and finally that of the law-writer himself. The chapter has the added interest of containing a central clue about Esther's history—a clue that will reveal the identity of her father, but that at the present moment lies concealed in the name of the chapter itself.

"The Law-Writer" broaches directly the issue of the proper name under the unlikely sign "Guster." While Guster and Mrs. Snagsby are, from the viewpoint of personality, sheer opposites, Dickens questions the notion of the proper name by suggesting that Mrs. Snagsby is a Guster: "This proper name [Guster], so used by Mr. Snagsby, has before now sharpened the wit of the Cook's Courtiers to remark that it ought to be the name of Mrs. Snagsby; seeing that she might with great force and expression be termed a Guster, in compliment to her stormy character" (x, 117). Such a passage calls into question what we mean by a proper name and by names in general. While a proper name is supposed to designate a particular individual, here it overflows traitorously into the world beyond the individual self, seeming to designate two different people at the same time. "Guster" is a common meaning, fixable at various points to various characters. In this light "Guster" hardly seems to identify Guster. We must recall that "Guster" is only a makeshift name, a fabrication; it suggests an origin that cannot be quite read, an original act of naming that is unknown. She is "by some supposed to have been christened Augusta" (x, 117). The so-called proper name, then, is only a nickname (like Esther's many nicknames), or a fragmentary or partial name, like "Jo": "Don't know that Jo is short for a longer name" (xi, 134). "Guster" is the abbreviated form of some unknown whole, the fragment out of which a human history may some day be deciphered. In this way Guster reminds us of the kinds of names orphans and bastards characteristically bear. I recall the apparently fatherless Pearl, who embodies the sign of such fragmentariness and unreadability in the letter A. Guster's name is fragmentary in a second way: it carries with it no family name to help fill out the riddle of her identity. Guster is like the orphan Jo, or even Mr. George, the self-orphaned man who takes his first name as his last—all three characters "Don't know that everybody has two names" (xi, 134).

In "The Law-Writer" Dickens shows us that in naming, the loss of our proper or individual identity may also entail the loss of our humanity. He does so by laying bare a process he himself typically uses to name the characters of his novels. The domain of the human is threatened in *Bleak*

House by personified ideas, ideas that become humanized by being given names. For example, allegory, a particular kind of naming, becomes itself allegorized into "Allegory" (x, 119); and before our very eyes in a single paragraph, "rumour" (itself a power of words able to scandalize the highest person, as in the case of Lady Dedlock) undergoes a subtle metamorphosis into the capitalized, and named, "Rumour" (x, 118). Such allegorizations make us realize all the more how "Guster" is no proper name, and how the process of naming is a process of making common, of allegorizing. I mean that in such names—Allegory, Rumour, and Guster—individual identity disappears precisely through the process of naming. But the effects of such allegorizing on a person and on an idea differ. In "The Law-Writer" human beings are dehumanized by allegorical names (such as Guster) while ideas are humanized by allegorical names (such as Allegory and Rumour). This double movement makes us see the darker side of what we often take to be a simple and happy equation of identity, where there is no distance between signifier and signified, where name and idea or person simply coincide. Such an equation, however, lies outside the realm of human history, and invades it only to belittle it. This kind of naming confuses subject and object, consciousness and matter: "Gallows," "the Brick," and "Young Chisel," for example, make up the young, orphaned, and nameless population of Tom-all-Alone's, where impromptu names function to dehumanize these children, to name them as no more than equipment in a hopeless pattern of life and death.

I have already described the way in which names are allegorized in other novels: "Clarissa" is transformed into "a Clarissa" (just as in *Bleak House* we comically learn the consequences of becoming "a Guppy" or even "a Krook"), while in the name "Pierre Glendinning IV," "Pierre" functions as a common name, a familial essence, not a proper name at all. In such examples, the name comes alive as the sign of the triumph of language over proper identity, over humanness itself. As a technique in writing, allegory is double-edged: the writer's own verbal ability endows objects or ideas with life, but his human characters often shrink, comparatively, into mere fictive nothingness, mere "shades of names" (lii, 620). In a single chapter Dickens shows us how the ideas of allegory and rumor grow into characters, Allegory and Rumor, with gesture and movement, while two human characters seem no more than mere gusters—no more, in fact, than the air and wind of words (in an ironic version of the traditional comparison between words and breath).

We now begin to see the deepest function of place names in the novel. The example of the Bagnet family helps us here. The Bagnets extrapolate personal names and place names, and in so doing effect a comic solution to the problem of naming. The Bagnet family anchors its children to the places where they were born, Malta and Quebec being constant reminders to their parents, and to themselves, of their birthplace; such names function as a log or seaman's diary that records the military family's travels. Comical as such names are, they ironically echo "Tom-all-Alone's," where person and place become identical, with human subjectivity sinking into the thingness of impersonality. "Tom," with its personified houses and human vermin and dead-alive characters like Nemo, symbolizes such tragic confusions, and Dickens's comedy plays counterpoint to a tragic motif. We begin to see how place names do not simply function to introduce the problem of personal names, but actually compete with them and thereby put into question what it is to be human. As in *The Scarlet Letter*, the domain of the human depends on the names the characters bear, the names bestowed on them. This, after all, is the question with which I began my entire study: how does fiction meet the challenge of naming persons, and not simply ideas or things? In *Bleak House* we find demonstrations everywhere of the name undermining the humanness of the character. "Prince," as Caddy points out, "sounds like a dog, but of course he didn't christen himself" (xiv, 169), and this explains the charge against Mr. Turveydrop, Prince's father: "he wouldn't let his son have any name, if he could take it from him" (xiv, 173).

My claim that "The Law-Writer" illuminates the way in which naming violates the individual and the human, and the way in which the techniques the writer uses to name often undermine his own power, has its most potent support in the image that closes the chapter: the writer himself discovered nameless and dead. Moreover, these ideas about naming, by culminating in the figure of the dead writer, become part of *Bleak House*'s central family plot, Esther's plot. Ominous echoes of *Hamlet*, sometimes turned comic—in the image of Peffer's ghost hiding at the cock's crowing at dawn; in the theme of Tulkinghorn's indecision; in "bodkins" that remind us of a particularly relevant and celebrated passage from the play[4]—are clues from the beginning that "The Law-Writer" is about the dead father, or as we eventually realize, Esther's dead father. The theme of the dead father is introduced in the first paragraph of the chapter through the idea of one name displacing another: "*PEFFER AND SNAGSBY*, displacing the time-honoured *PEFFER* only," is simply the first step in the total effacement of Peffer's name, or what amounts to the same thing, Peffer himself—after all, the loss of name in paragraph 1 of "The Law-Writer" leads logically to the reemergence of Peffer as a mere ghost in paragraph 2. The complicated metaphor that describes the loss of the name has multiple implications. First, by wreathing itself around Peffer's name, the smoke "quite over-powered the parent tree" (x, 117); the loss of the name is at the same time the loss of the father. Second, the figure of "the affectionate parasite" (the smoke, renamed the London ivy) recalls my suggestion that the allegori-cal name parasitically swallows up the individual. We eventually recog-nize the relevance of this for the law-writer. He is the father who deliber-ately misnames himself to hide himself. He replaces "Hawdon" with the allegorical "Nemo," and as in the model we are studying, "Nemo" paras-itically eats away the parent name and the man it identifies, the man who authored the name "Nemo" in the first place. The end of the chapter thereby turns up the dead law-writer, where "the gaunt eyes," "the rusty skeleton," and "the starved man" (x, 124–25) are the effects of being bled dry of your own name and life. The father demonstrates the equation between allegorical names and namelessness that I have been exploring: "Nemo" means "No one."[5] And when, in death, Nemo "establish[es] his pretensions to his name by becoming indeed No one" (xi, 126), he literalizes for himself what the other characters in *Bleak House* expe-rience at least figuratively: dying to fulfill one's name.

A prominent source of the kinds of misnaming and unnaming I have been describing in *Bleak House* is the law; hence the significance of the father as the law-writer. "Nimrod," Mrs. Snagsby's comically incorrect rendering of the pseudonym "Nemo," suggests the conjunction between the language of the law and the language of Babel: "the beginning of his [Nimrod's] kingdom was Babel" (Gen. 10:10). Likewise, the punishment allotted to the builders of Babel is comically echoed in "The bar of England is scattered over the face of the earth" (xix, 232): "Come, let us confound their language, that they may not understand one another's speech. So the Lord scattereth them abroad from there upon the face of all the earth" (Gen. 11:8). Hence the diaspora of plot and character in *Bleak House*, the sharpest and most tragic form of which is the divided family—each member lost to the other, typically hidden by a false name. The builders of Babel declare, "Let us build a city and a tower . . . ; let us make us a name" (Gen. 11:4). Chancery likewise usurps the power of naming and builds an unreal city by establishing the precedent of false names, by rewriting and thereby disallowing the terms of kinship. The law, for example, denies Esther her aunt—"Aunt in fact, though not in law" (iii, 21)—and in this way contributes to Esther's namelessness, to the unknowability of her history. In Gridley's case, the law attempts to rob him of his rightful father: "the Master . . . inquired whether I was my father's son—about which there was no dispute at all" (xv, 193). With his paternal name in question, he is no longer Gridley but only the nameless "man from Shropshire" (xv, 193).

But *Bleak House* is not a simple attack on the English legal system, just as *The Scarlet Letter* is not a simple attack on Puritan law. In both works the family itself is the maker of discord and division, of false names and false identities; hence the law-writer as the father (to reverse the emphasis now). Chancery is an especially powerful image that focuses such acts, and makes a business out of them. The family member as writer (and especially as law-writer) connects the family plot and the Chancery plot. In Esther's case, Dickens insists that her obscure origin has behind it a writer—not simply Dickens himself, nor even just the law-writing father, but finally Miss Barbary: "the writer had bred her in secrecy from her birth, had blotted out all trace of her existence, and . . . if the writer were to die before the child became a woman, she would be left entirely friendless, nameless, and unknown" (xvii, 213). Writer and text repro-duce—and in this case, displace—two familial roles: the all-powerful parent and the entirely dependent child. The writer has complete author-ity over identity; she is in fact the author of identity, and makes, keeps, and discloses its secrets. It is in this sense that the writer is the law of his or her own creation—a version of the classical view of the father as law-giver. In Miss Barbary we see how the writer uses her ink in two ways. First, paradoxically, she erases or "blot[s] out" all traces of exis-tence. Second, she creates a substitute or fictional life for herself and her creation. She does so by renouncing her sister Lady Dedlock and by taking for herself a new name at the same time that she invents for Esther—her niece/goddaughter/mock-daughter/literary creation—a new name. Like Pearl in *The Scarlet Letter*, Esther shows us the child as fictional product, a mysterious and unreadable text to which the child herself does not have the key of interpretation.

By using names to hide her own identity, and by betraying another (usually a family member, especially a child) into anonymity and the confusion of false names, Miss Barbary commits the central crime of *Bleak House*, thereby repeating the crime of the father. The crime of the parent coincides with that of the writer: to fail to put one's name to one's deeds and words, to misname. The law ironically becomes the medium of such crime. Krook's "crooked mark" (v, 55), the mock Lord chancellor's attempt at writing, suggests that the law makes possible a certain criminal use of language—a crooked (that is, erroneous and criminal) classifica-tion of fathers, mothers, daughters, and sons. All of London seems to experience "diving through law and equity, and through that kindred mystery, the street mud, which is made of nobody knows what, and collects about us nobody knows whence or how" (x, 123). The law muddies our understanding of our origins, making each of us an obscure nobody, thereby contributing to the deepest "kindred mystery" in *Bleak House*. At the same time the law exalts, and thereby misuses, the powers of representation, writing and naming: this is the worship of the letter of the law. As a writer, Miss Barbary honors the written word over the child whom she takes as her charge. She warns Esther to heed the letter of the law, to "pray daily that the sins of others be not visited upon your head, according to what is written" (iii, 19). By keeping from Esther the names of the child's parents, Miss Barbary (as her name suggests) is, like the legal bar, the bar between child and parent. She is the sole law of the child's universe, her "carved" (iii, 21), unresponsive face a reminder of the stony tablets of the merciless law.

In Esther's family plot, then, the family member is the writer who, in unnaming and misnaming, breeds a fictional product: the father unnames himself and breeds a nameless, apparently orphaned child; the aunt breeds the fictional product "Esther Summerson" (and symbolically murders and buries "Esther Hawdon"). In such ways identity is hidden under the stain of ink—even literally. We recall that Esther's introduction to London and the law is Guppy, "a young gentleman who had inked himself" (iii, 28). Richard's entire absorption in the law takes the form of a "commentary . . . indelibly written in his handsome face" (li, 612). The "black drizzle" that covers London in the novel's first paragraph, we eventually realize, is the drizzle of ink, or what Dickens will later call "a rain of ink" (x, 124), covering the characters and their dwellings (I am thinking especially of Nemo, Gridley, Richard, Charley, and Caddy.) What the ink covers, in *Bleak House*, is at once one's familial identity and one's humanity. Caddy's "inky condition" (v, 57) is an especially good example here. Ink becomes the means by which Mrs. Jellyby symbolically orphans her own daughter, to become mother to the entire tribe of Borrioboola-Gha. Caddy no longer even seems human (doesn't her name designate her pure instrumentality?): "I am only pen and ink to *her* [Ma]" (xiv, 169), a complaint that underscores the way in which "Esther Summerson" is only pen and ink, no more than the fictional product of a writer. By obscuring identity, ink becomes the cause of death. This is the meaning that Jo's malapropism, "Inkwhich" (xvi, 200), inadvertently detects, but which goes unheeded in the law's inquest into the law-writer's death. In Hawdon's case, the name under which he hides makes him "no one," and so undoes him. The law-writer, then, almost literalizes death by ink. We recall that he "lived—or didn't live—by law-writing" (xi, 127).

This association between the ink of writing and death (or suicide) recalls how prominently the stain of ink turns up, first on the law-writer's desk and then in the graveyard where he is buried. I remember that Clarissa's coffin is her writing desk, the place at which she writes herself to death (perhaps not literally, as her doctor fears, but by entering the correspondence that misnames and unnames her). Hawdon's desk, "marked with a rain of ink" (x, 124), is the workplace of the crimes of language, of unnaming and misnaming. In her secret visit to Hawdon's graveyard, Lady Dedlock, the mother of his child, fears the "deadly stains contaminating her," but she is unsuccessful in her attempt to avoid "the spot" (xvi, 202)—"the spot" (lix, 713) that, by the end of the novel, becomes her place of death, for she has learned that everywhere she travels becomes a "deserted blighted spot" (lvi, 674); she is the woman who carries with her "the stain and blot" (xli, 510).

As the sign of illegitimate breeding, of fictive reproduction, the ink stain shows up most palpably in the form of Esther's disfiguring disease. In this way the law-writer redefines the father as the engenderer of disease and death, "sow[ing] . . . in corruption" (xi, 137) and "propagat[ing] . . . infection and contagion" (xlvi, 553). Like the carved face of her aunt, Esther's face becomes a text, and, in fulfillment of the prediction of Miss Barbary the writer, a text that seems to record how the sins of the father are visited upon the children. While Esther innocently thinks her disfigurement will hide her parentage by obscuring her resemblance to Lady Dedlock, Esther's marked face becomes an ironic version of the way in which the father's traits are traceable in the child (as in *The Scarlet Letter*). I mean that the "scars" and "deep traces of her illness" (xliv, 539), the effects of the disease she catches from Jo (whose constant haunt is the law-writer's stained, infectious graveyard), are what she inherits from her father.[6] In the same way Caddy's baby has "curious little marks under its eyes, like faint remembrances of poor Caddy's inky days" (l, 599)—but as Esther's "namesake" (l, 602), this baby reproduces as well Esther Summerson's source in ink. In both *The Scarlet Letter* and *Bleak House* (and in *Pierre*, as I showed) the sin of the parents is visited upon the child as a half-intelligible writing that the child's body displays—half-intelligible especially to the child because, like Pearl, Esther cannot read the text of who she is.

"No one" and "Every one" in fiction

I will now argue that, by writing her own text, Esther finally overcomes her inability to read the text of who she is. Esther's lengthy narrative is an extended form of naming, her deepest weapon against anonymity. In this light, Esther's narrative act cancels the single-minded quest after the proper name by publishing an entire life story. In this way Esther rises above a dominant figure within the novel—the person serving a name, sacrificed on the altar of a name, dying to secure and fulfill his or her pretensions to a name. I will begin by showing how Esther's role as a writer is founded in the family plot of which she forms the enigmatic center. Esther takes her method and object in writing from what she learns in the complicated drama of veiling and unveiling that she and her mother perform, a drama that will lead to my calling Esther's act of narration, her extended form of self-naming, an unveiling of the text of who she is.

Esther's power "to read a face" (lxiv, 750), situated ironically within the plot which has her unable to read her own story, is further complicated by Dickens's portrayal of Lady Dedlock as the veiled woman. I refer here not simply to the mother's disguise as Mademoiselle Hortense when Jo takes her to the graveyard, but to the disguise or mask she wears every day as "Lady Dedlock." Esther's ability to read the text of her own face depends on her learning to read her mother's face—that is, on being able to lift the veil. I have already taken up, especially for Dickens's early novel *Oliver Twist*, the way in which identity is unravelled through a reading of the face as (family) text. In *Bleak House*, during their first meeting, Esther mysteriously experiences seeing Lady Dedlock face to face as seeing herself in a mirror: "But why her face should be, in a confused way, like a broken glass to me, in which I saw scraps of old remembrances . . . I could not think" (xviii, 225). As in *The Scarlet Letter*, the bastard child sees itself outside itself, first in a mirrored image that is at once familiar and strange, but then even further outside itself, in the face of another, the parent who is unknown and in some sense disguised. We recall that the child's face in *Oliver Twist* is the perfect copy of the mother's; likewise, the face of Lady Dedlock figures for Esther as a mirror because it is the face in which she can see her own. But Esther does not in fact recognize herself in Lady Dedlock (even though Mr. Guppy does). What keeps Esther from recognizing her mother is the symbolic veil that makes her "Lady Dedlock."[7]

It is this veil which is drawn when, after learning that Esther is in fact her daughter and that she is ill, the mother unguardedly rushes to her side in "Chesney Wold." Esther sees "a something in her face that I had pined for and dreamed of when I was a little child, something I had never seen in any face, something I had never seen in hers before" (xxxvi, 448). During this encounter Lady Dedlock moves back and forth between simply showing the mother's face and drawing "her habitual air of proud indifference about her like a veil" (xxxvi, 450). This is the only face-to-face encounter that Esther is allowed while Lady Dedlock is alive; in fact, what succeeds this moment of unveiling is a series of prohibitions—the law of the mother—that reveils the parent and secretes her permanently behind her false name and false face. It is perhaps the most painful moment in the encounter, when all the prohibitions that had been undeliberate (because Lady Dedlock believed Esther dead) become the law the mother knowingly enforces: "We never could associate, never could communicate, never probably from that time forth could interchange another word, on earth. . . . I must ever more consider her dead" (xxxvi, 450). Lady Dedlock discovers her daughter is alive, but Esther must act as if her mother were dead. Esther finds her mother, only to learn what it is to lose her. Lady Dedlock unveils herself, only to instruct her daughter that she never will remove that veil again.

The symbolic value of this reveiling is made especially apparent when Lady Dedlock leaves Esther with a document in which the child may read about her origins. The flesh-and-blood face that speaks the love of the mother dissolves into the power so persistently represented in *Bleak House*—pen and ink, the "dead letter." Lady Dedlock's letter represents the letter of the law: the mother owns the daughter in print, while fleeing from her in the flesh. Esther understands she must burn the incriminating letter as soon as she reads it. She is placed in the unnatural position of destroying the evidence that proves her a daughter, with human origins. Esther must bury the secret that has just been unmasked, and this means symbolically burying the child that has just been brought alive—a symbolic suicide that has its echoes in the deaths of the father and the mother. Esther understands the corollary proscription as well: after this interview, "At no time did I dare to utter her name" (xliii, 521). So, while the child fulfills the mother's wish in *Oliver Twist* by pronouncing her name, in *Bleak House* the nameless child sees as one of her primary functions the concealment of the mother's name. In this way Esther becomes an accomplice in the family plot of unnaming and misnaming.

These unveilings and reveilings of the mother play counterpoint to Esther's own, for throughout *Bleak House* Esther's progress toward self-discovery is measured by her views of herself in the mirror—by the knowledge she has of her own face and by the willingness she has to expose her face to view. It is no accident that, upon her arrival in London (in other words, at the start of her long and circuitous journey toward self-discovery), Esther is presented with a "looking-glass, . . . in case you should wish to look at yourself" (iii, 29). Here, at the entrance to

Chancery, Esther takes a last look at her innocent face, the face ignorant of the crime that stands behind it, the face as yet unmarked with the knowledge of good and evil. During her disfiguring illness, Esther's looking-glass is taken away from her, and only some time later does she have the courage to look at herself face to face:

> For I had not yet looked in the glass and had never asked to have my own restored to me. I knew this to be a weakness which must be overcome, but I had always said to myself that I would begin afresh when I got to where I was. . . . My hair had not been cut off, though it had been in danger more than once. It was long and thick. I let it down, and shook it out, and went up to the glass upon the dressing-table. There was a little muslin curtain drawn across it. I drew it back and stood for a moment looking through such a veil of my own hair that I could see nothing else. Then I put my hair aside and looked at the reflection in the mirror, encouraged by seeing how placidly it looked at me. I was very much changed—oh, very, very much. At first my face was so strange to me that I think I should have put my hands before it and started back but for the encouragement I have mentioned. (xxxvi, 444)

The distance between the reflection in the mirror and Esther—"it" looks at "me"—is exactly the distance between two faces, one entirely innocent of its orgins and the other on the brink of knowledge, for only a few pages later in the same chapter ("Chesney Wold") the mother unveils herself to the child. At first, then, the scarred face is mysteriously a foreign face, the face of another. Lady Dedlock brings its story; in unveiling herself she lifts the veil of mystery from the new face. Lady Dedlock's letter serves as the key to interpretation for "the old words" of the Old Testament law. Esther learns "the new and terrible meaning of the old words, now moaning in my ear . . . , 'Your mother, Esther, was your disgrace, and you are hers. . . . Pray daily that the sins of others be not visited upon your head'" (xxxvi, 453). Esther experiences the sin of the parents visited upon her head as if the sin becomes a part of her, a feature of her body or head, like the scars on her face—"I felt as if the blame and shame were all in me"—readable to everyone: "I had a terror of myself as the danger and the possible disgrace of my own mother and of a proud family name" (xxxvi, 453). Esther fears that everyone, like Charley, will be able to read "the secret in my face" (xxxii, 390). The chapter that opens with Esther's hesitant unveiling of herself and moves to the mother's hesitant unveiling and final reveiling of herself leads to Esther's terror of, and flight from, herself: "I ran from myself" (xxxvi, 454).

The chapter ends with Esther afraid and embarrassed, hiding her altered face from Ada's view, until she sees in Ada all the fondness and love unchanged, and finally yields to Ada's "holding my scarred face to her lovely cheek, bathing it with tears and kisses, rocking me to and fro like a child, calling me by every name she could think of, and pressing me to her faithful heart" (xxxvi, 456). This final scene in "Chesney Wold" is a crucial turning point. The literal mother, whose flesh-and-blood face disappears behind the veil of the letter, prohibits herself, and so gives way to the symbolic mother, merely another orphan girl, not empowered to bestow the proper name, but who in love and faithfulness bestows "every name." The encounter with the mother makes Esther feel that blame and shame are in her, part of her body, while the encounter with Ada bathes her, baptizes her in the spirit, and makes "every name" possible, especially the name that will overturn the stigmatized name of the lawless father and mother, the name "bastard," or the name the mother leaves with Esther again, "orphan." The deepest irony of *Bleak House* explodes the discovery of one's proper origins in anticlimax. Esther's personal anticlimax recalls the failure of those suitors in Jarndyce and Jarndyce who hope to be rewarded once their name is discovered on the genuine will, once they are discovered to be the rightful heirs. Esther burns the document that declares her the daughter, and discovers no more proper identity than that which she finds in the bosom of Ada, in a plethora of tender names, all of which have the same meaning by authenticating her here and now.

The climactic moment in the drama of veiling and unveiling between mother and daughter occurs when Esther finds her mother dead. Before this moment, Esther has seen her mother through a broken glass, and then face to face, as if recalling the famous passage from I Corinthians: "When I was a child, I spoke as a child, I understood as a child, I thought as a child; but when I became a man, I put away childish things. For now we see in a mirror, darkly; but then, face to face; now I know in part, but then shall I know even as also I am known" (I Cor. 13:11–12). The face-to-face meeting between Lady Dedlock and Esther, when the mother unveils herself, brings the daughter the knowledge of her identity but keeps her a child—in fact, a child in bondage to the law of the parent. The scene is in fact an ironic revision of the New Testament passage: Esther knows, and is known, but then this knowledge is cut off, prohibited, and Esther is returned to an enforced state of blindness (when she can see). It is not until Esther finds her mother dead that this pattern is resolved. Esther finds her mother with her face characteristically turned away and hidden: "I lifted the heavy head, put the long dark hair aside, and turned the face. And it was my mother, cold and dead" (lix, 714). Esther performs for her mother the same act she earlier performs for herself, the act that Lady Dedlock so dreads, finds so impossible to perform for herself. The child becomes parent to the woman. In this way the discovery of the dead mother signals Esther's liberation into her own womanhood, into the freedom of her own personhood; it is the movement beyond the child obeying the parent as her lord god, as the law.

At the same time the moment painfully makes us realize that Esther's final meeting with her mother face to face does not bring with it the recognition that Esther desires and that the New Testament passage suggests. The knowledge it brings is almost too painful to bear, certainly too painful for Esther to contemplate. The mother has ceased to be alive, to be human: "*it* was my mother." Moreover, the dead face literalizes what the veiled face has been all along. The recognition scene reads as a definition that is for all time, and so recapitulates what the mother has been in life: "it was my mother, cold and dead." In this way the dead face that does not respond brings us back not simply to our earlier views of Lady Dedlock, but to Esther's first orphaning when the creator of "Esther Summerson," the sister of Lady Dedlock, dies: "Many and many a time, in the day and in the night, with my head upon the pillow by her that my whispers might be plainer to her, I kissed her, thanked her, prayed for her, asked her for her blessing and forgiveness, entreated her to give me the least sign that she knew or heard me. No, no, no. Her face was immovable" (iii, 21). This immovable face, with no sign, with no kindred feeling—a face that blocks reading—is the face that Esther must move beyond.

The mother and daughter's drama of veiling and unveiling, at the level of plot, instructs us in the entire rhetorical structure of the text because, quite simply, Esther's lengthy narrative act is an extended form of unveiling. In a novel laden with biblical allusion, I recall that lifting the veil is a figure for the hermeneutical act itself: "for until this day remaineth the same veil untaken away in the reading of the old testament: which veil is done away in Christ" (II Cor. 3:14). In *Bleak House* this veil is done away in another symbolic child: the daughter Esther. Like the stain of ink, the veil is an omnipresent sign of obscurity that marks London: "Over all the legal neighbourhood, there hangs . . . some great veil of rust, or gigantic cobweb" (xix, 233)—the veil of the Mosaic legislation, the veil that Moses himself wears (II Cor. 3:13). To see Esther as the unveiler of her mother and the unveiler of herself is to realize the way in which Esther becomes the reader of her own face and, as I will show, the writer of her own text. The Chancery plot that runs parallel to Esther's story in *Bleak House* suggests another way of stating this: to see Esther as the unveiler is to realize the way in which she supersedes the law of the old will and testament and makes her own inheritance.[8]

The most potent effect of the final unveiling of the mother is to make Esther's entire narrative possible. The death of the mother releases Esther from the bondage of secrecy and silence; Esther is free to tell her story only after the discovery of the dead mother, only when in death the daughter unveils the mother once and for all. I understand Esther's act of narration as a kind of self-exposure that both her parents dread. Writing, for both Esther's parents, is a form of self-naming that brings with it a dreaded self-exposure. We recall that the love letters incriminate them, give them away, assigning the name Hawdon to Nemo, and the ironic (but no less incriminating) name Honoria to Lady Dedlock. One could say that the father lives and dies to escape such writing; as the law-writer he performs the most anonymous kind of writing, copying, where no personal signature is required, and where he gives as his professional signature "Nemo" or "No one." What he writes, as the copier, is not his own. The entire story of the mother in *Bleak House* instructs her in the dangerous consequences of writing. Her first significant act in the text, when she asks about the identity of a writer (who turns out to be her former lover), becomes the first step in the unravelling of her secret. Lady Dedlock's terror lies in being known, in having her name become a public sign: she fears "her shame will be published" (lv, 665), "chalked upon the walls" (xli, 508); with horror she learns that "her name is in these many mouths" (lv, 665). It is no surprise, then, that at the end Lady Dedlock avoids writing, and especially putting her name to her writing. Her poignant death notes, written for the unnamed "dear one" (still withholding Esther's name), are themselves deliberately unsigned. She is the no one who authors this final note: "I have nothing about me by which I can be recognized. This paper I part with now" (lix, 710). Her final act is to seek the kind of anonymity to which her former lover now shows her the way. She travels, veiled and unnamed, to the common burial ground to die the death of no one. If Esther did not unveil her, she would have been discovered as a poor common creature and been given the burial allotted to the nameless. In a moving reversal, the child performs the act of recognition that saves the mother from utter namelessness.

The narrative act that tells one's story from beginning to end, and signs one's name to it, is the direct antithesis to the parental act of writing. Esther's act of narration defines her position beyond her parents: it is the child's publishing of the family plot which the parents obfuscate and try to erase. At the same time a peculiarity in Esther's narrative calls into question such a view. Esther tells her story not strictly as her own: "I don't know how it is, I seem to be always writing about myself. I mean all the time to write about other people, and I try to think about myself as

little as possible . . ." (ix, 102). I wish to call such a moment in Esther's
text a narrative self-effacement to enable us to ask the following question. Is this kind of narrative self-effacement an example of mere modesty, or is it more troublingly an example of what I have been calling the
act of veiling, a self-silencing that obscures and even disguises? Such a
question brings us to the issue that has so occupied modern readers of
Bleak House: Esther's excessive modesty.[9] Modern readers, in reacting to
the modesty of Esther as if it were merely stilted and even coy, often
neglect that its sources lie in the lessons she learns from the beginning:
that she is no one, that she is a disgrace, that she should not have been
born. But I wish to emphasize, beyond such facts, the way in which what
I will call characterization by anonymity complicates and deepens Esther's self-effacement. The modesty of Esther's conscious personality is
extended and deepened by Dickens's view of a kind of anonymity that
plays counterpoint to the idea of her parents as "no one." We have
glimpses of this anonymity at the level of plot, in certain highly symbolic
events, as well as at the level of narration, in Esther's self-conscious—and
self-effacing—reflections on the telling of her tale.

Perhaps the best chapter in which to see this view of character at work
is "Nurse and Patient." At the exact center of the novel, in the tenth
installment, "Nurse and Patient" is the chapter in which Esther contracts
the disease that will disfigure her. The title of the chapter announces, we
realize in retrospect, a series of character doublings. "Nurse" and "Patient" are names that symbolically become exchanged and shared in the
course of the chapter: Esther nurses Charley, and Charley nurses Esther;
Charley nurses Jo, and Liz and Jenny send for medicine for Jo (recalling
that he had once done the same for them); Jenny nurses Liz's child as if it
were her own ("her child, but I call it mine"). Jo mistakes the veiled
Esther for the veiled woman (Mademoiselle Hortense) who impersonates
Lady Dedlock (who impersonated a servant, Mademoiselle Hortense), so
that for Jo the chapter is not simply the scene of doubling but of tripling:
"Is there *three* of 'em then?" (xxxi, 383). In short, "Nurse and Patient" is
a chapter in which women and children exchange roles. The deadly fever
creates a symbolic circle where each character loses one identity to gain
another, or to gain a common identity. The fever affects the characters by
deadening their sense of their own identity, so that Jo, for example, is
"strangely unconcerned about himself" (xxxi, 383), "looking on at what
was done, as if it were for somebody else" (xxxi, 386). This symptom of
the disease is the channel through which proper identity is left behind and
common identity is achieved. The feverish hallucination of "night melting
into day, and . . . day melting into night" becomes the charitable dis-

placement of ego, so that Esther feels "a little beside myself, . . . as if I were becoming too large altogether" (xxxi, 390–91)—almost too large to contain the identities that melt into her: Charley, here called "little old woman"; Jo, the symbolic orphan; Lady Dedlock, the veiled woman; the child who belongs to "the mother of the dead child"; Ada, whom Esther calls "my own Pride" (xxxii, 391). Dickens deepens, qualifies, and problematizes character not by extensive psychological notation of the proper personality (as Henry James does, say), but by those symbolic exchanges that extend character into ranges of identity beyond personality. This is the deepest value of those apparently inexhaustible variations on a theme that make up the multiple plot in Dickens's novels and that explore the nature of an identity that is intersubjective, multiple. It is a method of characterization whereby what we call Esther's personality—especially her sometimes cloying self-effacement—has below the surface a common ground where she intersects with the characters around her.

In this light "Nurse and Patient" shows us how Esther's story ultimately becomes a revision of the double threat that, first, one's proper name is common and, second, the name "no one" inextricably binds together namelessness and literal death—a revision, that is, of the problems of naming and writing I set forth in the first part of this chapter. "Nurse and Patient" arms the self against the ironic explosion of what I have called the notion of familial identity: to find oneself in one's family, to be recognized, named, and given one's proper identity. Esther discovers the self beyond herself, the life beyond death, the life that comes of death that neither parent finds. She makes us see how we all come together not merely in the grave of literal death—"that last shape which earthly lodgings take for No one—and for Every one" (xi, 131)—but in the further life that comes of the death of the ego, where no one is everyone. The mirror that shows her herself as another at last has a deep and benign meaning.

"The Appointed Time," the chapter that succeeds "Nurse and Patient," draws up an antithetical view of that anonymity which will lead us to our final view of Esther's act of narration as self-naming. The dissolution of the ego in "Nurse and Patient" has its grotesque analogue in "The Appointed Time." Esther's dissolution into the no-oneness of everyone, her sublimation of death into the death of the ego, is juxtaposed by Krook's horrifying dissolution through spontaneous combustion. In "The Appointed Time," in the room formerly inhabited by "No one," Jobling and Guppy await their meeting with Krook at the midnight hour of the mock Lord Chancellor's birthday, the moment at which the fate of Krook in fact becomes the fate of "No one." The metamorphosis into other human identities that occurs in "Nurse and Patient" becomes the metamorphosis into nothingness, or mere thingness, that occurs in "The Appointed Time," when the almost entirely dissolved remains of Krook are discovered.

From these two forms of anonymity, two forms of writing follow. One could say that, like Esther's father, Krook literalizes the death of the self, the idea of being no one. The men who live by the letter die by it—die in certain grotesque acts of literalization. Esther takes what the father dies by, and lives by it. She does this by fictionalizing (instead of literalizing) the idea of no-oneness and namelessness. She begins by thinking to herself, "I was no one" (iv, 45), where all this means is her lack of identity. But in the course of *Bleak House*, she converts her self-naming as no one into a profounder meaning. And finally it is Esther as writer who enacts such meaning. It is for this reason that Esther initiates those events in "Nurse and Patient" that formulate the revisionary concept of anonymity in *Bleak House*—a life lived through the life of others—by teaching Charley to write in her copy-book the letter "O," the symbolic zero at which the different identities in the chapter meet. While Esther teaches Charley a symbolic writing that inscribes a universal identity, in the succeeding chapter Guppy and Jobling seek the letters that will incriminate Hawdon and Lady Dedlock—the letters that name them, give them their literal or proper identity, and thereby indict them. "The Appointed Time" names the time at which the letters will be given over, but the moment set for identification, for the revelation of proper identity, turns into the ironically apocalyptic dissolution of Krook.

It is in Esther's act of narration that the delicate balance between proper and common identity—between her name and everyone's name—is most significantly achieved. Now I can explain the function of Esther's narrative self-effacement. The narrative act that publishes her story and signs her name to it is balanced by certain crucial narrative self-effacements that have the ultimate effect of showing that her story is not simply her own, but another's, many others'—a variation on what I called, in chapter 4 on *The Scarlet Letter*, telling your own story as another's. Esther's reaction to the prohibitions Lady Dedlock places on her identity appropriately signals such a moment of narrative self-effacement, as if the daughter here begins to know how to rewrite her obscurity into some value:

> It matters little now, how much I thought of my living mother who had told me evermore to consider her dead. I could not venture to approach her or to communicate with her in writing, for my sense of the peril in which her life was passed was only to be equalled by my fears of increasing it. . . .

It matters little now how often I recalled the tones of my mother's voice, wondered whether I should ever hear it again as I so longed to do, and thought how strange and desolate it was that it should be so new to me. It matters little that I watched for every public mention of my mother's name; that I passed and repassed the door of her house in town, loving it, but afraid to look at it; that I once sat in the theatre when my mother was there and saw me, and when we were so wide asunder before the great company of all degrees that any link or confidence between us seemed a dream. It is all, all over. My lot has been so blest that I can relate little of myself which is not a story of goodness and generosity in others. I may well pass that little and go on. (xliii, 520–21)

This remarkable narrative confession works through negation, especially self-negation. It tells, and tells most poignantly, by undermining its own significance: "It matters little." Self-effacement—in a sense, what amounts to a disregard for her own story—gets translated at the end into Esther's statement of narrative purpose. Whatever Esther's own sufferings—and she lets us know these by denying them (though their effect is certainly not lost on us)—her story is the story of others. Esther reaches the same point after the discovery of her dead mother—in other words, after the last unveiling reveals the face permanently veiled in death:

I proceed to other passages of my narrative. From the goodness of all about me I derived such consolation as I can never think of unmoved. I have already said so much of myself, and so much still remains, but I will not dwell upon my sorrow. I had an illness, but it was not a long one; and I would avoid even this mention of it if I could quite keep down the recollection of their sympathy.

I proceed to other passages of my narrative. (lx, 714)

The words here constitute the opening of the chapter entitled "Perspective," and with this title in mind we see the perspective in which first-person narration proceeds in *Bleak House*—through a form of self-exposure that is at the same time self-cancellation, one's own story told as another's.

Another, perhaps simpler way of making this point underscores two prominent features of the narrative structure of *Bleak House*. First, Esther's story is in fact never in the foreground for long, because of the diffusion of plot and character in *Bleak House*; the story of the first-person narrator is embedded in a complicated web of other, parallel, competing stories. Second, the first-person narrative in *Bleak House* is embedded within the omniscient narrative. I recall that the epistolary form of *Clarissa* makes possible the publishing of letters that contain facts about Clarissa's own story that she herself never knows. Similarly, in *Bleak House* we realize that one's life is never simply one's own when we see an entire world—sometimes including intimate details of what I am calling Esther's family plot—which Esther herself never sees. Esther's own story, in fact, can never be completely told by herself; it requires completion from another, auxiliary narrator. In this way narrative strategy in *Bleak House* consistently displaces the "subject" characteristic of first-person narratives. Everyone, as much as no one, occupies center stage in *Bleak House*.

In the second part of this chapter, I have viewed Esther as the instructress of writing, as we see her instruct Charley at the beginning of "Nurse and Patient," and as we see her perform her act of narration in the chapters she writes. I have seen in her text a revision of the kind of writing that succeeds at masking and concealing through a system of misnaming and unnaming—the view of writing we had reached at the end of the first part of this chapter. As a writer in a text already overpopulated with writers, Esther succeeds at a kind of writing different from that of her father, or Krook, or the law—in fact, a writing meant to supersede the rain (or reign) of ink that the law represents: "Forasmuch as ye are manifestly declared to be the epistle of Christ ministered by us, write not with ink but with the Spirit of the living God; not in tables of stone but in fleshy tables of the heart. . . . [F]or the letter killeth, but the Spirit giveth life" (II Cor. 3:3–6). Dickens uses "the great wilderness of London" (xlviii, 583), that "immense desert of law-hand" (xlvii, 567), to recall the Old Testament desert, with the law-writer "as dead as Phairy" (xi, 126) and the Jarndyce will as the "dead letter" which the child will supersede with a new kind of writing. Jarndyce characterizes Esther's effect on Bleak House as a sacred cleansing and renewal, a baptism into new life: "It rained Esther" (vi, 61). The metaphor at least in part is the sign of the succession of houses or reigns. The rain of Esther proceeds as a rain of ink, but one that alters the motives and ends of writing in the ways I have been describing.

Finally, Esther alters the way in which all writing is copying. The literalist is par excellence the copier of the letter, whether he be the law-writing father or Krook, the mock Lord Chancellor who says of himself: "I have a turn for copying from memory . . . though I can neither read nor write" (v, 55–56). The letter of the law is a blind copy, without meaning or spirit, a mere "dummy" (xxxii, 399). But Esther, when she instructs Charley in the copy-book, teaches a new form of copying. By copying the marks on her face onto the page, she transforms the enigmatic signs into a personal history; this is the writing that giveth life. The text she writes becomes as well a copying of her parents' nameless deaths, but she changes their motives and so gives us a new meaning for namelessness and death, one that makes Esther the ultimate human copy in the novel. In this way, she transforms the enigmatic signs on her face, which originally mark her as the outcast criminal child, into a universal meaning. Like the marked heart in *The Scarlet Letter*, the marked face in *Bleak House* tells the story of everyone. The legal system throws up its hands at reading the face or heart not inscribed specifically with the letter of the law. Mr. Vholes rhetorically asks Richard Carstone (while eliding his client's name), "Who can read the heart, Mr. C?" (xxxix, 487). But Esther performs this finer reading, of herself and others, and understands mercifully the way in which every person becomes, in Mr. George's self-naming, "a marked . . . man" (lii, 620). In these ways we see the maturity Dickens achieves over his earlier novel, *Oliver Twist*. *Bleak House* transcends the naive fable that pits the entirely unmarked face of the good child (Oliver) against the marked face of the evil child (Monks). The distance between the two novels is that between an identity based on the mother's name, and the devotion accorded to that name (*Oliver Twist*), and an identity based neither on the mother's name nor on one's own name (*Bleak House*). Jo is our guide here. When reciting the Lord's prayer by repeating Woodcourt word for word, at a crucial moment Jo makes a significant omission, as if understanding the danger of valorizing names; his last words, "Hallowed be—thy—" (xlvii, 572), give the deepest blessing, the one that goes beyond the name. In short, in *Bleak House* Dickens transcends the fable which makes the name the necessary endpoint of the entire narrative project.

6

The Mill on the Floss

In *The Mill on the Floss* the family is defined—and divided—along the lines of discourse. The story opens with the father making plans to educate his son to "talk fine and write with a flourish" (9).[1] The son becomes the tool by which the father hopes to preserve himself. Once educated, the son is enlisted in the father's battle with the law, a battle against words that eventually deprives the family of the Tulliver land of several generations, the ground of the father's being. While the father proposes his plan to educate his son, his daughter sits reading in the background. But it is precisely the daughter's voracious reading (culminating with *Thomas à Kempis*) that brings her into the foreground of the plot and makes her a significant threat to the family. Into the Tulliver household Maggie deliberately brings words, the symbolic entity that ruins the father in his role as property holder and confounds the son in his role as scholar. *The Mill on the Floss*, then, opens with a splintered family plot that takes its cue from the father's apparently contradictory desires: the father plans Tom's education in reading and writing at the same moment that he orders Maggie to "shut up the book" (17). It will be the daughter's success at words, and the father and son's failure at them, that will determine the ultimate contour of this family plot.

The specific division of the family in *The Mill on the Floss*—father and son on one side and daughter on the other—suggests the way in which gender assumes significance within this family plot. The attempt of father and son to maintain the land of several generations represents the safeguarding of the male power of regeneration. For this reason Mr. Tulliver's failure in the law and Tom's failure at his studies are both figured as a kind of maiming and emasculation. In the first part of this chapter I will examine the unmanning of father and son under the rubric "education," or what the second book of the novel calls "School-Time." In the second part, I will take up the education that Maggie conducts on her own, teaching herself how to move beyond the desire to keep self and name secure—the unswerving patriarchal principle of duplication. The clearest symptom of this principle is the desire to maintain and perpetuate the family name. For this reason the father's attempt, after he has lost his legal battle, to "retrieve his name" (244), becomes Tom's obsession to lift off "the obloquy of debt from his father's name" (285), to help in "regaining his honest name" (311), while every relationship that Maggie makes outside the family threatens "a family that has a good and honest name to support" (303); as Tom tells her toward the end, "You have disgraced my father's name" (426).

Maggie countervails this system of duplication through the family name by formulating, like Esther in *Bleak House*, a version of naming that does not perpetuate the self but cancels it—a symbolic version of the literal death the parent dies. Although not an actual writer like Esther, Maggie achieves nothing less than a complete revision of the discourse of the family, from the crucial terms of its diction to the most basic structures of its rhetoric. In both novels the daughter becomes the repository of meaning. And in both cases the law represents the literalism of the letter, precisely what the daughter brings her revisionary power to bear against. Because both Esther and Maggie discover a method of naming that allows them to escape literalism, they represent, inside the plot of the novel, the force of fiction that lies at the source of the novel. This pattern assumes added power insofar as the question of naming, and fiction as a particular form of naming, play such a prominent role in the life of "George Eliot." But at this point I wish merely to suggest that in *The Mill on the Floss*, as in *Bleak House*, the daughter discovers a form of self-naming that represents a particular narrative strategy for the novel at large, and in so doing illuminates the motives and ends of the entire fictional enterprise.

The education of father and son

In the beginning is the father's word: "'What I want, you know,' said Mr. Tulliver—'what I want is to give Tom a good eddication; an eddication as'll be a bread to him'" (8). By initiating the novel's action, the patriarchal voice aspires to become the story's First Cause, equal to divine fiat. But we cannot fail to hear how the father's own words, even before we meet the man who speaks them, undermine his authority. The circumlocution and the repeated mispronounced word remind us of Mr. Tulliver's own confession, "it's puzzling work, talking is" (10), and the doggedly repeated "what I want" begins to sound pathetic as it reappears a fourth and fifth time in the novel's opening pages. Only in retrospect do we recognize the full irony of the father's position: as the consistent spokesman against the artifice of words, he initiates the story with a speech on educating his son in talking fine and writing with a flourish. The story of *The Mill on the Floss*, then, begins by showing the father's awkward attempt to use words to make his will the law. In the course of the novel we will see that he is a match neither for the law that Wakem practices nor for the law to which his wife unwittingly supplies a quasi-theological gravity: "The law was the first beginning" (440). So much for the father's attempt to bolster his position at the origin.

Mr. Tulliver's announcement of his intention to educate his son in reading and writing undermines the position of the father at the origin in another, more palpable way. The father (or biological maker) puts his son into the hands of the educators to be remade. And the tools of civilization will, like the master builder's, repair and reconstruct where nature has bungled. Mr. Tulliver, afraid that Mr. Stelling's education of Tom will not be practical enough, is reassured by understanding that "when a workman knows the use of his tools, he can make a door as well as a window" (20). What will he make out of Tom? The desire of the father—"what I want" repeated again—is narrowed to a plan to correct his own work of engendering: "Now, what I want is to send him to a school where they'll make him a bit nimble with his tongue and his pen, and make a smart chap of him" (18). Tulliver's desire rests fixedly on his son's advancement in the uses (and abuses) of words, but flies in the face of nature if we trust the father's own evaluation of the boy: "But he's slow with his tongue, you see, and he reads but poorly, and can't abide the books, and spells all wrong, they tell me, an' as shy as can be wi' strangers, an' you never hear him say 'cute things like the little wench" (18). With his daughter in possession of all the brains that his son should have, Mr. Tulliver seems to have no alternative but to correct such "mistake[s] of nature" (12) by turning Tom over to the schoolmaster.

Mr. Tulliver would not have to make such allowances for mistakes in nature if words (especially the words of lawyers) had not invaded nature and divided him from the world of things: "Not but what, if the world had been left as God made it, I could ha' seen my way, and held my own wi' the best of 'em; but things have got so twisted round and wrapped up i' unreasonable words, as aren't a bit like 'em, as I'm clean at fault, often an' often. Everything winds about so" (18). Tulliver stumbles through the maze of words, and dreams of the time when he might have walked through the Eden of things. Mr. Tulliver rails against the language of lawyers, but even his own speech, especially when it accidentally slips into metaphor, consistently entraps him, as when Mrs. Tulliver takes literally his analogy, "You'd want me not to hire a good waggoner, 'cause he'd got a mole on his face." While she argues elaborately that not only does she have no prejudices against moles, but she rather likes them (after all, her beloved brother had a mole), Mr. Tulliver throws up his hands at the difficulties of words: "I didn't mean justly the mole; I meant it to stand for summat else; but niver mind" (10). Mr. Tulliver has calculated correctly that words often work through indirection, but he has yet to master this power, at least as far as communicating with his wife is concerned.

On his guard against the pitfalls of figurative language, Mr. Tulliver characteristically uses definitions that are simple linguistic equations in order to unravel what is wrapped up in words: "a river's a river" (137), for example, and "water's water" (14); in fact, "the principle that water was water" (135, 139, 140) may be the first principle for Mr. Tulliver. The father's definition of himself as an honest and substantial man of nature depends on this practice of naming by tautology—his use of substantives that are equal to themselves by virtue of the law of irrefutable equations. The corollary here is Tulliver's mistrust of new names: the old names are better because they are closer to the original things. "'Why, Pivart's a new name hereabout, brother, isn't it?'. . . 'New name? Yes—I should think it *is* a new name'" (136). The newness of his name disqualifies Pivart from interfering with the river (and infringing on the father's own use of the water), especially since "a river's a river"—a primal fact that has existed for generations under the Tulliver eye, and perhaps more importantly under the Tulliver name. Mr. Tulliver's practice of naming casts the bourgeois father in the role of the owner of property, the proprietor of nature. Tulliver sees himself as the Adamic first father who, if not the bestower of the original names of things, is at least their keeper. But he finds that the things of nature are being robbed from him in the name of the law, or, more particularly, in the name of Pivart. Mr. Tulliver's exasperation at this new name and what it portends takes the form of uprooting it, making it into a verb which Tulliver empowers himself to define as an act of aggression: "But I'll *Pivart* him!" (136). In a novel where the family name is the badge of honor, Mr. Tulliver turns Pivart's name on the man himself, as an execration.

As the keeper of the original names for things, Tulliver sees himself as the man of nature, victimized from without—by words, especially the artificial words of the lawyers. But "a river's a river" in Tulliver's lexicon makes the river his own, and I would argue that his appropriation is an impertinence against nature. It is Tulliver's decision to educate his son that most clearly undermines his view of himself as the natural man. First, it betrays his own son into what Tulliver sees as the artifice and dishonesty of words: "I want him to know . . . how to wrap things up in words as aren't actionable . . . [to] let a man know what you think of him without paying for it" (20). Second, it seeks to subvert nature's most basic design, the law of Oedipal displacement:

> "if I made him a miller an' farmer, he'd be expectin' to take the Mill an' the land, an' a-hinting at me as it was time for me to lay by an' think o' my latter end. Nay, nay, I've seen enough o' that wi' sons. . . . I shall give Tom an eddication an' put him to a business, as he may make a nest for himself an' not want to push me out o' mine." (15)

The "winding about" that seems to Mr. Tulliver the crookedness of civilization is in fact an especially apt image for the cyclic and turning pattern of nature. Doesn't his own knowledge that sons displace fathers inadvertently recognize such a pattern? Educating his son, then, is an attempt to stop the natural flow of time, or at least to sidetrack his impalpable double, "father Time" (134). Even the mill that the father works is a symbol of change; "the unresting wheel" (8) represents the twists and turns to which everyone, even fathers, must yield. In short, Tulliver's naming tautologies, and the simple view of nature they propound, naively misunderstand (or deliberately resist) the fact that "Nature has the deep cunning which hides itself under the appearance of openness" (29).

Nature and language seem to work hand in hand in Tulliver's defeat, despite his claim that language (except when it is held to simple equations) is the contrary of nature. We can see this best when we understand that Tulliver's first principle, "water is water," exposes Tulliver's willful attempts to oversimplify nature as well as language. Tulliver sees water as the solid ground on which he tries to build his life, but water is the fluid medium of change that pulls him down, like the fluid medium of language itself. Hence "water" appears in the text in the service of a series of linguistic tricks played on Mr. Tulliver. First, there are the half-comic idioms showing the different threatening sides of water, as in Aunt Glegg's warning that Tulliver is "getting into hot water" (111), or Aunt Pullet's diagnosis, "I doubt it's the water got on his brain" (182). Second, there are those metaphors suggesting that water is a bottomless hole whose depth Tulliver fails to gauge, the opposite of the ground of being on which he can establish himself and his family: "Wakem, to his [Tulliver's] certain knowledge, was (metaphorically speaking) at the bottom of Pivart's irrigation" (139). It is Tulliver himself (and not Wakem) who drowns in these symbolic depths, in the bottomless hole of metaphoric speech. The water that Tulliver tries to hold onto in his useless tautology ("water is water") is the water that drowns his children and uproots the Tulliver home. Water becomes the metaphoric medium by which the rhetorical design of the text undermines Tulliver's simple equation between names and things, and the patriarchal view such an equation is meant to ground.

The consequences of Tulliver's educating Tom are comically suggested at the beginning of "School-Time," when the father's use of metaphor—namely, that Tom's education will "be a bread to him"—backfires. School turns out to be no bread, literally, or at least no pudding and no roast-beef. In the first case, "the difficulty of enunciating a monosyllable in reply to Mr and Mrs Stelling was so great that he [Tom] even dreaded to be asked at table whether he would have more pudding"; "a new standard of English pronunciation" (117–18) paralyzes the boy, and Tom goes hungry on account of words. In the second case, "when Mr Stelling said, as the roast-beef was being uncovered, 'Now, Tulliver! which would you rather decline, roast-beef or the Latin for it?'—Tom, to whom in his coolest moments a pun would have been a hard nut, was thrown into a state of embarrassed alarm that made everything dim to him except the feeling that he would rather not have anything to with Latin: of course he answered, 'Roast-beef,' whereupon there followed much laughter" (119). Roast-beef and Latin are alternatives, and Mr. Stelling's fine talk and Tom's miscomprehension add up to no food. We realize that in *The Mill on the Floss* the home is literally the child's source of nourishment; it is the mill. In this light, school is a substitute for home, words for food. Even the metaphor that calls a pun "a nut" precipitates, in the midst of the larger joke, the way in which metaphoric language teases us by holding out (while holding back) the thing itself—in this case, food. Tom's education begins inauspiciously, with the son's stomach going empty and the father's metaphor going awry.

To decline roast-beef for Latin is innocently to allow oneself to be force fed a foreign idiom that literally changes one's being. Tom is being remade from the inside. After all, *"der Mensch ist was er isst."*[2] "School-Time" tells the story of an alteration in Tom that becomes a perversion of his nature. Tom's consumption of irregular verbs has the unusual side effect of producing an irregularity in his otherwise common boyish nature: it "gave him something of the girl's susceptibility" (124); "at that epoch of irregular verbs" Tom "had never been so much like a girl in his life before" (125). While Tom is stumbling over irregular verbs, Mr. Tulliver is creating his own ("I'll *Pivart* him"). In this light, the highly irregular verb *pivart* looks like a form of *pervert*, a word that George Eliot uses in the text to explore "perverting or mutilating one's nature" (363). The boy who starts out as the veritable mold from which all boys are made, with "a physiognomy in which it seems impossible to discern anything but the generic character of boyhood" (29), becomes like a girl under the auspices of Latin. Before "School-Time," Tom has the generic boy's understanding of genus: "He knew all about worms, and fish, and those things; and what birds were mischievous" (35). But listening to him recite his Latin lesson, we wonder where his natural understanding has gone: "*Sunt etiam volucrum . . . ut ostrea, cetus*" (130). For the genus "flying creatures," Tom lists oysters and sea-monsters; and as the lesson proceeds, for wild beasts he lists oysters again. For the father, water is water and a river a river; for the son learning Latin, an oyster is a flying creature and a wild beast. Neither father nor son can name with meaning. Tulliver's simplistic tautologies go nowhere, and Tom's Latin trespasses the boundaries of nature. Tom's Latin becomes meaningful only if we construe it as hyperbole or metaphor (as in the narrator's naming Uncle Deane the "oyster" Tom opens), but the boy who shrinks from puns neither intends nor understands such meaning.

Tom's mistakes in genus, via the foreign idiom of Latin, underscore how Tom himself becomes an unknown genus, or at least an unknown gender. By being remade (or educated), he is alienated from his own nature. Mr. Stelling uses metaphor to mask the act by which he violates his student: "Whence Mr Stelling concluded that Tom's brain, being peculiarly impervious to etymology and demonstrations, was peculiarly in need of being ploughed and harrowed by these patent implements: it was his favourite metaphor, that the classics and geometry constituted that culture of the mind which prepared it for the reception of any subsequent crop" (122). The violation of Tom is figured in those conventional metaphors used for the male's penetration of the female. Irregular verbs suggest the irregular use of Tom's body and mind, but Mr. Stelling disclaims having to do with "anything abnormal" or with "irregularly educated people" (121–22). I have already suggested that the remaking of Tom is a substitute reproduction; but the "culture of the mind" comes dangerously close to being the perversion of the natural instincts and appetites of the body. Mr. Stelling's figurative language makes Tom's stupidity into a bodily weakness: "A boy born with a deficient power of apprehending signs and abstractions must suffer the penalty of his congenital deficiency, just as if he had been born with one leg shorter than the other" (148), making Tom the symbolic brother of Philip, the physically deformed son of Wakem. Even when Tom tries to reassert his masculinity, to show his body's powers, he mutilates himself by almost cutting off his leg during his sword performance. Mr. Tulliver wants Mr. Stelling to make Tom equal to the men of the law, and appropriately "Mr Stelling was not the man to enfeeble and emasculate his pupil's mind by simplifying and explaining" (124). But "School-Time" ends with Tom almost emasculating his body.

The deepest meaning of the perversion and mutilation of the son depends on understanding the Tulliver relationship to home and land. The scholar fed an exotic diet of Latin (when he once was the child fed at the mill) has his powerful double in the father who praises home and property as the source of his own natural nourishment: "He [Tulliver] couldn't bear to think of himself living on any other spot than this, where he knew the sound of every gate and door, and felt that the shape and colour of every roof and weather-stain and broken hillock was good, because his growing senses had been fed on them" (229). What has fed Mr. Tulliver has naturally become part of him: "he felt the strain of this clinging affection for the old home as part of his life, part of himself" (229). Tom's declaration toward the end of the novel has the force of a literal truth, when he explains to Uncle Deane his desire to win back the mill: "I'm attached to the place" (350). The narrator corroborates the father and son's feelings: "There is no sense of ease like the ease we felt in those scenes where we were born, where objects became dear to us before we had known the labour of choice, and where the outer world seemed only an extension of our personality: we accepted and loved it as we accepted our own sense of existence and our limbs" (133). In *The Mill on the Floss* the loss of home means the loss of limbs, and dislocation becomes mutilation. But the narrator places the feeling of primal unity in the past, in an epoch that she surveys over the gulf of time—the primal scene of childhood, where the objects of home are the home of being. To be attached to home may be what we call natural, but to be turned out of home, to lose the source of one's natural nourishment, and even to lose oneself, may be the kind of education that nature exacts from us.

The language of the law is the instrument by which Tulliver loses his home, and Latin—the language on which the law is based—presents Tom with a lesson that predicts this loss. The single question in syntax that we actually see in Tom's Latin textbook is a paradigm for the Tulliver downfall, and in this way education represents the fall from innocence into disgrace, unmanning, and death. For the category "*Nomen non creskens genittivo*," Tom must give the answer "*Mascula nomina in a*" (131). As an answer, "masculine names in a" is ominously oracular, pointing (like irregular verbs) to emasculation. In Tom's Latin, case in grammar (like genus in natural history) spells a disorder in nature: "A name not increasing in the genitive." Tulliver is such a name. Father and son die in the novel, and the family name fails to increase (Tom is childless, and both he and Maggie die the deaths of the stillborn child, strangled in the waters of creation). The laws of Latin syntax, then, run counter to the Tulliver practice of naming, where the Tulliver name is prior to "Pivart," and hence entitled to the land of generations. Tulliver's failure in the "genitive"—"a grammatical form of substantives . . . chiefly used to denote that the person or thing signified by the word is related to another as source, possessor, or the like" (O.E.D.)—suggests the way in which grammar and rhetoric write up the fall of the substantial man, the man who tries to secure his position at the beginning, as the possessor—a definition of the patriarch and his mutual powers of regeneration and ownership. "Tulliver," the patriarchal name, must take its place with other names in a system of laws that puts "Pivart" first. To educate means to mutilate and emasculate for the Tullivers, a lesson spelled out in English but owing its cutting edge to the ancient language from which such cognates come.

In *The Mill on the Floss* school-time is an awesome epoch that no character, not even the father, can neglect or escape. In fact, the denouement of the story of father and son occurs as a revelation of the father's own education—and illness, impotence, and death. We see, for example, how the father's "breaking down in the world" (171) is the tragic echo of the schoolboy's "breaking down in a demonstration" (204) in Euclid. The father's fate is written up, in words as alien as those of Latin, in a language that arrives on the scene as a death notice. Tulliver is "struck as if it was with death when he got the letter as said you'd [Wakem] the hold upo' the land" (217); "It was the letter with that news in it that made father ill" (176). "Gore's letter" (where the name has a deadly meaning, ironically undermining the man who tries to control the meanings of names) is the letter that killeth, the same letter of the law we saw in *The Scarlet Letter* and *Bleak House*. In all three cases the father fails in his attempt to stand above it. The news this letter carries revitalizes the father's practice of naming by tautology, but entirely to Wakem's advantage: "[Wakem] knew quite well that the majority of substantial men then present were perfectly contented with the fact that 'Wakem was Wakem;'

that is to say, a man who always knew the stepping-stones" (219). The linguistic equation that Mr. Tulliver has made his hallmark, the sign of his own identity, now serves his arch enemy as a formula for permanence and weight, a self-evident equation that represents the indisputability of Wakem's being. At the same time, the simple equation of identity (Tulliver is Tulliver) no longer holds true for the man who is no longer himself. During the illness caused by Gore's letter, Tulliver is "not himself" (166), and in every temporary revival he is seen as "becoming himself again" (212), something Tulliver never entirely achieves.

Tulliver's defeat requires his rewriting of the simple equation of identity: "I'm nought but a bankrupt" (228). Tulliver is no longer Tulliver, and his nothingness, his loss of self, is written out like the figure zero in a bankbook. This equation has its source in Tulliver's understanding that the self is equal to the property it owns: "they've sold me up . . . they've sold me up" (227). Mr. Tulliver shows himself unable "to maintain himself and his family" (171), where the verb *maintain* suggests the conjunction between remaining oneself and financing one's identity— "remain[ing] Mr Tulliver of Dorlcote Mill" (171). The genitive here suggests not the father as possessor, but the father possessed by the property that owns him. Similarly, the man who builds his life on the substantive theory of naming, and on those substances that cannot support him (in Tulliver's case, water), "was held to be a much more substantial man than he really was" (67), where the idea of "a man of considerable substance" (67) suggests Tulliver as a man whose vitality is equal to his property, his money. Tulliver's death therefore comes as "A Day of Reckoning." Tulliver may be no "mere book-man" (20), but his history, summed up at nought, is drawn up by the books, by what in another passage is called "book-keeping . . . and reckoning" (202). The father has "failed" (213) at words and figures, and the consequences are considerably worse than what the schoolboy in a similar position suffers.

The self that can be "sold," the self that can be a "bankrupt" and a "nought," seems very far from the natural self that Tulliver has envisioned for himself. The final version of Tulliver's equations of identity at first seems to restore the man to the simple world of nature: "I'm a tree as is broke—a tree as is broke" (232). Tulliver no longer defines himself through tautology; in the world of self-division and pain he now inhabits, it is metaphor he requires, to describe the mutilated self, the self torn in two (but still at one with the objects of nature). The broken tree recalls an Edenic self to which he can never return: "what's broke can never be whole again" (226). But Tulliver's elegiac cries over a lost natural innocence are cancelled in the modern idiom of bourgeois society: "it's true as the master's broke" (210). Tulliver's metaphoric association between himself and the tree of nature, once exploded, looks like the kind of fine talk Tulliver distrusts, a metaphoric mask for the actual basis of his identity: money. The duplicity of words, the double meaning of "broke," keeps Tulliver honest, in another example of the way in which the rhetoric of the text revises and corrects the language of the patriarch. Finally, "I'm a tree as is broke—a tree as is broke," like "they've sold me up . . . they've sold me up," is the sign that the father's voice has become an entirely impotent and paralyzed echo of itself, of "what I want . . . what I want." His desire to keep the origin secure and grounded is mocked in a speech pattern that is a paralyzed repetition, a failure to develop—a redundancy that is the logical consequence of his tautologies.

In the final winding about that nature executes, the broke master becomes the child. The father's illness puts him in "a childlike condition of dependence" (242), with an "infantine satisfaction in Maggie's near presence—such satisfaction as a baby has when it is returned to the nurse's lap" (175). With the nourishing mill lost, the father begins to feed off his own children in what becomes a deadly psychic parasitism. First, we recall that the father himself is a devoured man. The narrator suggests how, as if it were a law of nature (and not simply the law of lawyers, or of metaphor), "the pike [Wakem] is likely to think nothing further even of the most indignant roach [Mr. Tulliver] than that he is excellent good eating" (219). In turn, the devoured man devours his children through shame, guilt, sorrow, and substitute living: "And Maggie's graces of mind and body fed his gloom" (257). Tulliver's loss of home in this way unmasks what the father's inordinate desire ("what I want") has been from the beginning: the child's fear of losing his home, of being abandoned. Aunt Pullett's maudlin prognostications—"he'll most like be childish, as Mr Carr was, poor man! They fed him with a spoon as if he'd been a babby for three year" (182)—cuts deep when we remember the motive behind Mr. Tulliver's decision to educate Tom to a business different from his own: "I shan't be put off wi' spoon-meat afore I've lost my teeth" (15). Paralyzed, Mr. Tulliver loses the use of those limbs that have represented the power of manhood. Mute, he loses the use of the voice that has represented the patriarchal power of naming. In the end, he is a man with neither deeds nor words at his command. "[N]ot able to speak for himself" (191), the father must have Tom speak for him, and thereby the father at once fulfills and undermines his goal in educating Tom. On the one hand, the son's education trains Tom to use words so that he can defend his father to his uncles and aunts; on the other hand, it prepares Tom to take his father's place, to speak in his stead.

The father awakens from his paralysis to put to use what he purchased with his money—namely, the son's ability to write. The son's function is realized in blind obedience to his father's command: "Do as I tell you, Tom. Write" (233). The patriarchal voice at the beginning fulfills its desire by turning potency to destruction through a deadly inscription: "Now write—write as you'll remember what Wakem's done to your father, and you'll make him and his feel it, if ever the day comes. And sign your name Thomas Tulliver" (233). For the unmanned father, the "straight" son and pen (like the sword earlier) become weapons, measuring rods of the father's potency: "Wakem 'ud be fine and glad to have a son like mine—a fine straight fellow—i'stead o' that poor crooked creatur!" (309). The curse is for all time, inscribed in the Bible alongside the births and deaths and marriages of the family. It extends across the generations, and thereby defines what it means to be a Tulliver. Tom's life is cut out for him. Tom is bound to obey, by understanding that only in writing is he allowed to be his father's son: "you never forgive him, neither, if you mean to be my son" (232). The signature of his name (Tom is told his name, in case he should doubt or forget it) ensures not only his obedience to his father, but also the only identity he has ever known, an identity he is powerless to transcend. The child once awkward with tongue and pen now writes his identity in the words of a curse.

While Tom writes the curse in the Bible and signs his own name, he acts in strict obedience to the letter of the law, the father's law. Tom's identity is abridged, once and for all, by writing his father's words but signing his own name to them. This act suggests the ultimate consequences of the father's language of tautology. The son's identity is cancelled in the father's; this is the equation Tom never gets beyond. All the son's goals are the father's: to pay back the debts, to own the mill again, to take care of Mrs. Tulliver and Maggie, to retrieve the family name. Tom's barrenness, then, stems from the fact that "he espoused his father's quarrels and shared his father's sense of injury" (135). This marriage (as the Latin cognate reminds us) prevents any other. Similarly, in his return to the mill, Tom returns to a food source that has darker consequences than the son realizes: "prejudices come as the natural food of tendencies which can get no sustenance out of that complex, fragmentary, doubt-provoking knowledge which we call truth. Let a prejudice be bequeathed, carried in the air, adopted . . . these minds will give it a habitation" (401). In *The Mill on the Floss* the patriarchal inheritance is prejudice; the barren son, in adopting his father's prejudice, makes it a substitute child and proceeds to feed on it (in the manner of the father's feeding on Maggie's graces). The familial metaphors here redefine home as a habitation of barrenness, parasitism, and even cannibalism. Using the same metaphoric framework, the flood that was "the nightmare of her [Maggie's] childish dreams" (455) is finally realized at the end as a representation of the way in which the family, like the river, is a nightmarish incubus, "a hungry monster" (36) that feeds off and finally devours the children—in short, a psychic inundation. The mill is the home in which the archetypal son "Télémaque was mere bran" (250). Still, in perhaps his most perverse definition of all, Tom sees his obedience to his father's memory as "manly feeling" (479).

"Living twice over" in fiction

While the father's voice booms in the foreground, announcing his plan to educate his son, Maggie sits reading quietly in the background. But it is precisely Maggie's activity at self-education that haunts the Tulliver household, as the father hints in his description of Maggie "allays at her book!" (15). Maggie's reading constitutes the counterplot to the education of father and son in *The Mill on the Floss*. Any reading or writing not directly in the service of the family (as Tom's education is meant to be) is a threat to the family. Hence the father commands Maggie to "shut up the book" (17) at the same time that he plans Tom's education. Even as a young child Maggie explains the value of reading in such a way that it threatens the narrow family circle. The child encourages Luke to read about people from different countries—about Dutchmen, for example— because "they're our fellow creatures, Luke—we ought to know about our fellow creatures." Luke's answer characteristically rebukes the widening circle of reading: "There's fools enoo—an' rogues enoo—wi'out lookin' i' books for 'em. . . . That's what brings folks to the gallows— knowin' everything but what they'n got to get their bread by" (27). Luke transforms Mr. Tulliver's dark augury about Maggie's reading, "it'll turn to trouble" (15), into a vision of the gallows. For both men, reading threatens the attempt to live the insular life of the mill, to live by bread alone. After all, Tom's education is meant to be quite literally a bread to him, a new means to secure old ways, the safeguarding of the nourishing mill.

Maggie's wide reading gives her the power of naming and in so doing situates her between the extreme positions of father and son, with the balance that gives her words the power of meaning. Maggie explodes her father's simple tautologies, where each name is naively equal to itself, but she does not go so far as her brother's senseless mistranslations, where name and thing are unreasonably, even perversely, divided. Quite simply,

Maggie opens up the domain of words so that they have more than one meaning. This power of Maggie's is announced in a subtle variation on Tom's comic mistranslations when Maggie mistranslates "*bonus*" as "gift," but recoups with a lesson in words that Tom never grasps: "It may mean several things—almost every word does" (127). From Maggie's understanding of the multiple meanings of words flows a series of new meanings that allows the plot of the daughter to subvert and transcend the plot of the father and son. Maggie's "bond of friendship" (267) with Philip, for example, revises the monetary "bond" (114) her father owes to Philips's father. Maggie opens up the meaning of words at the same time that she opens up the question of heredity, breaking down the simple equal sign between names ("Wakem was Wakem") and between parent and child (Wakem Sr. equals Wakem Jr.). Maggie's friendship with Philip actually originates in her reading, not simply because both enjoy reading, but also because in reading Maggie learns a lesson that is prohibited in the Tulliver household: "He couldn't choose his father, you know; and I've read of very bad men who had good sons, as well as good parents who had bad children" (155). After instructing Tom in the multiple meanings of words, she instructs him in the multiple meanings of sons, a lesson that falls on deaf ears, given Tom's investment in the life of tautology, the life whereby the son is a copy of the father.

Maggie escapes the plot of tautology, in which the child simply recapitulates the parent, by taking the entire Tulliver–Dodson language of money and recoining it. The "purchase-money of pain" (287) buys new meanings that escape the literal, the strictly monetary and legal. In the course of the novel Maggie's pain and suffering purchase, in the form of Christian ransom, freedom from the letter of the law, and thereby "the new life" (442) for which Philip thanks her. Philip's gratitude for the "gift of transferred life" acknowledges her power to "give a new and blessed meaning to the foregoing pain" (442–43). Maggie's mistranslation of "*bonus*" as "gift," then, has its own power, its own truth; it is a redefinition that occurs through raising meaning to a new level. The terminology of bond, debt, claim, promise, and breach constitutes the discourse of the family in *The Mill on the Floss*, underpinned at every turn (as in "broke" and "substantial") with legal and financial meanings. Maggie "mistranslates" such terms, and uses the language of the family only to revise it. She takes Mr. Tulliver's brand of honesty—"You [Tom] must see and pay everybody" (195)—and makes debts and bonds and laws for herself. She tells Stephen, for example, "If the past is not to bind us, where can duty lie? We should have no law"; and "we owed ourselves to others, and must conquer every inclination which could make us false to that debt"

(416–17). By showing how almost every word may mean several things, Maggie enlarges the family's "narrow notions about debt" (244) into a humane terminology that surpasses the letter of the law. Maggie's life rewrites the family history, and in this way the plot of Maggie's story recapitulates the story of father and son by altering it. Perhaps the sharpest irony of *The Mill on the Floss* shows the way in which, by escaping literalism, Maggie successfully escapes the letter of the law—the ultimate law to which father and son lose their lives.

It is with the help of a crucial text that the child's clever defense of her mistranslation of "*bonus*" develops into the young woman's recoining of the terminology of debt and law. Once again Maggie's reading widens the difference between her life and the plot of father and son. The last sentence of Book 3—"'Be quiet, Maggie!' said Tom. 'I *shall* write it'" (233)—couples the familial silencing of the daughter with the son's decision to write the father's curse in the family Bible. But Book 4 strategically closes with another book and another writer in a symbolic displacement of the father. The words that Maggie reads in *Thomas à Kempis* double back with ironic precision on her father's history, revising the terms by which he lives and dies: "If a man should give all his substance, yet it is as nothing [unless] . . . having left all, he leave himself, and go wholly out of himself" (253). The father, who strives to be the man of substance, never willingly goes out of himself; in fact, as we recall, his division from himself is precisely the illness that finally kills him. Afraid of the symbolic life, Mr. Tulliver defines going out of oneself (the ultimate erasure of his equation of self-identity) solely as death. While reading her book, the daughter takes as her goal what the father defines as death, and therefore she begins her life where his ends: "for the first time she saw the possibility of shifting the position from which she looked at the gratification of her own desires—of taking her stand out of herself" (254)—a revision of the father's first words, his self-centered "what I want."

The Mill on the Floss bases an entire scheme of historical progress on this difference between father and daughter, the difference between the generations that Tom elides. The parent who is unable to "begin life anew," unable to accept and make new meanings, is like "certain animals to which tenacity of position is a law of life—they can never flourish again, after a single wrench" (173). The narrator's metaphor describes how Tulliver lives his life, and loses it—by the letter of the law, the stubborn law of his own nature (and not the law of lawyers). Tulliver becomes an extinct species lost in the Darwinian gulf of time. The Darwinism of *The Mill on the Floss*, however, is not based on the laws of nature, but on the laws of morality—those laws that Maggie draws up for herself. Maggie's ability to change her position (in exact antithesis to her father's tenacity of position), so that she can stand outside herself, is a moral choice she makes. This choice ensures her role in that historical progress which, however apparently obscure, the narrator chooses to record in *The Mill on the Floss*: "young natures in many generations . . . in the onward tendency of human things have risen above the mental level of the generation before them. . . . The suffering, whether of martyr or victim, which belongs to every historical advance of mankind, is represented in this way in every town, and by hundreds of obscure hearths" (238).

Maggie's power to name becomes a historical advance precisely insofar as it expands a local language into a universal definition—in other words, insofar as she takes the family's narrow notions of debts and laws and in expanding them gives us a definition of humanity. I have shown how she takes the laws of lawyers, of literal debts and bonds, and revises them. But she also takes the laws of nature, and by revising them gives us a definition of what it means to be human. Throughout the text, in an exercise that is at once ironic and sympathetic, the narrator compares the characters in *The Mill on the Floss* to animals. We recall Mr. Tulliver playing the roach to Wakem's pike, or Uncle Deane as the oyster Tom opens, or even the generalized metaphor of those animals for whom tenacity of position is a law of life; we see as well Mr. Stelling compared to a beaver in an extended comic simile, and Mr. Riley and Mr. Tulliver compared to "a parasite on an animal towards whom she has otherwise no ill-will" (23). Such metaphors sometimes represent human relations as a Darwinian struggle for survival (as in the case of roach and pike); more often, they are a call to forbearance, to accept human behavior as natural (even when it is not especially noble, as in Mr. Riley's selfish advice to Tulliver). But Maggie's power of naming often works in the opposite direction. Maggie redefines nature in order to make it human, or at least to tell us what in nature needs redefining so that we know what to call human. She counters Stephen's plea for the naturalness of their love, for example, by arguing with his terms: "Love is natural; but surely pity and faithfulness and memory are natural too" (395). Maggie's redefinition of the species "man" is in effect a paradox: she makes natural those qualities that are essentially found only in man at the same time that she sees man's special power in his ability to deny these most natural instincts. While it is natural—and even "natural law" (417), as Stephen calls it—for Maggie and Stephen to love each other, it is natural (but only as part of the highest human laws) for Maggie to give him up—as natural as "pity" and "faithfulness" and "memory." To be human, then, is to break the limits of one's own nature, to leave oneself behind.

Perhaps the most telling realization of this ability to step outside oneself occurs toward the end of the novel when Maggie relinquishes her claim to Stephen. At this point we witness an act of self-revision. We must recall that the young child's suffering makes her selfish (though understandable) consolation take the form of wishing she were Lucy: "She was fond of fancying a world where the people never got any larger than children of their own age, and she made the queen of it just like Lucy . . . only the queen was Maggie herself in Lucy's form" (53–54). This is the child's imaginative leaving of herself behind in order to fulfill her wish. After all, her brown skin and straight hair make her mother reiterate, "I'm sure she's [Lucy's] more like *my* child than Sister Deane's" (37); "I'm sure Lucy takes more after me nor my own child does" (12). But at the end of the novel Maggie exchanges her childish wish, even now that it is actually fulfillable, for experiencing Lucy's pain instead. When Lucy's lover falls in love with Maggie, the girls do change places, but Maggie gives Stephen up. She now puts herself in Lucy's place, not for self-gratification, but to experience her pain: "I see—I feel their trouble now: it is as if it were branded on my mind. *I* have suffered, and had no one to pity me" (419). To look through the text's underscored "I" is to look through the self, during the process of self-cancellation, to look through Maggie to see Lucy (and Philip too), and, as I will eventually suggest, to look through Maggie to see Marian Evans.

Tom's mind, we recall, was ploughed and harrowed by his teacher; Maggie's mind is branded by the sympathy she feels for Lucy and Philip, a lesson she learns from her own "Teacher" (254). Such images revise the tradition of British epistemological and pedagogical thought that the text invokes throughout, as in "call[ing] the mind a sheet of white paper or a mirror" (123). In *The Mill on the Floss* the perceptions of childhood are not neutral Lockean inscriptions but painful violations of consciousness whose most powerful signs are those marks that Maggie represents by driving nails into the head of her doll. This is why the text so consistently refers to the "brand" (132), the "burning iron" (420), the "touch of the torturing iron" (410). By insisting on the imagery of "wound" (295), "breach" (154), "scar" (459), "bruise" (198), and "lesion" (196), *The Mill on the Floss* revises the figure of the Lockean impression or "mark" and in so doing radicalizes the form of the *Bildungsroman*. At the same time, education in *The Mill on the Floss* is not simply mutilation and death— the view that the story of father and son suggests. Like the brand on the heart in *The Scarlet Letter*, which Hester makes into the sign of charity (so that her neighbors redefine the scarlet letter as standing for "Able"), the branded mind becomes the sign of Maggie's willingness to suffer for another. The deep impression is a violation that the male resists, and in this way such a figure suggests the female's superior educability. I recall that Tom's education "nullified his boyish self-satisfaction and gave him something of the girl's susceptibility" (124). The narrator metaphorically describes the father's "unreceptive surfaces" which prevent "the spiritual seed" (240) from being able to attach itself to him. In such ways the inviolability of father and son defines at once their gender, their unregenerateness, and their uneducability. Father and son seem never to receive on their minds anything deeper than first impressions or a set of "'first ideas'" (133): "he was a boy who adhered tenaciously to impressions once received: as with all minds in which mere perception predominates over thought and emotion" (145), Tom is unable to make that progress which "transform[s] our perception into love" (36). Maggie, on the other hand, educates herself in that sense beyond the mere senses of perception, in "that new sense which is the gift of sorrow—that susceptibility to the bare offices of humanity" (167). The emphasis on mutilation and emasculation, on the male limbs and organs of power, in the plot of father and son is undermined by the susceptibility of the daughter in her development of the "organs of her soul" (217–18). Such meanings make us see how the definition of the genus "man" requires revision. Tom's slander of Philip, "you're no better than a girl" (152), and Philip's heavily sarcastic retort to Tom, "It is manly of you to talk in this way to *me*" (303), begin to make us see how the "straight" (198) male, the crooked or deformed male (who was "brought up . . . like a girl" [370] and whose "nerves . . . were as sensitive as a woman's" [375]), and the girl who is a "mistake of nature" belong to a series of transvaluations of gender. *The Mill on the Floss* deliberately opens up a distinction between the genus "man" and the gender "male." Moreover, it issues a warning: father and son are not simply in danger of losing their maleness; their humanity is in jeopardy as well.

The branded mind, or the mind educated in suffering, shows itself through the face—in particular, the face that reveals a humanity so overwhelming that it lifts us above nature. This is the face Maggie envisions when she suffers for Lucy at the end: "she saw it face to face now—that sad patient loving strength which holds the clue of life—and saw that the thorns were for ever pressing on its brow" (413). Here the branded mind, like the branded heart in *The Scarlet Letter* and the marked face in *Bleak House*, represents the universal "pattern of sorrow" (254) that inscribes each of us like the stigmata that Christ wears for everyone. This face that holds the clue of life comes as the climax to a series of faces—or rather a history of defacement and self-effacement— that tells Maggie's story in short, from the "defaced" (24) doll, so marked with pain that it can barely represent anything human; to the idiot boy's face that Tom tells her to see in the mirror after she has cut off her hair (56); to the gypsy's face she seeks, like the brown one she sees in her own mirror (94); to the face she will not indulge, "steadily refusing . . . to look at herself in the glass" (257), when she facelessly hides from her pain in numbed anonymity. But at the end of the novel it is Maggie's own face that holds the clue of life, when she rescues Tom's spirit during the flood. It is not until "he [was] face to face with Maggie—that the full meaning of what had happened rushed upon his mind . . . it was such a new revela- tion to his spirit" (458). This face-to-face revelation recalls the well- known passage from II Corinthians in which, after seeing through a glass darkly, we finally know and are known face to face. Maggie's "beaten face" (458) is the embodiment and revelation of meaning, the meaning that is the mark of the spirit. The narrator's caution—"the lines and lights of the human countenance are like other symbols—not always easy to read with a key" (216)—goes unheeded by the Tullivers and Dodsons, who look in the face merely for the signs of the family lineaments. The deeper key lies not in conformity to the family line and mold, but to the human face we all share.

The universal "pattern of sorrow," where the branded mind represents the conjunction of one's own suffering with another's, defines what "the purchase-power of pain" in fact buys: the "superadded life in the life of others" (205), "that enlarged life which grows and grows by appropriat- ing the life of others," the "gift of transferred life" (443). But at the outset our most immediate response to the power of pain does not suggest it as an instrument used in our behalf, but rather as something from which we suffer, especially when we meet it in the repeated simile that makes a bodily pain represent what we find difficult to name, the heart's pain: "like a horrible throbbing pain" (420), "like an aching nerve" (250), "like an aching limb" (291), "like a sharp bodily pain" (306), "like a patient . . . without his opium" (380). Such descriptions make clear the narrator's sensitivity to pain, and become part of a humane forbearance that forgives us our weakness in the face of pain: "The leap of natural longing from under the pressure of pain is so strong, that all less immediate motives are likely to be forgotten—till the pain has been escaped from" (452)— in other words, the narrator sympathetically catalogues another one of our weaknesses as entirely natural. At the same time I would argue that one of the deepest narrative motives of the text challenges us to bear pain, as if to teach us that our endurance of pain is precisely the measure of our deepest humanity: "Only those who have known what hardest inward conflict is, can know what Maggie felt . . .—only those who have known what it is to dread their own selfish desires as the watching mother would dread the sleeping-potion that was to still her own pain" (448). In such a passage we turn from sympathy for our own selfish desire to escape pain, to wonder and admiration for the person who dreads such a weakness more than pain itself. Moreover, the opening clause sounds the note of challenge, making me name myself either as an initiate in the experience of pain or as an outsider. Such a challenge comes even more directly in another narrative aside that begins to characterize more clearly—or at least more personally—the generalized narrative voice, at the same time that it makes me question myself: "so it comes that we can look on at the troubles of our children with a smiling disbelief in the reality of their pain. Is there any one who can recover the experience of his childhood, not merely with a memory of what he did and what happened to him . . . , but with an intimate penetration, a revived consciousness of what he felt then . . . ?" (57–58). My tolerance for those who naturally seek to escape pain now seems to lie at a more superficial level in the text's multilayered goals; at a deeper level I find the call to revive pain, to reexperience it, and in that way to realize its benignant power to make me one with another. The revival of my former self carries with it the bonus of the superadded life of others. Such narrative asides in the text convince us that the narrator, often cerebral and wryly ironic, feels intimately the severity of pain; they are the narrator's credentials to tell the story of Maggie, but what is more, they suggest the deeply personal nature of the entire enterprise of *The Mill on the Floss*. In short, they are chinks in the armor of the omniscient and distanced narrative posture. We begin to feel palpably, behind the double or revived consciousness of Maggie, a similar consciousness at work. Just as Maggie draws on her own memories to recast her life as another's (Lucy's, say), this voice has done the same; in fact, the reader begins to suspect that Maggie is the very product of that sympathetic recasting.

I wish to formulate this relationship between Maggie Tulliver and George Eliot by understanding the way in which naming becomes a fictive act that extends beyond the limits of the story proper of *The Mill on the Floss*. But before doing this, it is necessary to gauge precisely the differences between the father's and the daughter's practices of naming in *The Mill on the Floss*. We saw that the father's definition of the things of nature through tautology had its source in a tautology of self, a patriarchal equation of personal identity that is really a version of the godly "I am that I am." Similarly, Maggie's reinvention of the literal law, the laws of nature, and finally the species "man," has its source in a redefinition of herself. Taking her stand outside herself breaks the equation of identity to which the Tullivers are wed. It is almost as if Maggie takes Tom's comic mistranslations—fish and wild beasts that fly—and turns them into a profound truth about herself and the world of the human: "I am not equal to myself." In the words that George Eliot translated from Feuerbach (and to which she signed the name "Marian Evans"), "Man is himself at once I and thou: he can put himself in the place of another."[3] This is what makes the human the only species that is defined through a form of antidefinition, named through a form of anti-naming. Finally, one could say this is what makes the human the only species for which equation is superseded by metaphor. Following the text's permutations in the rhetoric of identity, I am arguing that instead of tautology and mistranslation (the rhetorical modes of being that father and son represent), metaphor is the key to identity for Maggie. The text defines metaphor as the power to "declare what a thing is . . . by saying it is something else" (123). Suddenly we realize that the apparent verbal trickery of metaphor (in Tulliver's view) may hide its profound usefulness for representing a world that surpasses mathematical equation, a self that is historical insofar as it seems always to be surpassing itself.

I now can ask outright the question I have been approaching with hesitation: what is the relationship between George Eliot and Maggie Tulliver? This familiar question usually calls forth a convincing series of biographical conjunctions (such as the sister's early passion for her brother, or their eventual alienation, or the three maternal aunts) and some discrepancies (such as the daughter being the father's favorite child).[4] I wish to reformulate the question: what is the significance of Marian Evans's, or Mrs. Lewes's, or George Eliot's retelling her life as Maggie Tulliver's?[5] By reformulating the question in this way I hope not to eschew the question of biography but to shift its emphasis. I wish to open up the ways in which fiction functions to name the self even beyond the text proper. By pressing the series of names the author bears, I hope to read the name Maggie Tulliver as one name among others. This makes accessible the way in which the joint activities of naming and fiction-making function with equal force within the text of the novel and within the life of "George Eliot." Finally, in restating the question, I wish to make clear that the activity that characterizes Maggie's role in the story of *The Mill on the Floss* has its sharp and telling analogue at the authorial level of the text. We learn from Maggie the deepest power of fiction and the way in which its source lies in naming. By placing in the foreground Maggie's power of naming as revision (whereby she revises such names as "law," "debt," and "bond," and in so doing breaks the naive equation of self-identity), we enlarge our sense of the consequences of George Eliot's fictional renaming of herself and her world in *The Mill on the Floss*. Breaking the limits of one's own nature occurs through telling one's own life but rewriting it as another's—in short, through fiction. In both cases—in Maggie's case as well as George Eliot's—renaming empowers one with the superadded life of others.

Another way of formulating this relationship between character and author is by understanding the drawbacks of autobiography for George Eliot, and perhaps for the writer of fiction in general (Hawthorne, Twain, Hardy, and Conrad come immediately to mind). The fiction writer's argument with autobiography often slides between a native antipathy or temperamental distrust on the one hand and a philosophic indictment of autobiography as a particular form of discourse on the other, both of which informed my analysis of the double structure of *The Scarlet Letter*, in which the "autobiographical" "Custom-House" and the "fictional" tale overlap. George Eliot deliberately refused to write her autobiography, and responded personally at several points in her lifetime to particular autobiographies that came into her hands. At Harriet Martineau's, for example, she declared, "it deepens my repugnance—or, rather, creates a new repugnance in me—to autobiography, unless it can be so written as to involve neither self-glorification nor impeachment of others."[6] Such a statement finds in autobiography the antithesis of what I have been defining throughout my study as the motives and effects of fiction. One could say that in autobiography George Eliot fears that memory will be enlisted to glorify the self and attack another, while the act of memory we have studied in *The Mill on the Floss* revives personal pain and suffering precisely in order to pity another. This distinction recalls the way in which I characterized the two kinds of discourse in *The Scarlet Letter*: writing as a form of accusing another as a criminal versus fiction as a form of acknowledging a common crime in which we all share. In the first case writing functions as the letter of the law; in the second case as the merciful spirit that pardons us all. A similar model exists within the double plot I have described in *The Mill on the Floss*. I refer to the scene in which Tom, following the patriarchal command, inscribes in the family Bible the curse against Wakem. In this scene memory and writing join in the service of punishment: "Now write—write as you'll remember what Wakem's done to your father" (233). But "write as you'll remember," of course, underwrites the entire project of *The Mill on the Floss*, and I am arguing that the deepest motive in the text functions as a countermovement to such a scene. Writing becomes fiction precisely insofar as memory becomes sympathy: "Sympathy is but a living again through our own past in a new form."[7] Finally, one could say that every exaggeration, invention, omission, distortion—in short, every discrepancy between a life and its representation in fiction—functions ideally as a protection against the glorification of oneself and the accusation of another. It is precisely in the distance between fact and fiction that the possibility of mercy can be actualized. This is the bonus that comes of freedom from the letter of the law. Hence the danger of reading *The Mill on the Floss* autobiographically in a conventional way, and thereby reducing it to the kind of text George Eliot sought to surpass.

The name George Eliot is shorthand for the entire fictionalizing process I have been describing. Already in renaming herself George Eliot, Marian Evans has taken that step beyond herself that the fictionalized portrait of Maggie Tulliver accomplishes in another, more extended way. A particularly relevant analogue that traditionally characterizes the fiction writer's complication of his or her role as author is spelled out in the convention of the author as editor or translator, various versions of which exist at the beginning of the novelistic tradition in such works as *Don Quixote*, *Robinson Crusoe*, and *Clarissa*—a tradition that gets refurbished with particular relish in the twentieth century in such works as Conrad's *Under Western Eyes* and Nabokov's *Lolita*. And I have analyzed Hawthorne as the "editor" of his tale in my discussion of the problematic relationship between autobiography and fiction in *The Scarlet Letter*. In George Eliot's declaration that a force beyond herself wrote the best pages of her novels, we have an especially telling version of this disequilibrium between author and fictional text: "George Eliot told me that, in all that she considered her best writing, there was a 'not herself,' which took possession of her."[8] Such a statement suggests that even the fictive identity "George Eliot" is insufficient to rename the author, to describe how, in writing fiction, one breaks the limits of one's own nature, taking a position outside oneself.

This apparent negation of the (authorial) self takes a special form in fiction: a series of selves that diffuse identity and layer the space that exists between the "not herself" who writes and Maggie Tulliver, the final product of that writing. One might expect this splintering and layering of selfhood to exaggerate the distance between author and character. On the contrary, each "self" that exists between the fiction writer and Maggie functions as a mediator, another layer of self, another gradation of identity that brings into relationship the "not herself" and Maggie, though this relationship is never ultimately knowable, or at least never finally named in the sense of labelled, fixed, held stable. Within the text itself I have suggested that precisely insofar as Maggie transforms herself into Lucy we see the power of the fictional act. But everywhere in the text we see this splintering and duplication, and Maggie herself stares it in the face when Philip makes her see a picture of herself that he did many years before, so that "Maggie saw her old self leaning on a table" (264). At such a moment, in a way characteristic of fiction, doubling is doubled. Maggie sees her old self, her other self, at the same time that she represents what George Eliot is doing in seeing Maggie.

But even such a pattern does not comprehend the extent to which the splintering of the self takes place in the text of fiction. The young girl leaning on the table, looking out from the portrait at Maggie, recalls the narrator's posture in that curiously haunting prelude to the story proper in chapter 1—that narrator who is herself splintered in an especially complicated way, with arms leaning on her chair, watching in her dream her younger self (leaning her arms on the bridge) watching a little girl—Maggie. In a dream, then, the narrator looks inward where she sees her earlier self; but more than this, within the dream her earlier self sees the little Maggie, and the two are symbolically associated by being engaged in the same act, watching the "unresting wheel" of time that turns the self, making it and remaking it over and over again. The narrator's vision of herself as another, as her former self—whom she can watch in the special domain of the dream—mediates the second version of herself as another, as little Maggie. It is only by looking through a projection of herself as another that she is rewarded by a second projection of herself as another. The dream here is the analogue of fiction. The dream allows us to look through a multilayered "I," so that when the narrator awakens she has the sense of being two "I's," two (perhaps even three) people at once, in two different places at the same time: "I have been pressing my elbows on the arms of my chair, and dreaming that I was standing on the bridge in front of Dorlcote Mill" (8). At the beginning of the text, then, we look through "I" for the first time, and see a process of self-cancellation that is at the same time a process of self-perpetuation. The dream (or fiction) in which I lose myself rewards me with multiple selves—a kind of breeding that stands at the beginning to supersede the family system of exact and barren duplication and tautology. For this reason, this scene strategically comes first in the overall design of the novel, preempting the father's plan to educate his son (at the beginning of chapter 2). It is this opening scene that achieves the status of "the first beginning," to revise Mrs. Tulliver's apothegm about the law. In this scene George Eliot gives us a striking vision of the self outside itself, allowing us to watch, as if some veil has been drawn, the fiction-making process at work. The opening scene in *The Mill on the Floss* becomes the first beginning by showing us what it means to live twice over in fiction, an idea which the father fails to grasp and which therefore lies at the heart of his lament, "I shall never live twice o'er" (226).

7

Tess of the d'Urbervilles

Tess of the d'Urbervilles is the novel that Hardy claimed was "the beginning of the end of his career as a novelist."[1] It is also the novel that, in light of the paradigmatic naming plots with which I began, signals a crucial rupture in the novelistic tradition. *Tess* reverses perhaps the most characteristic plot of fiction by beginning with the traditional end: the discovery of a name that brings with it the discovery of an entire family history. Hardy uses this reversal of plot to ironize the central myth of the bourgeois novel, the story of the child's happy discovery of his or her family inheritance. The novel that begins by discovering for Tess a lofty name and noble blood ends by showing these to be forms of disinheritance. As the beginning becomes the end, the plot of comedy turns to tragedy. We realize how precisely *Tess* has reversed a traditional plot when we see that the child whose true name is disclosed at the beginning becomes the child who is lost through a surplus of names at the end. I am referring here to Angel's search for Tess at Sandbourne at the end of the novel. First he looks for her under the name of Mrs. Clare, then under "her maiden name, . . . Miss Durbeyfield"; the postman recognizes neither name, but does know "the name of d'Urberville"; but then Angel is surprised to find the landlady referring to Tess as "Mrs. d'Urberville" (and to make the irony complete, referring to him as "Mr. Angel") (311–12).[2] In Hardy's hands, then, the traditional comic plot of fiction, in which the child wins his or her name and family history, becomes an ironic moment within the larger plot in which Tess ultimately loses her name and identity. In short, Hardy reinvents the plot in which the name is found (*Oliver Twist*) as the plot in which the name is lost (*Clarissa*). In this way *Tess* is an ironic look back at an entire tradition—the beginning of the end not only of Hardy's career as a novelist, but also of the novel's career as a comedy of inheritance.

But perhaps the most revolutionary goal Hardy set for himself in novel writing centered on the characterization of his heroine. Hardy announced that "the doll of English fiction must be demolished,"[3] and Tess Durbeyfield in many ways seems a perfect fulfillment of his injunction. With Tess the dairymaid Hardy attempts to uncloset the heroine of English fiction by giving her a body. In so doing he demolishes at once the bodiless and doll-like heroine (whose quintessence comes in heroic proportions at the beginning of the tradition with Clarissa) and the tradition of English fiction based on such heroines. We recall Esther and her alter-ego, personified as Dolly (and that ultimate personification of the doll as alter-ego, Ada), and Maggie, whose brutalization of her doll quite logically turns into the young woman's self-effacement and self-sacrifice, an entire renunciation of the body and its will.[4] But in *Tess* Hardy does something quite puzzling: the story of Tess the field-woman, the girl with ripe mouth and womanly bosom, the heroine of sexual longing, still repeats the traditional fictional plot in which the proper identity of the child and the female is cancelled. Such a plot, as we will see, confirms Tess's own shrewd anticipation of her entire story: "I am one of a long row only—finding out that there is set down in some old book somebody just like me, and . . . know[ing] that I shall only act her part" (107). Is Hardy asking us to view Tess's life as a "belated" (195) repetition of the story of the first great heroine of English fiction? In the context of his remark about the doll of English fiction, Hardy complained that "justice has never been done to such women in fiction." One has to wonder how such a complaint is met by the ironic "justice" that the President of the Immortals metes out to Tess in the novel's last paragraph.

I can state the paradox of *Tess* in the following way: Hardy gives us a palpable woman, a heroine of flesh and blood, but in so doing he explores the ways in which the female body actually facilitates Tess's dissolution. The source of this paradox lies in what I have been calling the family plot. Tess's body becomes the crucial tool by which she is subjugated because it is a body in the service of a name, the family name. Hardy's understanding of the belatedness of the novel in his own day, then, actually undermines the project of making the heroine of English fiction palpable: "Novel-writing as an art cannot go backward. Having reached the analytic stage it must transcend it by going still further in the same direction. Why not by rendering as visible essences, spectres, etc., the abstract thoughts of the analytic school? . . . The Realities to be the true realities of life, hitherto called abstractions. The old material realities to be placed behind the former, as shadowy accessories."[5] In such a comment Hardy foretells the end of the realistic novel. His own role in this historic moment occurs through his version of the family plot, so that the specters made visible in the case of *Tess* are the heroine's ghostly ancestors—not merely made visible, I should add, but reified into "alabaster people" (108). It is against such a background that the palpability of Tess dissolves. In *Tess*, the family name shines through the flesh, so that the Platonic—or, in Hardy's vision, the ancestral—essence is embodied and reembodied in the family flesh. In this way *Tess* becomes an ironic revision of the naive myth we saw in *Oliver Twist*, where the child is the happy reembodiment of the parent. Hardy ironizes this tradition in all three of his last novels. In *The Well-Beloved* the protagonist falls in love with three generations of the same woman—over and again with the "perfect copy" of his first love, christened always with the same name, with each new "edition" taking up "her abode in the living representative of the dead."[6] This morbidly comic plot of family repetitions takes the form, in both *Tess* and *Jude the Obscure*, of a tragic family curse in which the dead master the living.

I mean by these introductory remarks to make clear that the theme of personal belatedness within *Tess* merges with Hardy's reaction to traditional forms of the naming plot and the family plot. My first topic in the following pages will be *Tess* as a naming plot in which the child is sacrificed in the name of the family. My second topic will be *Tess* as an act of fiction-making that is best understood through the crucial idea of confession. These two topics are in fact one: the act of naming, especially self-naming, expands quite logically into the act of confessing, of disclosing the secret truth about oneself. While the first topic is meant to bring full circle the issue of naming plots discussed in Part One of this book, the second topic is meant to do the same for the issue of fiction and family discourse discussed in Part Two, returning especially to my analysis of confession as motive in *The Scarlet Letter*. When reading James's book on Hawthorne, Hardy copied passages from *The Scarlet Letter* into his notebook.[7] He must have been struck even before this time with the similarities between himself and Hawthorne. Obsessed with family curses and an ancestral past in need of expiation (or, failing that, mere escape), both wrote of the temporary and ultimately unsuccessful escape from the fatal claims of the family, especially the ghostly but nonetheless potent family body: "A mortal symptom for a person, being sick, to lose his own aspect and take the family lineaments, which were hidden deep in the healthful visage";[8] "that old mortal symptom in him not mentioned by Hippocrates, that is, to lose his own face, & look like some of his near relations."[9] What I wish to emphasize in bringing together Hawthorne and Hardy is not so much the similar ways in which they view the family, or even the kinds of structural similarities shared by *The Scarlet Letter* and *Tess* (with a heroic but sexually stained woman at the text's center, flanked by two antithetical but nonetheless uniformly weak men). Instead, I will explore the ways in which both writers—morbidly self-conscious, reticent, and even secretive—exploited fiction as a medium in which the truth could be at once concealed and revealed. Despite the clear convergence of theme and structure in the two novels, I have read *The Scarlet Letter* as a novel exemplary of the successful mediation between confession and fiction, self and other, while I will read *Tess* as a novel exemplary of a series of inevitable disjunctions—between confession and fiction, between private self and public self, between self-sacrifice and self-preservation.

"In the name of the Father"

A comic prelude with tragic undertones, the opening scene of *Tess* is a curious ceremony, both baptism and burial, like that makeshift baptism that falls on the eve of the burial of the infant Sorrow. With everything slightly askew, down to a biased gait and a wandering tune, Hardy's characteristic realism presents us with a chance encounter, issued in by a series of indefinite articles (an undistinguished evening, a middle-aged man, an elderly parson, and a gray mare). But we soon learn that this chance encounter functions in order to fix identity, to name. The encounter begins with an apparent linguistic mistake that broaches the question of personal identity for the entire text: "what might your meaning be in calling me 'Sir John' these different times, when I be plain Jack Durbeyfield, the haggler?" (5). Durbeyfield's question arises from what I have called in previous chapters a naive equation of personal identity, like the tautologies that, in different circumstances, both Pearl and Mr. Tulliver use. Durbeyfield (like Tulliver) sees himself as the man of plain meaning, the father assured of his own identity, and the antiquary (like Wakem) as the harbinger of a kind of linguistic confusion. But the antiquary announces himself as the man of simple self-possession at the same time that he taunts Durbeyfield for not knowing his own true name: "I am Parson Tringham, the antiquary, of Stagfoot Lane. Don't you really know, Durbeyfield, that you are the lineal representative of the ancient and knightly family of the d'Urbervilles?" (5). The father's place at the origin is preempted linguistically by a family name he does not recognize as his own. In this light, the father falls into the role of the child: he is the belated and passive recipient of the family name. The bestower of names, the man of power at the origin, is the genealogist, the man who sets in motion the entire story of *Tess of the d'Urbervilles.*

The antiquary's function in this scene—to fix identity, to name with accuracy—is in fact equivocal. The man Durbeyfield begins to disappear before our very eyes, first as he is merged with a corporate body, and second as he seems literally to lose his own body. The parson's direct address to Durbeyfield in the second person—"You declined a little in Oliver Cromwell's time" (6)—equivocates between singular and plural, on the point of making Durbeyfield quite simply dead: "You don't live anywhere. You are extinct—as a country family" (7). Once his name is corrected, the man who was simply "walking homeward" (5) at the outset of the scene seems homeless, living nowhere, a mere specter escaped from the ancestral vault; and by the end of the novel the Durbeyfields are in fact forced to leave their home and camp beside the family vault. Like Sorrow, named to be buried, Durbeyfield is given his name only to be buried—alive. His inheritance is an ominous dispossession of life itself. This is another way of saying that Durbeyfield's body is actually appropriated by his dead ancestors. Looking squarely at Durbeyfield, the antiquary tells him, "Yes, that's the d'Urberville nose and chin—a little debased" (6). Named and possessed of a family, Durbeyfield seems to have lost more than he has gained; he is a faint or debased copy, or still worse, he is only one of the living dead. A ghostly prelude, this scene functions to foreshadow the way in which Tess will yield to the family plot, the life of the living sacrificed to serve the ever-potent life of the dead.

Neglecting the darker implications of the parson's news, Durbeyfield rejoices in his good fortune. After all, he is the man who has been chosen to live the central fiction of the eighteenth and nineteenth centuries, the common man surprised by the discovery of his own noble name and blood. He therefore loses no time in putting his knowledge to its most potent use, in what turns out to be an ominous parody of the father's role as engenderer and name giver. His knightly name encourages him not only to issue orders to a passing youth, but also to elide the boy's name. The boy, properly offended, asks essentially the same question Durbeyfield has just asked the parson: why do you not call me by my correct name? "Who be you, then, John Durbeyfield, to order me about and call me 'boy'? You know my name as well as I know yours!" (7). Durbeyfield repeats the parson's act, but in reverse: he takes a name away. Power resides in names, even in names withheld—in the boy's misunderstanding that this is Durbeyfield (when it is really d'Urberville) and in the man's refusal to use the boy's name. Durbeyfield strategically springs his newly discovered noble name on the boy and exacts the proper obeisance. Durbeyfield's double victory consists, then, in unnaming the boy and in repossessing the power to disclose his true name himself. But the boy whose loss is Durbeyfield's gain is in his namelessness an ironic reflection of the man who, according to the antiquary, childishly does not know his own name. Furthermore, the father's abuse of the power of naming will be repeated by Alec, but turned against Durbeyfield's own name and blood. The spurious possessor of the d'Urberville name sires through Tess "a nameless child" (77) that recalls the "boy" the father flaunts with namelessness. This is the kind of reciprocal "justice" that gives *Tess* its persistent tone of tragic cynicism. It anticipates the narrator's later contemplation of the doubtful morality that "visit[s] the sins of the fathers upon the children" (63).

The naiveté of Durbeyfield's response to the parson's news can be gauged in another way: while Durbeyfield thinks he has acquired his true name, the novel's fabric is woven from the specialized rhetoric of the double name. Durbeyfield learns his name is d'Urberville, for example, in what the text's first paragraph calls "the Vale of Blakemore or Blackmoor" (5); and the history of Tess's journeys is marked by such place names as "the river Var or Froom" (87) and "Bulbarrow or Bealbarrow" (24–25). Such names show us that even places apparently as old as time itself are subject to the human power to name and thereby fall within the equivocal boundaries of two names, just as Tess's family name passes from d'Urberville to Durbeyfield. In fact, the entire world Tess lives in is subject to a process of double naming when we realize that Tess herself "spoke two languages; the dialect . . . [and] ordinary English" (17).

But place names in *Tess*, like those in *Bleak House*, have their deepest purpose in alerting us to a world inhabited by characters whose identity is double. The playful rhyme about farmer Crick suggests a dissociation of identity whose symptom, the double name, is shared by the major characters of *Tess*: "Dairyman Dick/ All the week: —/ On Sundays Mister Richard Crick" (90). Both of Tess's lovers are elaborate versions of this "Sunday" transformation, this dual personality signalled by a double or false name. Alec is "The Convert" who backslides, caught between two lives, recalling to us that he is the man whose family converts its name and history by annexing the d'Urberville name. Alec Stoke has two names, or a compound name, Alec "Stoke-d'Urberville." Tess's other lover, Angel Clare, has a "Sunday" name that is a misrepresentation: he is "misnamed Angel" (281), both in his heterodoxy and in his cruel treatment of Tess. Such details underscore Tess's realization that Angel, during the confession of his own dark secret (Angel's fall into lust and debauchery), is "her double" (189). Like Tess herself, both her lovers represent identity under cover, misperceived and misnamed. Alec d'Urberville is after all the spurious copy (or double) of Tess, the true d'Urberville, just as Angel in his secret fall is a copy of Tess, the impure woman. We will see that the double name in *Tess* measures an extraordinary range of identity, from the self deliberately masked and duplicitous to the self that is genuinely multiple, even unstable, and sometimes convertible.

The double names in *Tess* (Crick/Dick, Blakemore/Blackmoor, Durbeyfield/d'Urberville) are unusual because they do not, like many of the double names in *Bleak House* (Summerson/Hawdon, say, or Weevle/Jobling), lead to the discovery of the one, true name. In fact, because they are only marginally different, they dispute such an idea, and we will see that the single name is a misleading sign below the surface of which is always hidden another name, another identity. For Hardy naming suggests the inherently equivocal status of identity. First, people and places are consistently situated on the margin (reminding us of Hawthorne's use of this figure), and, second, the margin is consistently on the brink of elision. This first point makes us realize that the status of Tess's identity is reflected in the nature of the landscape that plays so prominent a part in her story. The double place names in *Tess* are a sign of a compound landscape, "a level landscape compounded of old landscapes long forgotten, and, no doubt, differing in character very greatly from the landscape they composed now" (92); "an essence of soils, pounded champaigns of the past, steeped, refined, and subtilized to extraordinary richness" (163). For all their differences, the novel's settings are essentially part of one symbolic landscape—a compound place, viewed "at the marginal minute" (40). At this minute of "neutral shade," "half-tones," and "spectral, half-compounded, aqueous light" (110), those characteristics that usually distinguish between different objects are elided (so that a compound name is appropriate). It is that "hair's breadth . . . moment of evening when the light and the darkness are so evenly balanced that the constraint of day and the suspense of night neutralize each other" (72). Precisely at such moments, time and again, Tess seems to live her life, caught by the eye of the narrator even as she is disappearing into some larger, neutralizing setting: "her quiescent glide was of a piece with the element she moved in. Her flexuous and stealthy figure became an integral part of the scene" (72). In this way Tess merges not simply with the landscape, but with the kind of woman whose compound nature gives her a compound name: "A field-woman is a portion of the field; she has somehow lost her own margin, imbibed the essence of her surrounding, and assimilated herself with it" (74). Such moments of apparent Wordsworthian harmony are darkly ominous in Hardy. After all, the field-woman's loss of her margin, her assimilation into something larger than herself, suggests Tess's loss of virgin purity, Alec's appropriation of her (whether in the primeval forest of the Chase or later at Sandbourne), and, more generally still, that loss of individual identity which Hardy describes as the assimilation into her ancient family, so that she is named Tess of the d'Urbervilles. For such reasons the ominous symbol that predicts Tess's future is a text without a margin: "the *Compleat Fortune Teller*, . . . so worn by pocketing that the margins had reached the edge of the type" (18), is the source Mrs. Durbeyfield consults in order to try Tess's future. But the book where words invade the simple blank of the margin tells more about the child's fate than Mrs. Durbeyfield can understand.

Tess's loss of margin is part of an elaborate series of figures that suggest how Tess's bodily presence often obscures rather than clarifies the issue of her individual identity. First, the work of the laborer makes the individual a member of a corporate body. Consistently we read about "the body of harvesters" (78), of how they "leave in a body" (55), of how they "formed, bending, a curiously uniform row—automatic, noiseless" (118), and we remember Tess's complaint: "I am one of a long row" (107). Similarly, the three milkmaids (Izz, Retty, and Marian) often form one body with Tess—"Four hearts gave a big throb simultaneously," "the whole four flushed as if one heart beat through them" (120–21)—because "the differences which distinguished them as individuals were abstracted by this passion, and each was but a portion of one organism called sex" (124). For Hardy, woman consistently loses her margin—to the field, to her co-workers, to her sex generally. The individual woman's body loses whatever individuality it may have by becoming representative, so that Tess is caressed and kissed in that poignant and mysterious scene in which the three other milkmaids use her body as a way to reach Clare; to kiss Tess is to kiss the woman "he" loves. Such a scene reveals that Tess's body is a vehicle not only for her lovers—for Alec's lust and for Angel's ideal search for purity ("a whole sex condensed into one typical form" [111])—but for the members of her own sex as well.

Tess is corporate, part of a common property to be used by others, in an even more significant and primitive way. Tess's body is almost literally a vehicle for the working out of the family history. Tess is, in her mother's naive words, "kin to a coach" (21). With so many of the journeys in the novel positioned equivocally between deliberate and unconscious activity, Tess often seems conveyed by a force larger than herself—the d'Urberville (and sometimes Durbeyfield) will—as in "her involuntary hold on [d'Urberville]" (44) during the frightening ride to Trantridge; or in her sleepy ride with d'Urberville in the dense fog on the night of her violation; or in Angel's unconscious sleepwalking during which the passive Tess is conducted to a coffin; or in her ride to her wedding (during which she "did not see anything, did not know the road they were taking"), in a "cumbrous and creeking structure" with "a decayed conductor" (metaphors for the corrupt d'Urberville body) who is " expecting the old times to come back again" (179). Even when Tess sets out on foot, to go to Trantridge where her parents send her to claim kin, she seems carried along by a will—or feet—not completely her own: "Her feet had brought her onward to this point before she had quite realized where she was" (31). Clarissa describes her fatal error in the same terms ("My FEET are guilty; but my HEART is free" [2.266]), and we recall the river current steering Maggie and Stephen toward passion and away from duty. In such cases, while the identity of the self is implied, it in no way is palpable or manifest; the body seems divided from the true, but vague and indefinable, self.

The deepest meaning of such a division has its source, for Hardy, in the family plot. The body complicates personal identity by returning it to a communal identity, the family body—to its features, its propensities, its urges, and thereby to a repetition of its actions. This explains why Tess's many journeys become one circuitous path. Such a meaning also accounts for the special form the idea of fatality takes in *Tess*—not a dark curse dropped from an abstract heaven above, but a destiny lived in and through the flesh that one inherits, the fatality of heredity. And perhaps this sense that Tess is dual, even multiple, accounts for the way in which both Alec and Angel study and puzzle over her, raising the issue of her existence to ontological status: "What are you?" (33), Alec asks her; "I don't know what you are" (200), Angel tells her. From one angle, such questions are an extraordinary anomaly. Tess the field-woman, the simple milkmaid, viewed almost entirely out of doors, the flesh-and-blood antithesis of her sexless, nervous, self-contradictory, and enigmatic successor Sue Bridehead, is nonetheless the center of a controversy in interpretation.

The best way to understand this controversy, in light of the family plot, is to recall from *The Scarlet Letter* that "What art thou?" is the question directed at the child who is viewed not as a person but as a product, the sign of someone else's making. In *Tess* Hardy shows us the child's makers, on the evening Tess has left the parental cottage for the first time, lying awake in bed, in the place where Tess was made, arguing over each other's contribution and share in the gamble and game that is Tess's life: "'What's her trump card? Her d'Urberville blood, you mean?' 'No, stupid; her face—as 'twas mine' " (43). Tess's compound nature exists from the beginning, like the adulterous self Hawthorne describes in *The Scarlet Letter*. Hardy continually reminds us that she has her mother's "prettiness" (86), say, and her father's self-contentment (88); and we recall the scene in which Tess sees "her fine features were unquestionably traceable in these exaggerated forms" (183), the d'Urberville portraits, the dead ancestors who symbolically stand between the newly married couple and the consummation of their marriage. Tess seems put together, manufactured out of different parts and pieces. Or, to put it another way, Tess is dual, even multiple, insofar as she is layer upon layer, compounded of ancestral traits long forgotten, like the compounded landscape she travels. In *Tess* the family myth that makes the child the reincarnation of the dead parent, so naively represented in *Oliver Twist*, turns tragic.

Tess shares her body with others, then, before her intercourse with Alec. This is why her violation occurs under the sign "d'Urberville." Hardy takes the double plot of *Clarissa* and shows the insidious merger between the family plot and the plot of sexual violation by a bold addition: he gives the central actors in both plots the same name, the patriarchal name of d'Urberville. When I say that Tess's body is annexed in the name of d'Urberville, I am talking at once of the family and of the lover. From this angle, Alec's appropriation of Tess's body is simply the fulfillment, or embodiment, of the earlier act by which the Stoke family stole the name. The errand to claim kin, then, appropriately ends in the d'Urberville violation of Tess, just as it begins with Durbeyfield confusing different kinds of flesh and different kinds of mercantilism, sending his child from home on an errand of seduction while honoring the carcass of old Prince: "I won't sell his old body. . . . I won't part from him now" (28). The father here confuses as well the living and the dead, a confusion that anticipates the way in which the ancestral body lives as Tess's body dies. By collapsing the family plot and the love plot, Hardy makes the sexual surrender of the female at the same time a forceful representation of the compound or marginal nature of the child, the child who serves the name of the family. The family plot in *Tess*, then, underlines Tess's violation with the uses and abuses of the child's body. We recall Tess's complaint to her mother, "I was a child when I left this house four months ago" (70), and to Angel, "I was a child—a child when it happened!" (194). Even when we see Tess as a mother, she has borne "a child's child" (80), and in naming and burying the child "in the name of the Father" (80) she performs an act that collapses into one moment the essence of what will be her own painfully extended history. Tess the child witnesses her own death in the dying infant of her own flesh. Such an event is the corollary to the father's naive rejoicing that he is "one flesh" (6) with the dead.

The confusion over the dead body and the body alive is enacted not just by Tess's father but also by both her lovers. When Alec d'Urberville seems to Tess an "effigy" come alive, "a living person" (302) come out of the d'Urberville family vault, he represents the way in which the dead family member rises, and haunts us, even to the point of living within our own bodies, shaping our own intentions and desires. The reciprocal act occurs when, at the house that once was the mansion of the d'Urbervilles, Angel picks up Tess's living body from the unconsummated marriage bed "with as much respect as one would show to a dead body" (207) and transfers it to a stone coffin. The two scenes mirror each other: in *Tess* the dead are taken for the living, and vice versa. In Tess's case, the dead threaten to live through her and, in this way, to exact her death. It is an idea common in kinship-based societies, and it is often given as the explanation behind the many taboos against speaking the name of the ancestor. In *Totem and Taboo*, a powerful meditation on the way in which "the dead . . . become stronger than the living," Freud attempts to understand the taboo on the names of the dead by examining the common belief that "the dead, filled with a lust for murder, sought to drag the living in their train."[10] In Hardy such an idea is ambiguously placed between the "savage's" naive belief that the dead family member will devour him and the "neurotic's" unconscious surrender to the family history (to use Freud's terms). What I am calling the family plot includes all the ways in which the family, Alec, and even Angel (as we will see more fully) ensnare Tess and use her in the name of the family. And beyond this there is Tess's willingness to surrender. How can we account for this willingness, even desire? Is Hardy working out the idea of the unconscious through the idea of the family, the ancestral body, and even the family curse? Hardy shows us Tess surrendering—in her work, for example—to an activity larger than herself, an activity that divides her from herself: "her arms worked on independently of her consciousness" (276). Does Tess's body go to death in the same way? In any case, we see through Tess's flesh—especially when Angel lays it in the tomb—to the family "skillentons" (8) that the father naively glories in having dug up. In *Tess* the child's body is cancelled, made impalpable—as in those scenes in which, at the neutral moment of twilight, Tess's body transparently disappears into the landscape—at the same time that the family specters are reified into "alabaster people" (108). Durbeyfield evidently does not understand that to be "one flesh" with one's ancestors is to be one flesh with the dead. In *Tess* death becomes the ultimate family member, the "cold relation" (84) toward whom Tess's journey to claim kin impels her, the dark and delayed sequel to the father's walk homeward in the novel's opening scene.

I have said that Tess seems manufactured out of different parts and pieces from the ancestral body. In this she is like all children. What makes Tess special is that she has been selected by her lover to represent just the opposite: "untraditional newness" (109). Hardy's compound landscape, and his compound woman especially, is an ironic commentary on Angel's search for purity, virginity, integral wholeness, the entirely "fresh" and "novel" (109). Nature does not allow the purity Angel seeks, and the child is the crucial sign of impurity: "Every desired renewal of an existence is debased by being half alloy." "Nature in not allowing issue from one parent alone"[11] makes every child an alloy, as we saw in *The Scarlet Letter*. Pearl's remark in *The Scarlet Letter*, "I am mother's child," is the child's confused half-truth that results from the parents' criminal concealment of the natural fact of the father. In *Tess*, the heroine's attempt to escape her d'Urberville blood by emphasizing her maternal inheritance is the child's wish, perhaps learned from others, for an ideal purity and simplicity of identity that is impossible. In *The Scarlet Letter*, the child appropriately carries the sign of adultery; in *Tess*, she bears the double name, or what Angel will call the name behind whose "manifest corruption" (159) lies another name and an ancient, corrupt history, the inevitable family history. It is to this double name—and to Angel's role in Tess's family history—that I now turn.

"In the name of our love"

Hardy undermines the difference between family and lover in *Tess* with startling swiftness during "Phase the First" (though, of course, it is an idea that he continues to develop throughout the novel). It is as if, by giving the lover the name of the family, Hardy brings to fulfillment with a bold stroke what it takes Richardson in *Clarissa* much longer to accomplish. But Hardy tells us in his "Preface" that his purpose is to emphasize the life of his heroine after her violation, something unthinkable in the case of Clarissa—"this novel being one wherein the great campaign of the heroine begins after an event in her experience which has usually been treated as fatal to her part of protagonist." *Tess* adds to Richardson's collapse of the plots of the family and the lover a new element: the plot of another lover, an alternate lover, an angel-lover. And it is clear that Hardy adds this new element in order to explore whether or not another lover will allow Tess to escape the family plot. The early phases of *Tess* explore her attempt to claim kin; the succeeding phases begin with her resolution to disclaim kin and to name herself: "There should be no more d'Urberville air-castles in the dreams and deeds of her new life. She would be the dairymaid Tess, and nothing more" (85). It is with such a resolution that she goes off to Talbothays, where she will meet Angel Clare.

There is an ominous consistency in the two love plots that places both of Tess's lovers, as different as they are, in the same position. This consistency recalls Hawthorne's subtle positioning of Chillingworth and Dimmesdale in the same role, each one desiring Hester not to make public his name. From one angle, *Tess*'s two love plots at least look different. The first love affair begins with Tess's openly announcing the name d'Urberville to Alec—it is, after all, her passport to kin—while the second has her deliberately keeping this name from Angel time and again. But a deeper unity dispels this difference: both Alec and Angel insist on naming Tess in a way that contradicts her own desire. Tess travels to Trantridge to claim kin, to reveal that her name is d'Urberville, but Alec will make the economic arrangement she seeks only if he remains in charge of what she is called: "I must think if I cannot do something. My mother must find a berth for you. But, Tess, no nonsense about 'd'Urberville'—'Durbeyfield' only, you know—quite another name" (35). The spurious d'Urberville, master of verbal dissimulation, keeps Tess's real name to himself, just as he writes in the third person (in his mother's name) to offer Tess a berth, where the awkwardness of the pun is underlined by the ostensible intent of Alec's remark—to disallow verbal confusion, to insist down to the letter on the difference between the two names. But when Tess travels to Talbothays, this time to escape her d'Urberville name, Angel insists that she keep it: "Tess, you must spell your name correctly—d'Urberville—from this very day" (159). When Tess resists, Angel's solution is simply another version of telling her what her name is or should be. In this way Angel undermines Tess's original intention in coming to Talbothays—to call herself "Tess, and nothing more" (85). In fact he uses her desire to escape her name in order to frighten and trap her into his own name, reminding us that the linguistic tricks played on Tess are part of a system of naming in which the male, whether father or husband, possesses the power to name. This is another way in which Hardy collapses the stories of the child and the female. Upon discovering Tess's family name, Angel responds: "Now then, Mistress Teresa d'Urberville, I have you. Take my name, and so you will escape yours!" (160). Angel's "I have you" underscores the way in which possession—economic, sexual, psychic—depends on knowing and manipulating another's name.

Angel's naming of Tess is the best indication of how he wishes to remake (unmake) her; naming becomes a form of deadly reproduction. With Alec to birth her and Angel to reproduce her, Tess is the child whose value depends on her name or, more precisely, on the ability to manipulate her name: "after I have made you the well-read woman that I mean to make you" (159), Angel tells her he will execute the plan of "triumphantly producing her as worthy of such an ancient line" (177). Angel then holds within his power the timely disclosure of Tess's name, "the grand card with which he meant to surprise" (177) his family. Angel is the double of Tess's father. Both see Tess's secret name as the trump card in the game of Tess's life, and both try to use this secret by controlling its timely disclosure for their own purposes. Such meanings darken Angel's apparent tenderness: "You are a child to me, Tess" (161). Repeating the pattern that we have now seen in so many novels, Tess plays the role of the child—to be made and remade, named and renamed. Tess becomes the subject of a linguistic game, and Angel becomes its master: "He called her Artemis, Demeter, and other fanciful names half teasingly, which she did not like because she did not understand them. 'Call me Tess,' she would say askance" (111). Such literary names refuse Tess the novelty and freshness Angel says he wants, and tease her into a dissociation of identity that unwittingly anticipates what Angel will eventually believe about her—that she is an impostor, that her apparently simple request to be called Tess is part of a moral disguise of the most serious kind.

At one level the question of Tess's duplicity is less a moral dilemma than a philosophical, especially a linguistic, conundrum. Is Tess, the woman Alec violates, the same woman Angel loves? It is as if in her confession Tess has suddenly entered the game of naming, only to take it over with a grim, unexpected stroke of her own. Angel tells her, "You were one person; now you are another. My God—how can forgiveness meet such a grotesque—prestidigitation as that!" (191). Angel reacts with satiric bitterness and "horrible laughter" as "he contemplated this definition" (191). Angel's nicety of definition in the midst of Tess's shrieks anticipates the way in which the new definition of Tess will eventually be turned to his further use, his further power. But for the time he has lost the particular Tess—or text ("tex," in the text painter's suggestive slur-ring)—he controlled by being the master interpreter: "con[ning] the char-acters of her face as if they had been hieroglyphics" (147), Angel has been in charge of deciding on Tess's meaning. "'She is a dear dear Tess,' he thought to himself, as one deciding on the true construction of a difficult passage" (183). Angel's reading here is similar to what I have been defining throughout this study as an equation of identity that makes the person equal to the name he or she bears. After the confession Angel rewrites the equation to label Tess "d'Urberville," where her proper name, and whatever is individual about her, are lost in a meaning typical and common. This is a form of classification that recalls Lovelace's attempts to classify Clarissa. In both cases it is classification as slander. We might see Angel's search after the pure woman as what distinguishes him from Lovelace (who seeks, by naming Clarissa "woman," to reveal her impurity), but in fact it is a telling symptom of that same "philos-opher's regard" (109) that will allow him to classify her as impure by the use of another generic name, d'Urberville. Angel reacts to the confession by reducing its words to the disclosure of Tess's secret name, as if what Tess has revealed is neither an accidental moment in her history nor a complicated series of events, but the master word, the true name by which she is to be called, known, possessed, undone, the solution to the riddle of what she is: "I cannot help associating your decline as a family with this other fact—of your want of firmness. Decrepit families imply decrepit wills, decrepit conduct" (195). His failure to guess Tess's secret name earlier—"I wonder that I did not see the resemblance of your name to d'Urberville, and trace the manifest corruption" (159)—now rebounds back on him. He has failed to give Tess's name the linguistic analysis that would have unlocked the key to another kind of corruption—the name as the sign of Tess's impurity. In short, Angel holds Tess to the name she has tried to escape, and turns her confession into a confession of her name. In this way, her second love affair becomes an ironic version of her first, with Tess again sacrificed in the name of the family.

Tess now finds herself in a special predicament. While the confession convinces Angel that Tess should bear the name d'Urberville, she in fact at this point bears the name Clare. Tess asks herself: "She was Mrs. Angel Clare, indeed, but had she any moral right to the name?" (181). Tess can answer the question in the affirmative only by a total surrender of identity. The first step in this surrender is a radical reinvention of herself through the words of Clare. If Tess's confession remakes her into an impure woman (in Angel's eyes), perhaps the patient and unswerving rehearsal of Angel's words will reconvert her to innocence and purity. In

"The Convert," Tess and Alec meet on the common if disorienting ground of preaching another's words. Alec, whose mission is "to preach the Word" (267), quotes St. Paul via Parson Clare, while Tess quotes chapter and verse of Angel's texts. In this light, "The Convert" names not only Alec but Tess as well. Both are empty vessels for another's words. Hardy recalls here Hawthorne's probing of Puritan conversion, especially the view that the words one speaks remake one, convert one's identity (I have shown the specious uses to which Dimmesdale puts such a belief). In Tess's case it is conversion by puppetry, a characterization that is made more than once in the novel (17, 64). Having learned what her own words of confession have cost her, Tess dies to be reborn in and through the words of Angel—an unorthodox version of the Christian's rebirth through the Word. In this way she fulfills Angel's deepest desire, even though in far-off Brazil he cannot know this, for hasn't Tess from the start been the student for whom reeducation would become remaking? Her admiration of Angel from the beginning "led her to pick up his vocabulary, his accent, and fragments of his knowledge" (148). But the impressionable girl in love, valued for her spirited ability to copy, becomes the abandoned wife, reduced to pathetic mimicry: "she replied in the same words, at the same time inclining her mouth in the way of his" (203); "she simply repeated after him his own words" (212). "Her acute memory for the letter of Angel Clare's remarks, even when she did not comprehend their spirit" (266), makes us see that in her worship of Angel, Tess serves another form of patriarchy, another form of the letter of the law.

In speaking of his words as a "seed" (141), Parson Clare reminds us that the Word is empowered to replace literal engendering, to give one another birth, and it is precisely such a rewriting of identity that Tess desires. In short, Tess's worship of Angel's words becomes part of a plot whereby Tess hopes to escape the name d'Urberville, part of a deliberate attempt to change identities that begins to look like a form of self-eradication. Tess adores the name of Clare while her own name remains anathema. In both cases the name assumes a critical role in Tess's destiny. By sacrificing herself to be worthy of the name Clare, Tess simply reenacts from a different angle what we have seen before: the naming of Tess as other than she is or feels. From start to finish, Tess experiences her life as a gulf between herself and a name (whether "d'Urberville" or "Clare"). And no matter how faithfully she manages to mimic Angel's words, Tess remains outside the name Clare until Angel will recognize her as such. She does not allow herself to use the name, and so the last phases of her story are the worship of a name that she bears only privately as a sign of her own shame and unworthiness. Tess repeats her poignant request to be called by her proper name, but now only to protect Clare's name: "Do not call me Mrs. Clare, but Tess, as before. . . . I don't wish to bring his name down to the dirt" (236). Similarly, Tess refuses more than once, during her many encounters with Alec, to reveal her husband's name. Tess gives over her life to the safeguarding and concealment of Angel's name. Such acts simply continue the deification of Angel that began when he was the god of the four milkmaids' universe, the "*He*" (236) whose name they dared not pronounce. Angel fixes Tess's identity through a name, and thereby exposes her, but Tess keeps Angel the hidden man–god without material manifestation, so that Alec, with appropriate irony, calls the ineffable husband "a mythological personage" (274). The secret name Tess kept hidden during the Talbothays idyll, in order to protect herself, changes to the secret name she now keeps hidden in order to protect her husband. Like Hester in *The Scarlet Letter*, Tess is the woman who keeps the secret name of the man. *Tess*'s double plot, then, can be explained in the following way: Tess's life fluctuates between two extremes, between serving a name she comes to hate (d'Urberville) and serving a name she reveres (Clare).

As the woman abused in the name of names, as the guardian of names, as the woman who finally is willing to die for a name, Tess brings Clarissa alive only to die another death. We recall that Clarissa dies for the name that supports an entire culture; at the same time she dies for the name that supports her own selfhood, the self sacred and essentially inviolable: "Clarissa" *is* "virtue." Tess does just the opposite: she dies for a name whose meaning is entirely private (and entirely misunderstood), a name whose power depends at least in part on its ability to eradicate her own selfhood—the name Clare. Tess takes as the center of her identity another's name, a name that she worships but feels unworthy to bear, a name that she hides as the secret center of all being. For these reasons Tess relinquishes, to the power of a name, her sense of the conventional boundaries of self and other, of life and death. This is the only way I know to account for two extraordinary confessions that Tess makes. In the first, Tess explains after her major confession that she has restrained herself from taking her own life (she tells Angel) because "I was afraid that it might cause a scandal to your name" (200). In the second, she explains the event that moved her to murder Alec: "He heard me crying about you, and he bitterly taunted me; and called you by a foul name;

and then I did it" (319). Tess lives a life she finds unbearable in order to protect another's name; with the complete logic of madness she takes another's life in the same name.

I am arguing that the plot by which Tess is sacrificed in the name of the family turns into the plot by which Tess sacrifices herself (and Alec d'Urberville) in the name of love. In this light what Tess takes to be an escape from the family plot is only a deeper surrender to it. When Tess worships the name Clare she unwittingly valorizes the way in which the family, Alec, and Angel have consistently used the name d'Urberville to control her. It is as if Tess has capitulated to the idea that her identity is carried in a secret master word or name. Tess thinks her life lies entirely in the distance she can place between "d'Urberville" and "Clare"; but the two names are equally invented, equally fictitious, equally private in the meanings they carry—and equally potent to destroy. Tess fails to look critically at the act that valorizes names and the act that makes serving a name a form of self-sacrifice. But my language here may betray a naiveté that Hardy's text ultimately attempts to rescind—namely, that the self, especially the self in love, is identifiable in any publicly or mutually recognizable way. We feel this in Tess's plaintive but useless cry to Angel: "I thought, Angel, that you loved me—me, my very self!" (192). Tess's attempt to reinvent herself as "Clare" and to eradicate herself as "d'Urberville" is symptomatic of her attempt to establish a self through a name, to conceive of herself as loved for herself, to imagine that, in love, she has a self that is sufficient to be named. Even Angel participates in this lover's illusion, but we hear in his avowal already the note of doubt as he tries to convince himself of Tess's substantiality: "It was for herself that he loved Tess; her soul, her heart, her substance" (139). In Hardy's world the self is impalpable, unrecognized—"She was not an existence, an experience, a passion, a structure of sensations, to anybody but herself" (77)—and in such a world the name is actively sought, held onto in desperation; it is the last illusion. The desire to name Tess, expressed by the family, Alec, and Angel, turns into Tess's own desire to be named, to have a self, if not in the public domain, then at least recognized in love, a self outside her own consciousness—a self that becomes all the more impalpable as the family, Alec, Angel, and finally Tess try to name it. Clarissa's attempts to save herself are often made in the name of virtue, a name that she soon sees Lovelace not only does not respect, but actively attempts to discredit. In any case, it is a name with a publicly approved meaning and value. But with *Tess* we turn to a world in which the self summons to its own defense a far narrower margin of meaning. Tess's attempt to save herself is based on a name whose meaning and honor she thinks Angel shares, a name whose meaning, for Hardy, is the most private, the most subjective, the most tenuous of all: "In the name of our love, forgive me!" (191). Angel, the man in charge of names and their definitions, responds by arguing with Tess's terms, by using a philosopher's logic (and a lawyer's knowledge of legal cases) to hold her to the letter: "O Tess, forgiveness does not apply to the case!" (191).

Coda: Confession in fiction

Angel's interpretation of Tess's confession repeats the act which we have seen victimize the characters of fiction over and over again: "to read human nature" (100) and thereby to valorize the act of reading over the human self. Hardy makes us see how human beings—not only Tess, but Angel and even Alec (as "the preacher of the Word")—serve the word. Only Mrs. Clare's maternal passion withstands its power: "What woman . . . believes the promises and threats of the Word in the sense in which she believes in her own children . . . ?" (304). In *Tess* the characters take their cue not from Mrs. Clare, but from the text painter who answers, when asked if he believes in the words he writes, "Believe that tex? Do I believe in my own existence!" (67). Angel and Tess lose their existence to the word, believe in the word beyond their belief in human identity. The words of Tess's confession become a text that displaces Tess, making her disappear before Angel's eyes. Her words are so powerful in Angel's mind that it is merely their disavowal for which he begs: "'Tess! Say it is not true! No, it is not true!' . . . He looked at her imploringly, as if he would willingly have taken a lie from her lips, knowing it to be one, and have made of it, by some sort of sophistry, a valid denial" (199). The mere words of Tess's confession—not her impurity—are reified into a barrier that stands between Tess and Angel. At the same time, when Tess refuses to retract her confession, Angel assumes the power of the interpreter. Robbed of the text he was in charge of creating, his power now lies in the act of interpreting the text Tess insists on rendering. The immense power of the interpreter lies in his ability to read in whatever way he wills, to assign Tess her—or his—meaning. The self I make palpable in the words I speak about myself is profoundly violable, entirely at the mercy of another who interprets their darker side, acts as if he knows their proper meaning better than I do. In *Tess* self-disclosure is the innocent act whereby the child places herself in danger of violation; it is Tess's "childish nature to tell all that's in your heart" (161). The interpreter remakes and, in a pattern that we have seen before, undoes. The tradition of fiction, from *Clarissa* onward, suggests that the sexual violation of the female, her undoing, is the violent act of interpretation. To undo, to open and unfasten, to bring to nought and destroy, has as its original meaning "to explain and interpret" (*O.E.D.*). The undoer, whether he be Lovelace or Chillingworth or Clare, is the man who opens the text of the heart's meaning and stands at the threshold in charge of it. In *The Scarlet Letter*, the job of undoing becomes especially public. The branding of Hester is a symbolic violation the community justifies as the ultimate expounding of the text of Hester's heart, a bringing to the surface of an otherwise hidden meaning.

From this angle Tess's confession begins to look like a fatal mistake; and *Tess* brings the argument of Part Two of this book full circle by exposing what in *The Scarlet Letter* is a frightening suspicion behind the form of the fictionalized autobiography of "The Custom-House" and the fictionalized confession of the minister: what it would be like "to tell all" (as Hawthorne puts it). For Hardy, as for Hawthorne, fiction is a form of defense in which sexual violation represents the most palpable version of a more general, and more terrifying, violation: to be penetrated, to be exposed, to be turned inside out, to have one's life placed in another's hands—in short, to have another as the interpreter of one's own life. Tess's confession is a model inside fiction of what fiction will not do, of what fiction guards against.

I would even argue that the disastrous consequences of Tess's confession function as Hardy's indirect justification to himself of what his biographers have called "a lifetime of extreme reticence and secrecy."[12] If we look at Hardy's life and the way he reconstructs it in the *Life*, we find a significant contrast to Tess's central act of confession. Hardy constructs his *Life* through deliberate omissions and artful exaggerations of the facts, just as he manufactures "The Hardy Pedigree" (almost after the manner of the Stoke family in *Tess*) with a crucial goal in mind: to remain the sole interpreter of his own life. Hardy even takes what I have called Hawthorne's (dis)qualification of the first-person pronoun in both "The Custom-House" and the minister's confession in *The Scarlet Letter*, and literalizes it, but not with Hawthorne's intent (where self-defense becomes a form of universal mercy). Hardy writes his own autobiography in the third person, and the first-person pronoun undergoes a kind of ban almost everwhere in Hardy's late writing—from the more or less conventional (but deeply telling) insistence, in the prefaces to the late poetry, that his use of "I" is fictional (to prevent recriminations and accusations from his wife Emma),[13] to the extraordinary and literal erasure of "I" through secret codes and symbols in certain personal documents.[14] One could say that *Tess* and the *Life* lie at those opposite extremes between which Hawthorne's *The Scarlet Letter* mediates by imagining a fictional self, fiction's neutral territory between "I" and "he." With Hardy's life (and *Life*) set at the opposite extreme of Tess's act of telling all, I would argue that for the man Hardy, Tess's confession is a rehearsal, within the protected world of fiction, of the consequences of self-disclosure; the more gruesome and tragic Tess's fate, the more justified is Hardy in a lifetime of secrecy. Tess's confession, then, is a privileged moment in fiction, a moment in which the writer gauges the motives of fiction, representing its boundaries by transgressing them through a fictional character. It is fiction turned inside out, a dropping of all fictions, an unveiling, a baring, inside fiction, so that the author can have it both ways.

I must admit that the antithesis I am pressing, between Tess's self-disclosure and Hardy's self-concealment, is neither simple nor complete. We do not read *Tess* simply as a practical warning against self-disclosure. Within *Tess* Hardy dramatizes at the same time his fear of violation (through Tess) and his concomitant horror of inviolability (through Angel). This last point redirects our view of Tess's violability, casting it in a new light, lifting it from a practical warning, purging it almost entirely of Hardy's morbid fear. And we realize that the text's deepest warning may be against the self-defended man and the barrenness he suffers. Hardy presses the shock given to Angel's sensibilities by Tess's confession, but Tess is equally shocked when she discovers a hidden side of Angel—not just an accidental event in his past (the weekend of dissipation he confesses), but a significant part of his character that until now has been hidden: "she was appalled by the determination revealed in the depths of this gentle being she had married" (206); "She was awe-stricken to discover such determination under such apparent flexibility. His consistency was, indeed, too cruel" (203). Angel blames Tess for being two people, or at least not the same person with whom he fell in love, but he too has a hidden self within his depths. Hardy carefully describes Angel's hidden self in terms that repeat, with a crucial difference, Tess's secret self, her violated female self: "Within the remote depths of his constitution, so gentle and affectionate as he was in general, there lay hidden a hard logical deposit, like a vein of metal in a soft loam, which turned the edge of everything that attempted to traverse it" (202). If Tess's secret is that she has been violated, Angel's is that he is inviolable. Sexual violation—and its opposite, impenetrability—are examples of character, perhaps even generic types, gender types. Isn't Angel's "hard logical deposit" his maleness? Isn't this why his hardness is described in terms of the traditional agricultural metaphor (especially apt for *Tess*, where Hardy describes the field-woman losing her margin as the fields are opened to the plow) of the male's penetration of the female? Like father and son (whose "unreceptive surfaces" [240] are impenetrable to the seed of the spirit) in *The Mill on the Floss*, Angel is the man who cannot be penetrated, even by the cry for mercy, even by the seed of the word that asks for forgiveness.

If Angel is the man whose remote depths are hard as metal, Tess is the woman who, in her mother's naive words, is "tractable at bottom" (22). Hardy accomplishes an extraordinary reversal here. Next to Angel's inviolability, Tess's violability—even her earlier "surrender" (69) to Alec, her "want of firmness" (195)—becomes part of an admirable generosity, a readiness to give herself to another that reaches its noblest moment in the description of Tess as Apostolic Charity: "she sought not her own; was not provoked; thought no evil of his treatment of her. She might just now have been Apostolic Charity herself returned to a self-seeking modern world" (202). Charity, for Hardy, is consistently, constitutionally female: "The intuitive heart of woman knoweth not only its own bitterness, but its husband's" (205). As Hardy says in the *Life*, woman is "one of the sex that makes up for lack of generosity by excess of generosity."[15] If woman's knowledge intuitively encompasses the desire of another, even as Angel reaches the farthest extremes of his sympathy for Tess (notably before her confession) he fails precisely in this regard: "Do I realize solemnly enough how utterly and irretrievably this little womanly thing is the creature of my good or bad faith and fortune? I think not. I think I could not, unless I were a woman myself" (183). Gender is the boundary Angel cannot cross. But by marking Angel with the "stains of hetero-doxy" (304), of "bad faith" not to God but to Tess, Hardy marks the inviolable man, and thereby transvaluates the conventional stain that marks the violated woman. By such an act Hardy attempts to revise a system of gender signs for an entire culture.

The figure of Tess as Apostolic Charity can help us recognize the way in which the loss of proper identity lies at the heart of the text of fiction. Fiction consistently gives its characters marginal identities, and the elab-orate series of masked and invented identities that characters assume in fiction seems to constitute the most basic element of the genre: fiction is about the fictions of identity. I have been investigating this idea through the figure of the child, and somewhat more tentatively through the idea of gender. The male figure in fiction assumes an invented identity in order to guard the male metal or ego, to keep it intact; such an identity ultimately signals the self wounded, and the male substance in dissolu-tion, with identity finally written up as a nought, as emptiness, barren-ness, and death. But the nought that describes the child and the woman at zero-degree identity—I am thinking of those "O's" that Charley copies at the opening of "Nurse and Patient," the chapter in *Bleak House* in which children and women exchange identities in a dizzying round—becomes the sign of a common circle of charity where no one and everyone meet.

Esther, the daughter, rewrites the value of her father's "No one," the father's bankrupt death-in-life. The male self travels a long path to a dead end, and becomes "no one," the end of the male line. The danger is always the threat to the male name, the name handed down from generation to generation. The female self travels a parallel path, but makes "no one" into a common self, a self that does not contract into nothingness, but expands into a flexibility and tractability of selflessness. The female name is sacrificed in the service of other names. The feminized man, Dimmesdale, unveils himself as a common center only when he shares the child's and woman's shame at the end (and the man dies in doing so).

Typically, the reinvention of woman as the "no one" of universal charity takes the form of extreme self-effacement, often literally enacted. In *Bleak House*, for example, Esther's scarred face is a literalization of the self-effacement that she practices throughout her life, pinpointed in the charitable nursing of Jo and Charley whereby she contracts her disfiguring disease. In effect, this act repeats the burial of her doll in the simple garden of childhood—that doll, we recall, "with her beautiful complexion" (iii, 17). In *The Mill on the Floss* the child's literal defacements of her doll allow Maggie the universal face of suffering and mercy at the end. Tess adds another chapter to the history of female self-effacement when she literalizes it by committing the act on herself. The "self-effacement" (245) by which Tess assumes the role of Apostolic Charity, the woman who seeks not her own, finds grotesque expression when Tess snips off her eyebrows and ties a handkerchief around her face, covering her chin and temples, and then works in a faceless landscape that mirrors her—"a white vacuity of countenance with the lineaments gone," "a complexion without features, as if a face, from chin to brow, should be only an expanse of skin" (237). Living one's life by a kind of anonymity, as "somebody" or "nobody," as the featureless universal face, converts the male fictional moment—of disguise and attempted self-preservation—into the self-sacrifice that grounds human identity at its pivotal point. The search for the proper name is superseded by the larger classification of one's humanity.

But the grotesque and cruel images of Tess's self-disfigurement make us ask, is Tess a woman who wins her humanity only to lose her womanhood? The silent and passive doll, forced to take whatever shape and punishment are given her, is never sufficiently demolished in *The Mill on the Floss* to allow Maggie her womanhood. In fact, one could say that Maggie purchases her humanity at the cost of her womanhood, that the near demolition of her doll is not Maggie's liberation into womanhood but her first exercise in the extinction of self-will. That such a purchase means a sacrifice of womanhood is made clearer in *The Scarlet Letter*, where Hester's becoming a "self-ordained . . . Sister of Mercy" (xiii, 117) goes hand in hand with her loss of her woman's nature, as Hawthorne remarks only a few pages later: "Some attribute had departed from her, the permanence of which had been essential to keep her a woman" (xiii, 118–19). The heroine's purchasing of her humanity at the cost of her womanhood, a transaction at the heart of English and American fiction from the time of *Clarissa*, is crystallized—and ironized most forcefully—in *Tess*. The novel's most disorienting irony is not Angel's failure of sympathy—what he calls his inability to be a woman— but the way in which the heroine ceases to be a woman. We feel, in the final description of Tess lying on the stone of sacrifice "like . . . a lesser creature than a woman" (328), Hardy's doubts. What are the limits of self-sacrifice and self-victimization? Is "woman" a classification of nought where the finest achievement is self-abasement and self-annihilation? What "The Woman Pays"—the title of Phase the Fifth—always seems too much in *Tess*. Tess's remark, "I feel what a nothing I am!" (107), is not the celebration of her universal humanity, but its dark and cynical echo. Finally, we must recall how consistently misguided Tess's self-sacrifices are, ending in her childish mimicry of Clare. Tess the convert winds up not at the center of humanness, but as the disciple and idolater of a false angel.

By focusing on certain prototypical characters and events in *Tess*, I mean to suggest the ways in which, inside the plot of the novel, Hardy explores and tests the enterprise of fiction: what it means to confess the truth or to hold it back, to victimize oneself or to interpret (and master) another; what it means to be the child who tells all, the man who preserves his metal by hiding it, the woman who sacrifices herself by becoming no one in particular. I am arguing that the central conflict between "self-sacrifice" and "self-preservation" (the terms, stated as an antithesis, are Angel's) within the plot of *Tess* is in fact the dilemma the author faces in fiction writing in general. Perhaps the best way to apprehend this dilemma directly is to return to Hardy's life, but now with an eye toward his famous campaign for candor in fiction. I find below the surface of Hardy's plea for candor a deep ambivalence. On the one hand, Hardy's powerful feelings are fueled by the sense that, if denied here, under the cover of fiction (in what Hawthorne calls "the neutral territory"), where will self-disclosure be allowed? As a rewriting of the family history, fiction does not (like the *Life*) simply erase; it allows the darker side to come to the surface in a defended form, and in this way becomes a more substantial record than the *Life*. The self, if it is to exist anywhere beyond the hinterland of its own secret consciousness, requires recognition, particularly in the publicity of words, especially those words by which we are known—names. The children born out of wedlock, the infant deaths, the recurring pattern of marital unhappiness, the embarrassing poverty—all exist in the fiction, rearranged, especially under the sign of the altered or reassigned name. Hardy first called Jude, for example, by the name of an actual Berkshire relative, Jack Head (and before this the manuscripts show that Hardy used Hand, the name of his mother's family), and even when he changed the name to Fawley, he was using the name of the birthplace of his Berkshire grandmother, Mary Head (whose name turns up in the text in the forms of *Mary*green and Bride*head*).[16] In *Tess*, he took Talbothays from the name of his father's farm,[17] and d'Urberville from the actual Turbervilles who were remotely connected with the Dorset Hardys.[18] Perhaps most telling of all is that moment in *Tess* when "the Hardys" (108) take their place alongside the Durbeyfields as one of those mighty families that have fallen. In short, when Hardy fights for candor in fiction, he fights for the right to tell his own story.

On the other hand, Hardy's own account of *Tess* suffering at the hands of publishers and reviewers is less than candid, and even a downright lie in significant ways. J. T. Laird's useful investigations into the manuscripts of *Tess* have brought to light that "by a combination of untruths, half-truths, and vague assertions Hardy, sometimes deliberately, offered his readers an account of events that was less than frank, and this has had the effect of obscuring, over the years, a complete understanding of the publishing problems he faced and the measures he took to overcome them."[19] Hardy uses, about the history of the text, the language of Tess's violation, as if he imagines at the authorial level a defense against violation, against "manipulators" who "pervert" and "mutilate" the novel, against the "dismemberment" of the "intact" text.[20] I would like to argue that Hardy to some degree displaces onto his publishers and reviewers his own lack of candor, so that he exaggerates how his work is censored from the outside when in fact the most interesting censorship of it occurs from the inside, under Hardy's own (if sometimes only half-aware) eye. From this angle the external censor is a thinly veiled disguise for the way in which the very act of writing fiction is self-censoring, self-manipulating, self-dismembering—acts that coexist alongside self-defense, and sometimes merge with it. The external censor is a convenient symbol for the complicated system of forces—some outside, some inside—that keep us from telling all. In other words, the deceptions of fiction—what Hardy calls, before her confession, Tess's agony of "trying to lead a repressed life" (106)—annul the self in apparently trying to preserve it. For Hardy, the self seems cancelled, or at least partially maimed, either way—in the self-concealment of apparent self-preservation, in the self-disclosure (and self-sacrifice) of Tess. Hardy was sufficiently self-conscious to know how deeply this dilemma affected him, and prints the following characterization of himself with approval: "A shrewd man who knew me at this time (aet. 26) said, Here is a man who, when he is silent will never begin to speak; & when he once begins to speak, will never stop."[21] This quandary over speech versus silence is dramatized everywhere in the text of *Tess*. The plot begins with a telling (like a birthing) that gives Tess a family and history, a telling the parson chastises himself for, just as Angel later does ("I think that parson who unearthed your pedigree would have done better if he had held his tongue" [195]); and, of course, one of Tess's worst agonies occurs when "she held her tongue" (109) about her d'Urberville background (first her family history, and then her violation); and, finally, over the text as a whole hangs Hardy's own curiously suggestive wish, "*Melius fuerat non scribere*" ("It would have been better not to write"), a reference to the subtitle ("a Pure Woman") that suggestively expands into the kind of regret that Hardy felt time and again about what he had written, that he had written. In one of the queerest ironies of his life the dilemma I am describing overtook Hardy when, by a slip of the tongue, he gave away the secret that he had written his authorized biography himself.[22] When it came to his fiction, Hardy solved the dilemma in his extraordinary self-silencing after *Jude*. In his last novels Hardy no longer saw in fiction a solution to this division, and in the end he closed even his career as a poet by declaring "He Resolved to Say No More,"[23] with the haunting sense that he already had said too much.

PART THREE

FICTION AND THE TRADITIONS OF NAMING

Whatever has come to be has already been named.

Ecclesiastes 6:10

The lordly right of bestowing names is such that one would almost be justified in seeing the origin of language itself as an expression of the rulers' power.

NIETZSCHE, The Genealogy of Morals

Needless to say, I have allowed no name to stand which could put a non-medical reader upon the scent; and the publication of the case in a purely scientific and technical periodical should, further, afford a guarantee against unauthorized readers of this sort. I naturally cannot prevent the patient herself from being pained if her own case history should accidentally fall into her hands. . . . Now in this case history—the only one which I have hitherto succeeded in forcing through the limitations imposed by medical discretion and unfavourable circumstances—sexual questions will be discussed with all possible frankness, the organs and functions of sexual life will be called by their proper names, and the pure-minded reader can convince himself from my description that I have not hesitated to converse upon such subjects in such language even with a young woman. Am I, then, to defend myself upon this score as well?

FREUD, Fragment of an Analysis of a Case of Hysteria

8

Lolita

Lolita, light of my life, fire of my loins. My sin, my soul. Lo-lee-ta:
the tip of the tongue taking a trip of three steps down the palate to
tap, at three, on the teeth. Lo. Lee. Ta. (11)[1]

In *Lolita* we learn at the outset that the erotic is embedded in the power
of words. The question becomes how to deploy this power, how to turn it
to our own erotic pleasure. Discourse in *Lolita* does not simply alert us to
this power, but forcibly and unequivocally educates us in the way to
make this power our own. Phonetics and syntax constitute a grammar of
the erotic by which we are guided on the "trip" whose destination is the
quintessence of the erotic: the erotic name. Without this originating trip,
Humbert's erotic travels across the body of Lolita and the body of
America would hardly be imaginable. The reader begins the text by being
introduced to a name that is the sequestered spot at the end of a sensuous
journey through labial *l*'s and dental *t*'s. "Lolita" is alpha and omega, the
beginning and end of all speaking and writing, literally the first and last
words of the text, enveloping all other words by giving them its meaning,
as if all other words were only an elaboration of the meaning "Lolita," as
if all other words functioned only in apposition to "Lolita," as they do in
the first sentences of the text. In fact, there are no sentences in the
opening paragraph of *Lolita*, only fragmentary repetitions of and directions to "Lolita." The name at the beginning overwhelms the syntax of
the proposition, making everything that follows fragmentary and supernumerary (except insofar as it may send us back to the beginning,
"Lolita").

The first paragraph of *Lolita* in this way becomes an invocation of
Eros that makes public the otherwise secret ritual of approaching the god
by accurately pronouncing the name. Hence the opening of *Lolita* is at

once a worshipful prayer and an erotic exercise, a sacred call to bring Lolita into being and a gymnastics of the tongue that tries to taste her sweetness while she is absent. At such a moment we are initiated into the magic of naming. It is in this sense that I speak of approaching Lolita— even supplicating her—through the correct pronunciation of her name: "The 'special god' . . . lives and acts only in the particular domain to which his name assigns and holds him. Whoever, therefore, would be assured of his protection and aid must be sure to enter his realm, i.e., to call him by his 'right' name."[2] The text of *Lolita* severely circumscribes the field of divine power by positing it on a single principle—the pleasure principle of the erotic. Hence Humbert's god is at once his "soul" and, in an ironic inversion, his "sin."

In uttering the syllables "Lo-lee-ta," Humbert crosses the ancient threshold of magic which, from the beginning of time, the neophyte has tried to cross by successfully uttering a name. By crossing this threshold with him, we arrive at the most ancient power attributed to naming. The magic that attends the utterance of a name is perhaps best understood as bringing into existence the object named. In ancient Egypt, for example, the creator god calls himself into being by uttering his own name: "the first god himself is held to have been created by the power of his own mighty name: in the beginning was the name, which from out of itself brought forth all being, including divine being."[3] With the god only the belated offspring of his own name, "often it is the *name* of the deity, rather than the god himself, that seems to be the real source of efficacy. Knowledge of the name gives him who knows it mastery over the being and will of the god."[4] In this context, the distinctly philosophic search with which I began this study—the search after the name which Plato describes in the *Cratylus*, and which becomes in science the way to apprehend all objects—has a more ancient form: the search after the name which magically bestows divine power. It is a search after not merely the power of things, but the power of the god behind all things. The successful attempt to seize such power is told effectively in the well-known story in which Isis outsmarts the god Re of his name. Re explains, "My father and my mother told me my name, and it has remained hidden in my body since my birth, lest some sorcerer should acquire magic power over me thereby." Isis insists on learning that name before she will cure Re of the wound he has suffered from a poisonous serpent: "Tell me your name, father of gods, . . . that the poison may go out of you; for the man whose name is spoken, he lives." Before finally yielding, Re uses a form of self-naming that I have been proposing as a paradigm for naming in fiction. He names himself in the third person—a model that we recognize from the Old Testament, when Yahweh names himself to Jacob, "I am he" (Isa. 48:12). But Re's "I am he" does not satisfy Isis, for precisely the reason that it so successfully supports the project of fiction: it does not designate identity literally. She asks again for the name, "for he shall live whose name is named." Re finally yields ("My name shall go forth from my body and over into thine"), whereupon Isis gains power over Re and all the other gods.[5]

In the beginning was the name Lolita, and in uttering it, Humbert moves the name from Lolita's body to his own, in an erotic version of the story of Isis and Re. When Humbert utters "Lolita," we recognize the power of holding the name of the beloved object in one's mouth (an idea that Proust makes even more explicit, as we will see). The name makes possible the consumption and absorption of the divine body. In this way the successful pronunciation of the name Lolita not only marks Lolita's body as the place of divine pleasure, but begins Humbert's control of that body. This is what the name Lolita signifies: "in my arms she was always Lolita" (11).

Precisely because the name contains a power that the god does not want published, we must wonder over Humbert's initial act of uttering it publicly. And when Lolita is unveiled as the pathetic twelve-year-old victim of Humbert's lust, we begin to understand why the magic of naming traditionally carries with it a long list of prohibitions and taboos to protect people from name-magic—prohibitions, one could argue, that Humbert breaks in publishing the name Lolita: "For even a person's ego, his very self and personality, is indissolubly linked in mythic thinking, with his name. Here the name is never a mere symbol, but is part of the personal property of its bearer which must be carefully protected, and the use of which is exclusively and jealously reserved to him."[6] The practitioner of name-magic believes that "injury will result as surely from the malicious handling of his name as a wound inflicted on any part of his physical organism."[7] With this in mind, one can read the promiscuous publication of the name Lolita at the beginning of the text as the initiating and master violation of Lolita. It is through his successive acts of naming that I wish to take up the way in which Humbert consolidates his power over Lolita.

By openly exploiting the ancient tradition of name-magic, *Lolita* gives us a crucial clue about its relationship to the traditions of naming and the tradition of the novel. *Lolita* exposes through exaggeration what often remains underground in the novelistic tradition. By this I mean that the signs of name-magic occur everywhere in the tradition of the novel, but in a vestigial form. *Lolita* helps us understand the process by which name-magic is domesticated within the realistic bounds of the novelistic tradition. In other words, *Lolita* suggests the way in which apparently rational systems of naming are used to master the object of desire—that is, the way in which, during the epoch of the rise of the novel, particular naming systems were developed to allow naming to retain its ancient capacity to control, only now under the sponsorship not of magic but of science. The text of *Lolita* turns on the pivotal encounter between the rise of the novel and the rise of powerful naming systems during the Enlightenment. As part of its gesture as parody, *Lolita* is an ironic reflection on this historic clash between naming systems in philosophy and the art of narrative in fiction, a clash whose consequences are still being felt today. *Lolita* makes possible a broad exploration of this clash by directly invoking other texts in which the valorization of the name, or of a naming system in general, threatens the entire narrative enterprise, and I have selected two such texts (*Fanny Hill* and *A la recherche du temps perdu*) to study this problem further. But it is to the novels that I have already examined that *Lolita* alludes most suggestively. *Lolita* recasts the plot in which the family erases individual identity, especially by the abuse of the (female) child in the name of the family. The sexual violation of the daughter in *Lolita* recapitulates the stories of Clarissa and Tess, and makes us see all the more clearly how such examples of sexual violation are part of a system of unnaming and renaming. After all, as the master namer who rapes to name and names to rape, Humbert reembodies the man who, at the dawn of the novel in England, imagines the name as the key to erotic pleasure and ravishment: "CLARISSA LOVELACE let me call her. . . . Her very name, with mine joined to it, ravishes my soul."[8]

The science of classification

The method, the soul of science, designates at first sight any body in nature in such a way that the body in question expresses the name that is proper to it, and that this name recalls all the knowledge that may, in the course of time, have been thus named.

LINNAEUS, *Systema naturae*

And when I thus think of *Lolita*, I seem always to pick out for special delectation . . . the tinkling sounds of the valley town coming up the mountain trail (on which I caught the first known female of *Lycaeides sublivens* Nabokov).

NABOKOV, *Lolita*

The science of classification is the central means by which Humbert takes charge of the meaning of Lolita (and *Lolita*). The power to classify is the source of his authority in the text: "Now I wish to introduce the following idea. Between the age limits of nine and fourteen there occur maidens who, to certain bewitched travelers, twice or many times older than they, reveal their true nature which is not human, but nymphic (that is, demoniac); and these chosen creatures I propose to designate as 'nymphets'" (18). From the first pages of this study, I have argued that fiction discovers the name for the human, but in such a passage Humbert countervails an entire tradition of fiction. Not only does *Lolita* show us how the general theory of classification dehumanizes, but Humbert designates the title character by a name that literally classes her as nonhuman. To present the story of his title character, Humbert does not choose as his model the biographer of a person's life; instead he chooses the natural scientist who, with a trained eye, founds and practices a science and thereby makes a specialized nomenclature (in which, we will see, "Lolita" attains a technical meaning). "The science of nympholepsy is a precise science" (131), and *Lolita* is addressed at least in part to "the student" (19) who wishes to learn more about the science devoted to the study of this class. Nabokov has taken the desire of the natural scientist and made it the novelist's—and maniac's—desire, as if the nymphs that Nabokov captured and named as a child[9] have been transformed into the nymphet that Humbert seeks to capture and name. "Nothing in the world would have seemed sweeter to me than to be able to add, by a stroke of luck, some remarkable new species to the long list of Pugs already named by others."[10] The question becomes, what does Nabokov achieve in extending the lepidopterist's language of desire to the realm of the human, and to the discourse of the novel, the discourse that takes as its goal the naming of the human? Why take the scientific classification of a creature and map it onto fiction's naming of a person?

The science of classification comes into being to place all objects and all creatures within a system of knowledge and under the classifier's dominion. I will argue in the first part of this chapter that *Lolita* deliberately draws upon a theory of naming that, during the Enlightenment, succeeds in reshaping philosophy into science.[11] There are, of course, examples of the science of classification before the Enlightenment (perhaps most notably Aristotle's *Historia Animalium*), but it is not until the Enlightenment that the desire for a scientific discourse informs an entire culture. By successfully capitalizing upon the science of classification, Humbert exposes at least one reason for the hegemony of scientific discourse from the Enlightenment to our own day: such a discourse realizes the dream that equates knowledge with power. In *Lolita* this power takes the form of constituting the erotic through the idea of the mastery of knowing, as Humbert comically suggests by lasciviously chuckling over "a book with the unintentionally biblical title *Know Your Own Daughter*" (176). In the fourth part of this chapter I will take up this subject in *Fanny Hill*, an erotic text written in the eighteenth century and therefore coterminous with the emergence of the naming system I am describing. For the moment, however, I wish only to pinpoint the strategy by which, during the Enlightenment, the science of classification seizes for its own purposes one aspect of the Adamic myth of naming. It does not claim the mystical or divine knowledge that inspired Adam; in fact, it demystifies the myth by fabricating a purely arbitrary language.[12] In so doing the science of classification draws up a nomenclature that will give man dominion over other creatures by classifying them. In such a view, Adam is the only man, man constituted as uniqueness itself, the man who names all other creatures by class names, just as in the Enlightenment the natural scientist draws up a system that has the power to allow nothing individual, nothing unique, for everything must find its way into his table of names.

In the course of these pages I have been interpreting the tradition of the novel by showing the ways in which it exposes the naming system of the family as a man's language, a patriarchal language. *Lolita* performs a similar function by exploring in detail the motives and uses of the science of classification. It is in this sense that *Lolita* is a modern version of *Clarissa*, ironized and radicalized. The plot in which the male hunter captures the female prey (a terminology that both novels share) takes its subtlest and most insidious form in the naming plot in which Lovelace–Humbert classifies Clarissa–Lolita. By engineering his marriage to Lolita's mother, Humbert in fact becomes the "name-father" Lovelace only pretends to be. The growing significance of the association between child and female in the naming plots of fiction, which reaches a crucial moment in Tess's repeated declaration that she was only a child when she was violated, finds its logical conclusion in the stepfather's sexual violation of the girl-child in *Lolita*. The idea of the child as an unknown entity is radicalized in *Lolita*, as if in characterizing (and capturing) Lolita in the discourse of science, Humbert merely lays bare the way in which the child assumes the role of specimen in a culture—say, the Freudian child (of which Lolita is an ironic version). Juxtaposing "photographs of girl-children" with "some gaudy moth or butterfly, still alive, safely pinned to the wall ('nature study')" (112), *Lolita*'s narrator defines the value of the female child as part of a "nature study" in which the science of classification pins the ultimate meaning, and in which the sexual exploration of the child is made out to be a necessary part of an experimental science. In sum, in the age of science the classifier takes over, in a powerful maneuver, the traditional roles of father and lover. At the same time, *Lolita* is a parodic exaggeration of the ways in which the father and the lover, from the beginning of the novelistic tradition, play the role of the classifier.

The authority of the science of classification rests on its capacity to produce meaning, even to monopolize meaning. At first, "Lolita" appears to be an entirely private designation—not simply eccentric, but the fantastic denomination of a madman. But the science of classification works to authenticate the significance of "Lolita"—that is, to universalize it, to win it a public meaning. In this sense the science of classification is an attack on the proper name. As the central specimen to be studied in an introduction to the science of nympholepsy, "Lolita" attains a technical meaning. In short, the definition of "Lolita" as a "nymphet" remaps the singular name into a class name. "Lolita" is the name by which the author signifies, and makes public, the hidden meaning in "Dolores Haze." The scientist supplants the father, not simply in remarrying the mother but in renaming the daughter. "Lolita" becomes an unveiling, a correction of the vision and nomenclature of the family, and of the layperson generally. The expert's piercing vision uncovers "the body of some immortal daemon disguised as a female child" (141). The science of classification, then, acts to make public a private significance. The special form such activity takes in *Lolita* is to pluralize—and thereby violate—a proper name. When Humbert imagines that a motel allows "no Lolitas" (149), he means that it bars its doors to the class "nymphet"; when Humbert imagines that the mountains "swarm with panting, scrambling, laughing, panting Lolitas" (226), he designates an entire school of creatures, like a pack of hyenas or a swarm of insects. We learn here how the most proper name of all, the most private and peculiar meaning, is vulnerable. We learn the power of the science of classification to make "Lolita" serve a general meaning, a meaning which, I would suggest, we do in fact recognize when we hear, even apart from the book's pages, the name pronounced. We know what someone means by "a Lolita."

"Lolita" acquires such meaning only by taking up a position in a meticulously ordered taxonomy. The classifier's central tool is a language that allows him to position the (apparently) particular within the more general. Names, as part of their syntactic function, make such a language possible. The science of classification comes into existence precisely insofar as it can control the contracting and expanding power of the name, the movement from (say) spaniel, to dog, to quadruped, to animal.[13] In such a series we see, through a practical application, the way in which the theory of the name specifies the grammar of the philosophic inquiry into the particular and the general. Moreover, this movement from the particular to the general recapitulates the entire history of the development of language—the movement from the proper names with which utterance is born, to the common nouns by which an ever elaborating and chaotic plethora of names is made into an economical system of communication and knowledge. In *Lolita*, Humbert must "itemize" (165), "survey" (250), and then "tabulate" (260). This is the process of classification by which he can designate Lolita a "nymphet."

The process of classification works simultaneously in two different directions: to synthesize and to differentiate. The classifier must synthesize the features that all the members of a particular class share, and at the same time he must differentiate the newly discovered and named class from all other classes. "Given a group photograph of schoolgirls," only the nympholept can "discern at once, by ineffable signs—the slightly feline outline of a cheekbone, the slenderness of a downy limb, and other indices" (19)—the nymphet in the group. He marks the telling features that at once constitute one class while distinguishing this class from other classes. But the nympholept is especially interested in the activity of differentiation because he is claiming that the group we normally take to be girl-children has hidden within it a very specialized, competing class. "Nymphet" comes into existence only insofar as the scientist (or nympholept) can distinguish her from other creatures with which she may be confused. The classification of a particular species involves one, then, in a global system, a field of investigation with expanding boundaries. The designation of "Lolita" as a "nymphet" requires that she be made part of a larger system of other designations which differentiate her from "human females" (20) and "terrestrial women" (20), say, or from "a young girl . . . [or] a 'college girl'—that horror of horrors" (67). Since the scientist's authority depends upon his microscopic power of discrimination, it is especially "human little girls" (19) from which Lolita must be distinguished, divided. It is in this sense that a classificatory system exaggerates the role of difference, and that "nymphet"—and its central specimen, Lolita—is less a creature than a sign in a carefully ordered system of signs. It is almost as if the sign "nymphet" is part of a problem in symbolic logic, part of a syllogism with which the nympholept goads us: "Between those age limits [of nine and fourteen], are all girl-children nymphets?" The answer, "Of course not" (18), taunts the layperson's ignorance at the same time as it puts the burden of proof on the classifier.

In assigning value to each of these classes—human little girls, college girls, terrestrial women—Humbert overhauls an entire cultural system. In other words, to become a classifier necessarily involves the nympholept in an argument, always implicit and sometimes explicit, with what he takes to be competing systems. There is, for example, the nympholept's system versus the anatomist's: "I was aware of not one but two sexes, neither of which was mine; both would be termed female by the anatomist. But to me, through the prism of my senses, 'they were as different as mist and mast'" (20). Whichever system of classification we accept, the girl Lolita is reduced to a verbal sign; she exists insofar as "the difference between mist and mast" exists—a vast difference of identity based on the subtlest differentiation in signs. In a similar vein, the nympholept's system competes with, and seeks to undermine, the nomenclature of the law: "in England, with the passage of the Children and Young Person Act in 1933, the term 'girl-child' is defined as 'a girl who is over eight but under fourteen years' (after that, from fourteen to seventeen, the statutory definition is 'young person'). In Massachusetts, U.S., on the other hand, a 'wayward child' is, technically, one 'between seven and seventeen years of age' (who, moreover, habitually associates with vicious or immoral persons)" (21). Is what we ordinarily take to be the perverseness of Humbert's own system no more than an extension of the law's system? Such passages from the text underscore the way in which the science of classification is not an unusual or eccentric activity peculiar to Humbert, but the ground of an entire culture. To enter the world of denominations is not to enter virgin territory, but to fabricate—and legitimate—a competing system. At the same time, by placing the competing systems—the anatomist's, the lawyer's, the nympholept's—beside each other, Nabokov relativizes the singular authority we often attribute to a classificatory system. The apparently neutral system we call classification is in fact always at work for some particular institution. When Humbert threatens Lolita that she would be "analyzed and institutionalized" (153) if she were to escape his guardianship, does he fail to recognize that the system by which he attempts to "naturalize" and legitimize his own erotic desires is no more than one more form of analysis and institutionalization?

The classifier's goal is to make public the distinguishing mark by which he identifies and names a creature. The nympholept's goal is to make publicly acceptable what appears to be a crime against the family and the law. In the nympholept's case, then, the goal of classification takes the special form of marking Lolita, and thereby winning her from the legal system and the family system within whose bounds she would otherwise fall. Only the discourse of science can attempt to compete with the authority of the law and the family. So often addressed to the jury that he expects to face, Humbert's text consistently shapes his self-defense in the form of the scientist's specialized evidence. He dismantles the legal system of classification by showing the arbitrariness of its boundaries. The law that prohibits sexual intercourse with the sixteen-year-old (in this state or in that country) does not make such a prohibition with regard to the seventeen-year-old. What is the difference? The difference between mist and mast? Along such lines of thought, Humbert authorizes his own lust, and makes legal, so to speak, sexual intercourse with the class of creatures known as "nymphet." In the same way the discourse of science competes with and undermines the family's system of naming, in order to win Lolita from Charlotte and Harold Haze and to rename her. The science of nympholepsy undermines the family's system of naming by showing that the two work in the same way, by showing that every naming system is an arbitrary authorization of power. The mark that classifies the child as a family member and no more (I am thinking especially of the names Pierre Glendinning IV and Tess of the d'Urbervilles) is simply exaggerated through parody into the mark that deindividualizes (and dehumanizes) the child by classifying her as a member of another family, the family "nymphet." In *Lolita* the mother actually classifies her child with her lilies—"'That was my Lo,' she said, 'and these are my lilies'" (42)—as if the parent is no more than a (negligent) scientific classifier. The science of classification is simply the scientific extension of, and improvement upon, the family system of classification of given names and surnames, and *Lolita* becomes a later stage in the novelistic tradition's exposure of the discourse of the family.

This is perhaps most apparent in the use Humbert makes of the distinguishing mark as name. With the aid of the science of nympholepsy, Humbert uses the tradition of the distinguishing mark to overturn the family's and the law's authority to name. From the beginning, the novel as a genre looked with profound ambivalence upon the simple fable of family recognition in which the distinguishing mark naively rewards the orphan-bastard with the family inheritance and the family name (and thereby with legal authorization)—an ambivalence I have gauged in Dickens's case from the naive acceptance of such a tradition in *Oliver Twist* to its bitter denunciation in *Bleak House*. In *Lolita*, Humbert imagines finding on Lolita such a mark: "as if I were the fairy-tale nurse of some little princess (lost, kidnaped, discovered in gypsy rags through which her nakedness smiled at the king and his hounds), I recognized the tiny dark-brown mole on her side" (41). In Humbert's hands such a mark is evidence against the family name "Dolores Haze" and against the humanness of "Lolita," against Lolita's legal rights. Science claims Lolita for its own, just as the wild children of the eighteenth century were claimed—and classified—in the name of science. Science supersedes the systems of the family and the law, and the darkest reaches of parody in *Lolita* explore the way in which all three systems abuse the child.

Humbert turns the distinguishing mark almost immediately into the lover's sign, the mark by which he designates the power of his desires, and hence the mark by which he can claim that Lolita is in fact a nymphet. He spies "a yellowish-violet bruise on her lovely nymphet thigh" (62), and soon he is himself the maker of "the purplish spot on her naked neck" (141). In this way he repeats the act by which Lovelace leaves his mark on Clarissa.[14] The sexual violation of the female (child) has its visible sign in the male's ability to mark her, to name her, hence to make her his own—to have his brand of possession on her (as the Puritan community does in Hester's case in *The Scarlet Letter*). In the case of both Lovelace and Humbert, empirical proof always turns out to be a projection of the scientist's—and a fulfillment of the lover's—desires. In this light the spot on the body is connected to the spot or stain that the scientist–philosopher uses to characterize the (erotic) crime and the (erotic) shame that is (so the argument goes) the nature of woman. The telling stain, the stain as evidence—it appears in conjunction with the female in *Clarissa*, *Oliver Twist*, *Pierre*, *The Scarlet Letter*, *Bleak House*, and *Tess*—writes up a semiotic system whereby woman is classified. In *Fanny Hill*, as we will see, the stain of female blood is writing itself, and functions directly as a class name. In all these cases the stain blocks the proper name—as in "the stain upon the name"—and thereby comes to stand in place of the proper name. Novels like *Clarissa*, *Tess*, and *Lolita* radicalize the idea of the child as the *tabula rasa* by exposing the act by which the male violator (typically in the guise of the scientist–philosopher) writes up his own meaning on the blank tissue of the female body. "Lolita" and "nymphet" are simply technical terms that exaggerate, by locating in the child (and not simply in the adult woman), what is taken to be the scandalous nature of woman in the novel from *Clarissa* to *Tess*, where "woman" functions as a stigmatized class name authorized by the discourse of the male scientist–philosopher.

There is a further way in which *Lolita* exposes and rewrites the naive tradition of the distinguishing family mark. *Lolita* shows us how the classificatory mark undermines narrative discourse, the form of discourse that makes the novel the life story of the title character. Once again *Lolita* undermines the tradition of the novel by exaggerating one of its features—in fact, by showing us how that feature undermines the genre of the novel itself. If the naive theory of the mark posits a life history that is fulfilled only in the moment of family recognition—a plot, that is, that moves with single-minded force toward the successful classification of the character (*Oliver Twist* is a perfect example)—why not simply replace the life story (so much unnecessary plotting) with the activity of classification throughout the text? Such an operation would expose the underlying end of the family plot, an end that is already fairly visible in *Tess*, where the name "d'Urberville" arrives on the scene in the first chapter, and where one can read the remainder of the text as the successful classification (and victimization) of Tess through this name. Similarly, the family name "nymphet" arrives on the scene early in *Lolita*, but with very little pretense to becoming part of the narrative of a life story. Humbert simply makes the remainder of his text the continued classification of Lolita.

While in the traditional fable the single mark is all that is necessary for the naming (or classifying) of a person, in the science of nympholepsy (as in any science) a series of marks or features is necessary. Perhaps the most striking symptom of this difference between fable-novel and *Lolita* can be put this way: in the procedure of itemization and tabulation, narrative discourse in *Lolita* is undermined by the rhetoric of the list. The series as narrative, as the sequence of events in a life story, is superseded in *Lolita* by the series as list. Given neither an inner life nor a history, Lolita is simply the locus of what appears to be a list of requirements necessary to fulfill the class "nymphet" or the subclass "Lolita." In this way "Lolita" has attached to it a series of other, subsidiary names that take the form of a catalogue, a list of material objects that she consumes, and that thereby make up "Lolita": "I bought her four books of comics, a box of candy, a box of sanitary pads, two cokes, a manicure set, a travel clock with a luminous dial, a ring with a real topaz, a tennis racket, roller skates with white high shoes, field glasses, a portable radio set, chewing gum, a transparent raincoat, sunglasses, some more garments—swooners, shorts, all kinds of summer frocks" (143–44). Lolita emerges between the lines as a piecemeal "Dolly" (another of her sobriquets). We work to put her together, to see her whole, through the fragmented description of her desires, or at least the desires attached to the class name by which she has been designated. The list, in which the order of itemization is not a determining principle, is a model of discourse that undermines the proposition, the building block of narrative itself—a discursive form that, unlike the list, works through subordination and coherence. Lolita is taken to be a creature of lists, of desires objectified and catalogued: "Sweet hot jazz, square dancing, gooey fudge sundaes, musicals, movie magazines and so forth—these were the obvious items in her list of beloved things" (150). We know the creature through the accoutrements that outfit her or through the objects she desires or through the vocabulary she uses—"'revolting,' 'super,' 'luscious,' 'goon,' 'drip'" (67)—or through the exacting measurements of her body: "hip girth, twenty-nine inches; thigh girth (just below the gluteal sulcus), seventeen; calf girth and neck circumference, eleven; chest circumference, twenty-seven; upper arm girth, eight; waist, twenty-three; stature, fifty-seven inches" (109), and so on. "Lolita" is the sum of her parts, quite literally; and the list is the instrument of these parts, in contrast to narrative, which is the instrument of the whole—the whole that is always larger than the sum of its parts. In *Lolita* the science of classification periodically overtakes narrative through a proliferation of lists, each one of which displaces a segment of narrative. Neglecting personal history, the science of classification takes as its field of investigation the life that can be comprehended in a list and specified in a name.

Etymology

There existed during the Enlightenment another popular theory of naming. Insofar as its procedures reversed those of classification, I wish to view it as a competing system. And just as these two competing systems of naming existed side by side within the same culture, they coexist within the text of *Lolita*. The science of classification investigated things, and attempted to name those things through a newly fabricated, arbitrary system of signs. Etymology, on the other hand, investigated names, in the belief that only in names—names already in existence, even names from the distant past—could things be understood. The title of one such etymological work, published by John Cleland in 1766, makes this clear: *The Way to Things by Words*. Despite the very large number of works which the theory of etymology produced, its popularity and influence have often been overlooked in the history of ideas because of the extraordinary influence that Locke's *Essay* enjoyed, with its powerful statement of the entirely arbitrary status of names.[15] In direct opposition to Locke's *Essay*, the etymologist's search for the original universal language has its source in the idea of a natural (as opposed to conventional) language, and hence reinstates the debate of the *Cratylus*. The model for such a language is Adam's act of naming in Genesis. Whereas the science of classification seizes from the Adamic myth the idea of man's dominion over other creatures through class names, etymology draws upon the long and important tradition of the mystical inspiration of Adam. One could say that if both theories of naming are utopian, the scientist's utopia lies in a man-made future, while the etymologist's lies in an Edenic past. Whichever theory of naming one chooses, Adam is made into a philosopher: "Adam came into the world a philosopher, which sufficiently appeared by his writing the nature of things upon their names."[16] But for the theory of naming to which we are now turning our attention, Adam is a very particular kind of philosopher: "One could say that the first man was also the first etymologist."[17]

In the science of classification every name functions in relationship to a system of names while each name has a discrete value, but in etymology each name is itself an intertext, the charged locus of other names that lie buried within it. The science of classification requires a transparent vocabulary by which it attempts to strip names of their associations and ambiguities, even to invent an entirely new nomenclature that is naked and pure by virtue of its having no history—in short, each name comes into being in the present, with a discrete significance. In contrast, etymology seeks not to strip a name of its associations, but to restore to the name its many historical associations, and thereby to bring into being all the names hidden within the name under investigation. In the science of classification the power of the classifier opens a temporarily closed system with a new name of which he is in charge, so much so that the new name often incorporates the name of its author (as in the case of *Lycaeides sublivens* Nabokov). The etymologist, on the other hand, is not the inventor or giver of names, but only their humble servant, and the system he serves never closes. In the science of classification the name is absolutely flat, two-dimensional, part of a horizontal grid; but in etymology the name is thick with historical significations, a single manifestation of a vertical depth that never touches bottom, for the original language is always just beyond its grasp. In Cleland's words, "to discover and establish . . . those Celtic primitives precisely at their point of divergence into other languages, before the adventitious variations, by syllabic combination, by convertibility of sound, and other incident disguises, render it extremely difficult, if not impossible, to ascertain them."[18]

Etymology is the unearthing of a forgotten discourse, and it is precisely this discourse, hidden behind but nonetheless sounded in a single name, that natural history during the Enlightenment began to devalue and eventually reject: "the whole of animal semantics has disappeared, like a dead and useless limb; the words that had been interwoven in the very being of the beast have been unravelled and removed." In Linnaeus's classification, for example, after name, theory, kind, species, attributes, and use, *Litteraria* lags behind in last position, an outdated appendage from an earlier period.[19] One could say that *Lolita* is literary precisely insofar as it recovers for scientific classification the store of names and figures, observations and imaginings, that constitutes a significant part of the study of a nymphet. Nabokov uses the term *lore* to designate this idea of the historical and fabulous documentation of the creature "Lolita," so that "Anna Lore" at one point in the text replaces Annabel Leigh, as if we find in the surname "Lore" the broadest (language) family from which Lolita is descended.

The theory of etymology, particularly the version we have of it in *Lolita*, shifts our interest from the classification of a creature, the nymphet, toward the (re)discovery of a name and the derivation of its meaning. The science of classification eschews history, describing in arbitrary (and even "new") nomenclature the visible structure and character of a creature. It does not provide a history of the species or of the particular subject under investigation, and thereby it neglects the model of biography. Etymology, on the other hand, is a research into time, into beginnings, and as such *Lolita* becomes the derivation of a name but still not the biography of a person. Etymology is a purely textual endeavor: as the derivation and definition of a name, it works through an investigation of texts. "Lolita" once again becomes only a sign in a system of signs— not in this case the designation of a creature, but the designation of an intertextual identity. Perhaps the simplest way in which to see this is by realizing that "Lolita began with Annabel" (16). There seems no end to the idea of precursorship in *Lolita*: Lolita derives from Annabel Leigh, who derives from Poe's Annabel Lee, who derives from Dante's Beatrice, and so on. I wish to emphasize two points in such a chain. First, the study of Lolita is textualized; fictionalized characters, characters in print, stand behind her—and with perhaps even more meaning than Tess, she could say, "What's the use of learning that I am one of a long row only— finding out that there is set down in some old books somebody just like me."[20] It is in this sense that Lolita is descended not from a human mother, nor even from the little human child (Annabel Leigh) that Humbert meets on the Riviera, but from a text: "my discovery of her was a fatal consequence of that 'princedom by the sea'" (42). Second, the study of Lolita becomes etymological when Humbert finds the identity of the various "Lolitas" at the level of the name, or the name's essential syllable. By rewriting Dolores as "Lolita," and Lolita as "Lo-lee-ta," he finds two Lee's—"Annabel Leigh" and "Annabel Lee"—as well as "Bea" from Dante's Beatrice. Even Poe's actual child-bride is written into the etymological equation of nymphancy: "Oh Lolita, you are my girl, as Vee was Poe's and Bea Dante's" (109).[21]

The kind of rewriting of names that Humbert performs in such examples is standard practice for the traditional etymologist. Therefore, what we may take to be parody has very little, if any, exaggeration in it. In fact, Cleland's etymological claims in *The Way to Things by Words* make Humbert's look tame. I offer here a sampling, before proceeding with Humbert's own etymologies:

1. To *batten* or to *fatten*, is the same word only with different initials.
2. *Prop.* A contraction from *Bear-up.*
3. *Wedding.* Is a corruption of the word *Bedding.* "With this Ring I thee wed," was a formulary, long prior to Christianity; it meant, "With this Ring I thee bed," or have a lawful right to admission to your bed.
4. *Token.* A substantive compounded of the particle *to*, and the verb *ken*, to know. . . .
5. In the common particle *If*, lurks the word *given*; *gif*, *if*.[22]

I wish to keep in mind such examples from Cleland—and I could have chosen similar examples from countless other Enlightenment authors—while looking at Humbert's etymological practices.

The etymology of the name Dolores produces one of the most persistent strands of discourse in *Lolita*, and reveals the way in which the text of *Lolita* is given over to a complicated and shifting panoply of linguistic activities that often take the place of action as we typically define it in novelistic plots and narrative sequences. The name Dolores is anatomized, and the whole of the name and each of its parts is shown to be pregnant with significance. Humbert finds in "Dolores" not a proper name that points to a single individual, but an intertextual identity; he hears in the name a phrase from Ronsard, and thereby "Dolores" seems derived from a Renaissance text (just as "Lo-lee-ta" is derived from Poe's text): "I felt *adolori d'amoureuse langueur*, to quote dear old Ronsard, as I reached the cottage where I had left my Dolores" (216). Precisely because "Dolores" ceases to name a person, and begins to name a quality, it comes to function as an adjective that underscores an essential quality of Lolita—"my dolorous and hazy darling" (55), Dolores Haze. And being in love with Dolores means catching this quality, being infected by it: "I spend my doleful days in dumps and dolors" (45). Taking the name apart, the etymologist finds hidden within it a crucial syllable which, when isolated, brings to the surface a host of other names and significances. The etymologist, in Cleland's words, is "convinced that the original elementary language must not only necessarily consist of mono- syllables, but be reducible to a small number of radicals; whence, in their infinite combinations and variations, it is capable of shooting forth, and expanding into all the dialects, however numerous."[23] In "Dolores" the originating monosyllable is "lo," the syllable that gives birth to "Lolita." One might call "lo" the ur-syllable because of its power to originate other names. Just as "Dolores" becomes the adjectival "dolorous" and "doleful,'" "Lo" reemerges in the text in such verb forms as "lolling" (194) and "lolled" (164). "Lo" also forms part of the adjectival "Loquacious Lo" (142), and functions as an exclamation in the cry of astonishment that sounds our wonder at the presence of Lolita, as in "Lo and Behold" (164), or "no Lo to behold" (225).

I am arguing that what we may take as no more than mere word play, random and comical at best, is predicated upon a traditional and highly influential theory of naming that we fail to recognize when we take too cavalierly the comic or parodic elements of *Lolita*. I would even argue that the most important philosophical questions asked about language during the Enlightenment are entertained in Humbert's naming practices. For instance, the question of the origin of language, one of the most prominent subjects of eighteenth-century philosophy, lies just below the surface of Humbert's acts of naming. In both eighteenth-century philosophy and Humbert's "philosophy," the entire issue of the origin of language grows out of the theory of etymology. The search for elementary roots and for the original language (be it Hebrew, Celtic, or some other) develops into a philosophy of the origin of language: how did language arise? During the Enlightenment this question often took the following form: in which part of speech did language originate? We find implicit in Humbert's naming procedures the popular answer of the Enlightenment: in *Lolita* the name, or noun, is the original part of speech, from which adjectives ("dolorous"), verbs ("lolling"), and interjections ("lo") derive. Undermining the sequential nature of narrative, *Lolita* asks us to see the essence of language not in propositions but in the act of denomination itself. I mean here that the text of *Lolita* trains the reader to find meaning not in a significant sequence of events but in a key name from which significance radiates in all directions. The text of *Lolita* values the name over both the microscopic and macroscopic rhetorical structures of the verb—that is, both the proposition and the sequence of narrative at large. We see this not merely in those activities of etymology that valorize the name, but in the actual interruptions of the structure of sentences, whereby the name, surrounded by dashes, is an island of meaning apart from the sentence itself. We see this as well in those "sentences" that are no more than the reinscription of the name itself, as if no proposition, no articulation of the various parts of speech, is quite equal to the careful sounding of "Lolita." The conventional sentence is replaced by the name sentence: "Lola, Lolita!" (52); "Lolita!" (86, 238). And even the formal unit known as the chapter and the lithographic unit known as the page are eaten away by the name: "Lolita, Lolita, Lolita, Lolita, Lolita, Lolita, Lolita, Lolita, Lolita. Repeat till the page is full, printer" (111).

In this light all linguistic activity seems collapsed inside the significant name, as if the name—the ur-name—contains the essence of being itself, the ur-verb, the copula. In Humbert's poem, for example, "Dolores" rhymes with, and contains within it, "is!" (258). All being (to which all becoming yields) resides in the significant name; this is the theoretical basis behind the eliding of narrative discourse in *Lolita*. Similarly, when we realize that "Lo" is the object which, when we behold it ("Lo and behold!"), excites us to cry out, we seem to witness the historical origins of utterance, when the primitive cry ("Lo!") crosses over into the act of denomination ("Lo"). "Lo" is the name in which we can hear the primitive cry that by a moment precedes naming, and thereby "Lo" allows us to come as close as possible to the origin of utterance, which is the origin of naming.

Allegory, meta-allegory, and parody

"Dolores" and its derivatives (Lo, Lola, Lolita) constitute a very special name group in the text of *Lolita*, but not because they are a name group charged with meaning. Perhaps the most peculiar rhetorical feature of *Lolita* is the way in which all the names in the text seem to be charged with significance. The name Dolores is special because it is the only name in the text that we know for certain is not a pseudonym: "While 'Haze' only rhymes with the heroine's real surname, her first name is too closely interwound with the inmost fiber of the book to allow one to alter it" (5–6). Only the name Dolores, then, can support the theory of etymology. This fact requires that we account for "Miss Opposite," who lives opposite the Hazes; and "Killer Street," on which Humbert expects to kill Lolita's kidnapper; and all such names. It is as if, in such names, Humbert mythologizes or fictionalizes the practice of etymology, and by so doing discovers for himself the literary mode called allegory. What the writer has discerned in Bea-Vee-Lee-Leigh-lee (a brief history of the idea "nymphet"), or in the ur-syllable Lo, he puts into practice everywhere, so that in *Lolita* each creature and thing bears a significant name. But the status of these allegorical names is fictitious, literary; such names are of a different order from "Dolores." For this reason no other name receives the kind of etymological embroidery, no other name focuses at once the author's attention and all the other words of the text, as "Dolores" does. Next to "Dolores," "Miss Opposite" is no more than a two-dimensional signpost, entirely fabricated, and performing the simplest of functions, simply drawing up the linguistic geometry around which "Dolores" or "Lolita" emerges with all its pregnant meanings. In the fallen world, Adam is reduced to being the author of allegory; but "Lolita" restores to the author at least the glimmer of Edenic innocence, when names still had their primitive power to make clear the essence of all creation, to make meaning visible, palpable, graspable.

Angus Fletcher's brilliant exploration of the psychological underpinnings of allegory is especially useful here. According to Fletcher, one of the most prominent features of an allegorical text is the character's obsession with one idea: "We find that he conforms to the type of behavior manifested by people who are thought (however unscientifically) to be possessed by a daemon."[24] It is precisely the demonic nature of character that leads to the denominations of allegory. The allegorical character is so possessed by one idea that he takes his name from it, he becomes the idea. In *Lolita* we have an especially interesting version of this. Not simply a character in an allegorical text, but the author of one, Humbert exposes to us the theory of the demon and its relation to allegory: a demon works to make you write allegory, to give everything allegorical names in relationship to itself. By explaining that Lolita is "not human, but nymphic (that is, demoniac)" (18), Humbert gives us the first cause behind the allegorical text he writes. What remains underground in most allegorical literature, part of the machinery that remains behind the scenes, becomes visible in *Lolita*. Again, by being at once a character in, as well as the author of, an allegorical text, Humbert exposes to us what it means to live within an allegorical universe. In *Lolita*, we see allegory as we rarely do—from the inside, even in process, as Humbert parenthetically remarks to us about the rhetorical quality of a particular phrase, or about the allegorical names that he is deliberately and openly constructing.

Allegory is a radical practice of naming that succeeds in turning the science of classification into an art. I mean here that, by neglecting proper or individual identity, allegory brings into the realm of art the class name that the scientific classifier uses. But with a crucial difference: the allegorist, because he seeks an idea ("Virtue," say), puts the name above the thing itself, and the name thereby takes up residence in the realm of the unreachable. In this way allegory follows the etymological search for the origin or, in this case, for the Platonic idea, for the place where all particular manifestations of the idea dissolve within the name. If, in the science of classification, the name turns the thing over to us, gives us possession of it, in the kind of allegory I am describing the exact opposite is true: the name makes the thing unreachable. Perhaps the best way to understand this is through the failure of the flesh, or the material world generally, to fulfill allegory's desires, so that the demon idea, the name, the noumenal always remains the goal we keep reincarnating without final fulfillment. It is as if Humbert's special curse is to seek in the flesh of Dolores Haze the final satisfaction of his idea "Lolita," just as Ahab's curse is to seek in the flesh of the whale the idea of evil; it is as if Nabokov has taken from Melville the idea of the special body, the body that is particularly unattainable (the nymphet body, the whale body), in order to exaggerate the form of allegory, the way in which the demon idea that is beyond realization drives us crazy. Aren't the bodies of Moby Dick and Lolita extended into the category of the special precisely because they are made to contain an allegorical, or demonic, idea?

Fletcher says that in allegory "the quest will often be presented under the guise of an eternally unsatisfied search for perfection, a sort of Platonic quest for the truly worthy loved object. . . . [D]aemonic agency implies a *manie de perfection*, an impossible desire to become one with an image of unchanging purity."[25] In this light Humbert is a parody of the Christian knight, and Lolita a parody of the chaste and unattainable maiden. But while the content of the conventional allegory is changed in this way, the form significantly remains the same. Allegory is about the unattainable; it is the literary mode of the unsatisfiable, the always unfulfilled. Again Humbert brings this feature of allegory to the surface by remarking about it, inspecting it, making us see that it plays a role in the text he is authoring: "There was in the fiery phantasm a perfection which made my wild delight also perfect, just because the vision was out of reach, with no possibility of attainment to spoil it by the awareness of an appended taboo; indeed, it may well be that the very attraction immaturity has for me lies not so much in the limpidity of pure young forbidden fairy child beauty as in the security of a situation where infinite perfections fill the gap between the little given and the great promised— the great rosegray never-to-be-had" (266). The flesh of Lolita only partially satisfies Humbert, and can partially satisfy him only for a brief span of years, because Humbert's desire for nymphets is in the nature of an endless quest for the idea "Lolita": "I could switch . . . from the thought that around 1950 I would have to get rid somehow of a difficult adolescent whose magic nymphage had evaporated—to the thought that with patience and luck I might have her produce eventually a nymphet with my blood in her exquisite veins, a Lolita the Second, who would be eight or nine around 1960 . . . ; indeed, the telescopy of my mind, or un-mind, was strong enough to distinguish in the remoteness of time a . . . salivating Dr. Humbert, practising on supremely lovely Lolita the Third the art of being a granddad" (176).

With Humbert's possession of Lolita's body at the end of Part I, allegory is temporarily and only superficially sated. Humbert becomes reduced to the rather "humdrum" (274) (his name, after all, is allegorical too) repetition of the impossible realization of his demon idea through Lolita's flesh, a quest that temporarily exhausts allegory (and almost exhausts Humbert), as he seems to alert us by suggesting that in the sequel "Lolita the Second" the renewed quest with an infinitely delayed goal will begin over again. Infinitely delayed because, true to his allegorical character, Humbert is "firmly resolved to pursue my policy of sparing her purity" (126) until Lolita's seduction of him changes the rules of the game and brings to at least a temporary halt the allegorical quest. I am arguing that the allegorical side of *Lolita* is in need of refurbishing once Humbert has intercourse with Lolita at the end of Part I. Hence Humbert is in need of another allegorical subject: Part II of *Lolita* finds in America its alternate (and of course parallel) subject, so that the trip across America takes our pilgrim on a quest across what he takes to be the vast virginity of America, the New World he hopes never to despoil even as he comes to know and name it, to possess it. America's newness is after all the equivalent of Lolita's nymphancy—"America, the country of rosy children" (29). In this pilgrim's progress, Humbert is the allegorist who seeks, in the land of opportunity, the chance to name, the chance to be the Adam of a new Eden. But Humbert finds the naming of America already accomplished before he turns up at the scene of the crime. He visits America some two hundred years after the moment that James Fenimore Cooper records as the violation of the virgin land through naming.[26] So, just as the pure nymphet turns out to have been seduced already, America turns out to have been named—and despoiled—already. The concept of the precursor backfires on Humbert. He finds "thousands of Bear Creeks, Soda Springs, Painted Canyons. . . . Our twentieth Hell's Canyon. Our fiftieth Gateway to something or other" (159). America has already had its allegorist; in fact, it has had far too many allegorists. It is not that the body, or the material world generally, fails to fulfill the allegorist's desire for the noumenal, for the transcendent name; that name itself has been ruined, despoiled, by being not Everyman's property but countless men's property. It is as if, in knowing twenty Hell's Canyons, Humbert meets face to face his own desire already executed, divided among the twenty men who have gone before him, who have beaten him to the act of naming. The name is thereby mocked; it no longer designates the transcendent spot. The allegorist no longer has any chance of winning the sacred idea by means of naming. The freedom of America suddenly comes to mean the freedom each man once had to name as he pleased; the vastness of America suddenly comes to mean the opportunity by which the name was so repeated and diluted and stretched out across three thousand miles that it no longer held any transcendent meaning.

Lolita is thus not mere allegory, but meta-allegory, allegory about allegory and about naming generally. It is precisely as meta-allegory that Nabokov's *Lolita* self-consciously watches those acts of naming that Humbert performs, and even watches those acts become frustrated. The last stage of meta-allegory in *Lolita* watches Lolita's escape from Humbert's power to name. During the trip across America—the trip that shows Humbert that America has already been named and violated by another (in fact, by countless others)—Lolita finally escapes his (naming) plots by being named and violated by another. She wins her ironic freedom on Independence Day, the Fourth of July. It is America's (second) victory over "the Old and rotting World" (93) (of Humbert Humbert); it is an ironic resistance to Humbert's names, not because America remains unspoiled and unnamed, but because both Lolita and America bear more names than he can manage, because both are more free and more vast than his names will allow.

Lolita escapes from Humbert through the successful employment of her own naming plot. In Part II of *Lolita*, Humbert increasingly loses the ability to name, to locate a crucial name that he needs when another person possesses that name and will not relinquish it to him; and Lolita plays a central role in Humbert's inability. I am thinking, for example, of the way in which Lolita handles Humbert's demand that she name the girlfriend she uses as an alibi for spending time apart from him during their second American odyssey:

"Yes? Whom?"
"A Beardsley girl."
"Good. I know every name in your group. Alice Adams?"
"This girl was not in my group."
"Good. I have a complete student list with me. Her name please."
"She was not in my school. She is just a town girl in Beardsley."
"Good. I have the Beardsley directory with me too. We'll look up all the Browns."
"I only know her first name."

"Mary or Jane?"

"No—Dolly, like me."

"So that's the dead end" (the mirror you break your nose against). (227)

Humbert's attempt to classify this unknown girl by the group to which she belongs, and to identify her by possessing her name, is foiled by Lolita's presentation of her own nickname, Dolly. Humbert finds in Lolita a cunning adversary, a mirror image of himself. What he finds when he discovers "two Dollys" (227) or "twenty Hell's Canyons" is his own defeat signalled by the entrance of another powerful namer into the plot. Lolita has evidently learned from Humbert the power of naming, and keeps what little freedom she possesses by defeating him in a contest of naming. If his power rests on his ability to designate her "Lolita," she exercises some measure of power by withholding the name of those people who have a part in what little private life she has, and in multiplying the number of people in her world who bear the name she herself chooses to go by. Moreover, the idea of "two Dollys" looks forward to the moment when Lolita's freedom from Humbert is at once legal and supreme; when, after having lost track of Lolita for a couple of years, Humbert recognizes her handwriting on an envelope addressed to him, the letter he reads finally bears the signature "DOLLY (MRS. RI-CHARD F. SCHILLER)" (268). Lolita escapes Humbert's naming plots—of classification, and etymology, and allegory—by renaming herself.

The interim plot that gets us from "Lolita" to "Mrs. Richard F. Schiller" shows us Clare Quilty's use of Dolly—and once again the way in which Lolita works a naming plot that deceives and ultimately defeats Humbert. In writing the play *The Enchanted Hunters*, and in successfully bringing Dolly into its orbit under the name Diana, Quilty begins the seduction and possession of Humbert's Lolita. Quilty authors a text that successfully renames—and thereby steals—Dolly from the text that Humbert authors in order to name her Lolita. Moreover, Quilty defeats Humbert by keeping his own name beyond Humbert's power. Humbert's search for the name of Lolita's kidnapper among countless names in 342 hotel registers shows Humbert now at the service of names, the slave of a master namer who outsmarts him. Quilty disarms Humbert of the powers of the science of classification (in which, for example, Humbert studies "the Chevrolet genus" [229] which Quilty drives in order to identify the car and the owner) and etymology (in which, for example, Humbert takes apart and reassembles numerous names in order to learn the "correct name" of Lolita's kidnapper [251]). And Lolita herself is, of course,

Quilty's accomplice in creating a fictional text with fictional names that deceive Humbert. She identifies the author of *The Enchanted Hunters* as "some old woman, Clare Something" (211), and later works the confusion between Clare Quilty and the dentist, Dr. Quilty (223). Not until Humbert arrives at Mrs. Richard F. Schiller's house does Dolly, in a final act of power, give Humbert the name he needs, the name that has succeeded Lolita's name as the charged locus of a search:

> "Come, his name!"
> She thought I had guessed long ago. It was (with a mischievous and melancholy smile) such a sensational name. . . .
> His name, my fall nymph.
> It was so unimportant, she said. She suggested I skip it. Would I like a cigarette?
> No. His name.
> She shook her head. . . . She said really it was useless, she would never tell, but on the other hand, after all—"Do you really want to know who it was? Well, it was—"
> And softly, confidentially, arching her thin eyebrows and puckering her parched lips, she emitted a little mockingly, somewhat fastidiously, not untenderly, in a kind of muted whistle, the name that the astute reader has guessed long ago. (273–74)

The plot that begins with Humbert's taking away from Dolly her name by classifying her as "a nymphet," and by etymologically rendering her as "Lo-lee-ta," ends with Dolly turning over to Humbert the name that he cannot possess on his own (and with Humbert still withholding this name from the reader). Moreover, as we will see, the name she turns over to Humbert is his own name—a new naming, or classification, of Humbert Humbert himself.

Quilty's and Lolita's successful manipulation of Humbert through the power of names is not merely a version of poetic justice. It also begins to instruct Humbert in the ways he has violated Lolita through naming. For example, Quilty's ability to make Humbert confuse "verbal phantoms" in hotel registers with "living vacationists" (253) and Humbert's desperate attempt to detect Quilty's pseudonyms among the "human" (250) vacationers begin to instruct Humbert in the abuses of which he himself has been guilty—the fictionalizing and dehumanizing of a person through naming. It is in this sense that "another Humbert" (219) steals Lolita from him, and in this sense that Humbert decides to murder "my brother" (249), his other self.

Humbert's long detective search after Quilty's name parodies the naming plot that seeks the criminal's name, especially when that search turns up one's own name (as in the case of Oedipus). In this context I recall that

Lolita is a confession. *Lolita, or the Confessions of a White Widowed Male* reflects back on the kind of confession we looked at in *The Scarlet Letter* and *Tess*, where confession becomes a form of self-naming that calls into question such antitheses as self and other, or subject and object. One could read *Lolita* as a parodic exaggeration of Dimmesdale's confession in the third person, and by implication the fiction writer's confession in the third person of fiction. Throughout his text Humbert alternates between naming himself as "I" and as "he," an equivocation that reaches its climax when he hypostatizes the criminal within himself as the criminal Quilty outside himself (who is nevertheless himself). This explains why the murder scene reads as a confusion of names in which the self, or subject, gets lost, a parody of the kinds of shifts in pronominal discourse that I have been describing as a way of naming from *Clarissa* onward: "he rolled over me. I rolled over him. We rolled over me. They rolled over him. We rolled over us" (301).

One could argue that the moment in which the subject is unhinged by being renamed as the other ("I am not myself, I am s/he") in such texts as *Clarissa* and *The Scarlet Letter* and *The Mill on the Floss* becomes in *Lolita* merely one more hallucination, one more projection of the self, so that Quilty, like Lolita, has no status except as the fiction of Humbert's mind. In this way the enlightening moment of fiction, when the self understands itself as other, carries with it the ironic suspicion that "the other" is already only a projection of the self.

But, then, who is the self or subject named Humbert, the criminal who confesses his crime in *Lolita, or the Confessions of a White Widowed Male*? I wish to suggest that the entire refraction and diffusion of the subject in such a scene as Quilty's murder is shorthand for the kind of naming we have been looking at all along in *Lolita*. In such a view Humbert is no more than the uneasy assemblage of a series of often contradictory naming systems: he is the scientific classifier, the etymologist, the allegorist, and, as he names himself, the poet, the murderer, the monster, the therapist, the father, the nympholept, and so on. But as I have shown, Humbert gets himself caught in Lolita's and Quilty's naming plots too. In *Lolita*, the coherence of the subject is split between the texts he can manipulate (all the naming systems he can control at once) and the texts in which he gets manipulated (all the naming systems that control him).

Another way to understand this is by recognizing the belatedness of the subject in *Lolita*, so that Humbert is no more than a filter for a series of traditions of discourse that have gone before him. He exists only as parody. In *Tess*, Hardy presents the subject's belatedness through what is, in the nineteenth and twentieth centuries, a growing vision of the parasitism of the family, a vision that reaches its apex with Faulkner in such novels as *Absalom, Absalom!* and *The Sound and the Fury.* In *Lolita*, Nabokov presents the subject's belatedness by showing us the self overwhelmed in discourse, in the discourses of the past. What else is parody? In both Hardy's and Nabokov's cases, this belatedness is, of course, textual; we see it through the ancient history of a name, or through the history of different naming systems, through a textual layering and compounding that make the subject impure, to use the sexual terminology by which both Tess and Lolita are characterized, each heroine standing at the end of what Tess calls "a long row." But perhaps the final irony of *Lolita* shows us that while Humbert manipulates "Lo-lee-ta" through such a system, the figure of the author itself turns out to be no more than such a layering and sullying. Isn't Nabokov's Humbert a brother to Beckett's characters, where the self seems only a space circumscribed by the echoing voices that fill it, where the "self" or "subject" is no more than a vessel for the discourses of others? In this sense the hero of Nabokov's work, like Beckett's, is the Unnamable. Humbert has chosen as his name "Humbert Humbert" after discarding "Otto Otto" and "Lambert Lambert" and "Mesmer Mesmer"; and he is "Quilty" as well; and he is "I" and "he" and "we" and "they." He is finally the Unnamable who attempts to build a self out of the naming systems he attempts to manipulate. It is not just Lolita, then, who is made up through the naming systems Humbert "creates"; "Humbert" is as well their creation. In *Lolita*, the subject is the object, just as Lolita herself, in the nightmarish landscape of American consumerism, is both: "She it was to whom ads were dedicated: the ideal consumer, the subject and object of every foul poster" (150), a fate she shares with "the author" of "Lolita."

The "science of pleasure" in *Fanny Hill*

Perhaps the most striking feature of *Lolita*'s rhetoric is the way in which the erotic functions not in antithesis to, but rather under the aegis of, certain rational systems of naming that we associate with the Age of Reason. *Lolita* demonstrates the attempt to control the object of desire, to transcribe it into discourse, to subsume it in a variety of systems of naming. Such a demonstration shows the way in which acts of naming can function to place the erotic squarely under the Enlightenment banner "Knowledge is power."

I hope to clarify this intimate relationship between the erotic and Enlightenment systems of naming by looking at *Fanny Hill*, a well-known libertine novel produced in the same era as the traditions of naming I have discussed in the first two sections of this chapter. Furthermore, *Fanny Hill* can help clarify a crucial problem in the history of the novel: the relationship between the act of naming and the act of narration. I would like to put the issue in the following way: what happens to the novel's naming of persons when the (erotic) name threatens to overtake and stand in place of an entire life story? Nabokov evidently regards the text I have chosen to discuss as an antimodel for *Lolita*. When he directly alludes to *Fanny Hill* in his Afterword, he acknowledges that those readers must be disappointed who "begin reading the book under the impression that it is something on the lines of *Memoirs of a Woman of Pleasure*" (318) (or, as it is better known, *Fanny Hill*). While *Lolita* and *Fanny Hill* differ in some of the ways in which they constitute an erotics of naming, they nonetheless both engage in the same enterprise. And both demonstrate how acts of naming undermine the narrative act that attempts to describe a human life—that is, how the science of classification is used to designate and control the object of desire, and thereby to depersonalize and dehumanize the beloved. Moreover, we have already met the author of *Fanny Hill*. Published in 1750 (one year after the last volumes of *Clarissa* appeared), *Fanny Hill* is the work of John Cleland some sixteen years before he turned his attention to *The Way to Things by Words* and two other books of etymology, *Specimens of an Etimological Vocabulary* (1768) and its sequel, *Additional Articles to the Specimen* (1769). A simple acknowledgment of the apparently antithetical directions of Cleland's work—erotic novel on the one hand and etymological philosophy on the other—makes an auspicious beginning for a study of the way in which the erotic and the philosophy of naming run side by side during the Enlightenment. Moreover, one could argue that what Cleland divided between two different texts, two different genres, Nabokov combined in *Lolita*.

Despite Fanny's use of the conventional metaphor of "re-plung[ing] into the stream of my history" (189),[27] as if her narrative were modeled on the flow of river to sea, the text of *Fanny Hill* is not grounded in a teleological narrative; instead, it is an apparently random picaresque of sexual adventures. But there is in fact a rule of order behind the apparent randomness: the goal of "narrative" in *Fanny Hill* is not to tell a story, but to make a catalogue. The end of *Fanny Hill* is the comprehensiveness of a classificatory system. The text is based on a scientific model of specimens and classification, in which the "inventory" (32) and the "survey" (64) are the chief activities, and the only rule is that each example be an addition to our store of (erotic) knowledge. The text, then, is not an organic development of a life story, even though the heroine is fitted with the traditional qualifications for such a story: she is "an unhappy friend-less orphan" (16). Like Nabokov after him, Cleland puts to different use this figure of the traditional novel. The text of *Fanny Hill* is organized through a process of accumulation whereby the system that it creates—the "science of pleasure" (147)—can be complete. The completion of such a system, of course, depends on that practice which seeks to place the proper name inside a common name; in other words, each new adventure is a type, an illustrative "experiment" (44), a species in itself. The lesbian, the sodomist, the sadist, the group, the simpleton—no one enjoys a special privilege; each simply takes its place beside another, in relation to another. Narrative in *Fanny Hill* is simply a disguised and elaborated list.

It is in this sense that the "narrator" of *Fanny Hill* is less storyteller than philosopher, but philosopher of a very special kind. Fanny's "natu-ral philosophy" (103) seeks to find that classificatory system that will comprehend all of nature—that is, every erotic act that the body is capable of performing. In this light one could say that in *Fanny Hill* we find a naming plot that runs counter to the naming plots of the tradi-tional novel. The plot that depends on the naming of the individual in *Clarissa* or *Oliver Twist* or *Tess* is undermined in the erotic text by a plot that catalogues not even types of persons so much as types of acts, acts that are performed by or on persons. In fact, in *Fanny Hill* "person" is neither more nor less than the body itself.[28]

In the typical experiment in *Fanny Hill*, each erotic adventure becomes part of a system of proofs whereby a general rule is proven by an individual test case. Erotic satisfaction blends, in the adventure with "the simpleton" (191), with Fanny's desire "to be satisfied, whether the general rule held good with regard to this changeling, and how far nature had made him amends, in her best bodily gifts, for her denial of the sublimer intellectual ones" (191). Fanny discovers in this case that the erotic act endows the simpleton momentarily with intelligence, writing up a mean-ing on what otherwise is the blankness of his face: "his countenance, before so void of meaning, or expression, now grew big with the impor-tance of the act" (194), while afterwards he falls again into that state of "no-meaning and idiotism" (196). The erotic bestows or uncovers mean-ing and value—and hence becomes the source of discourse. Can a system of naming be devised that will make this "meaning" available?

At the simplest level, the erotic in *Fanny Hill* is based on the titillation of the new. The textual goal is an inexhaustiveness of discourse that has its model in the erotic fantasy of the inexhaustible, the perpetually postponed climax. The erotic novel faces only one danger, "exhausted novelty" (184), so that genre and subject matter become one: the novel, the new, the next unnamed erotic act. Like the surfeited pleasure-seeker herself, or the scientist for that matter, the narrator must continually seek the "new species" (182). The titillation of the erotic pleasure-seeker joins the curiosity of the scientific observer. What more will the text be able to name? The author of the erotic faces the problem of any author of a classificatory system: will my reader become bored by a field so strictly circumscribed? "I imagined, indeed, that you would have been cloyed and tired with uniformity of adventures and expressions inseparable from a subject of this sort, whose bottom, or groundwork being, in the nature of things, eternally one and the same, whatever variety of forms and modes the situations are susceptible of, there is no escaping a repetition of near the same images, the same figures, the same expressions" (115). The "narrative" of *Fanny Hill* functions between the danger of exhaustion on the one hand and the fantasy that stands behind the erotic on the other: "pleasure is ever inventive for its own ends" (182). The erotic text, like the erotic act itself, depends on the inventiveness of the practitioner—or, as we will see, on a lively partnership.

The narrator of *Fanny Hill* records the way in which the actual language open to her in naming the erotic is severely bounded: she seeks "a mean . . . between the revoltingness of gross, rank, and vulgar expressions, and the ridicule of mincing metaphors and affected circumlocutions" (115–16). The most severe limit in *Fanny Hill*, then, is set by linguistic prohibitions that are cultural. Fanny avoids the direct name which designates the organ, as well as the overly artful circumlocutions by which the organ gets unnamed, so secreted that it is erased. The narrator therefore falls back on the repeated use of a limited number of predictable metaphors: "machine," "engine," "instrument," and "weapon" for the male organ, and "vale," "avenue," "gates," "hidden mine," "picklock," and "stronghold of Vartue" for the female organ. A full analysis of naming in *Fanny Hill*, and of naming the erotic in general, would have to take into account the cultural implications of such metaphors. I wish to emphasize the way in which *Fanny Hill* writes up a comprehensive science of pleasure by extending the act of naming not through breaking the ban on naming the sexual organs themselves, and not through inventing a radical new set of metaphors, but through drawing up a catalogue of erotic acts. What was to claim Cleland's interest some years later, the value and weight of the individual word, plays almost no role in *Fanny Hill*, where we rarely get an inventive exploration of what one might call the rhetoric of the erotic. As in science, the name is functional and becomes neutralized by mechanical repetition. Hence language falls short of its task, so that the reader's imagination must supplement it: "I must therefore trust . . . to your imagination and sensibility, the pleasing task of repairing it by their supplements, where my descriptions flag or fail" (115). The art of the erotic depends, then, on the actual rhetoric of the text falling short; it depends on the reader's active—and pleasurable—rewriting of the text by supplementing it. Hence the reiterated invitation to the reader, "Imagine to yourself" (29, 31, 58), "Think then! as a lover thinks" (215). What keeps the reader reading is not so much the language of any individual episode, but his or her contribution to each episode, or—when the limit there is reached—the "new species" (182) always about to arrive on the scene. What keeps the reader reading, then, is the system as a whole, and the erotic investment the reader makes in the "completion" of such a system.

I have distinguished between the kinds of naming that occur in *Fanny Hill* and in the traditional novel. But the crucial names of gender, whose use in such novels as *Clarissa* and *Tess* I have already discussed, are by no means taken for granted in *Fanny Hill*. In fact, if *Fanny Hill* has a narrative at all, it is propelled by two sets of oppositions, maiden/woman and man/woman. Do such names constitute a naming plot about personal identity that is traditional in any way? Do such names undermine the classificatory goal that neglects the individual for the type, and the person for the erotic act? While the narrator in *Fanny Hill* functions as the classifier of a broad range of erotic acts, a range that aspires to be comprehensive, Fanny at the same time enters the text as a character whose own story reaches a critical point when she passes from maiden to woman: "I had not time to consider the wide difference *there*, between the maid and the now finished woman" (64). If in such novels as *Clarissa* and *Tess* the classifier–lover stigmatizes the heroine on the basis of her passage from maidenhood to womanhood, in *Fanny Hill* "womanhood" seems a positive achievement. Instead of divided from herself, Fanny seems "finished," and there is in *Fanny Hill* even "a kind of title to womanhood" (132). *Fanny Hill* subverts the plot of the traditional novel in two ways: it reverses the conventional system of values implied in "maiden/woman," and it drastically reduces the narrative elaborations of personal history to focus on these two names, as if to underscore that this is the end by which people really interpret each other, that even in the traditional novel all of Lovelace's strategies go simply to prove Clarissa a "woman" instead of an "angel," and that all of Angel's illusions hang on Tess's proving herself a maiden. The act of narrative in *Fanny Hill*, insofar as it records a personal history at all, functions simply to make clear the heroine's movement from one name to another. The discourse of the erotic turns almost self-reflexive at one point, so that Fanny's story about becoming a woman gets subsumed in a series of narrations each of which tells the same story, the only story worth telling. Each of the four women of pleasure is asked to narrate this story for herself: "each girl should entertain the company with that critical period of her personal history in which she first exchanged the maiden state for womanhood" (121). In this way what we might have taken to be Fanny's particular story loses its individual weight by forming part of a larger (narratological) structure. Each story is only a variation on a theme, a species of a larger genus, and hence the key story of *Fanny Hill* is catalogued alongside the others while narrative—at least the narrative of an individual's story—is once again devalued. This suggests how the title *Memoirs of a Woman of Pleasure* challenges our penchant for the title with the proper name, *Fanny Hill*.

In *Fanny Hill*, the only name of consequence for an individual to bear is the name of his or her sex or, in other words, a class name. It should be no surprise that the tradition of the engraved soul, heart, and face, which I have been following in the novelistic tradition, becomes in *Fanny Hill* the body written up not with the proper name, nor with the family surname, nor even with the species name, but with the name of gender. In *Fanny Hill* the name of gender is not part of a classificatory system belatedly added on to us, fabricated by the classifier. The sign of one's sex is in fact a sign, the name that distinguishes man from woman or, perhaps more accurately, male from female. As a natural philosopher, Fanny's task is to read the writing on the body, to read the name and all the meaning that stems from it. The virgin blood that is spilled in the act of intercourse is seen as part of a natural system of "marks" (98) where the individual is no longer classified as "maiden" but as "woman"; such marks in fact become "bloody proofs" (165), so that the classifier can see "proof enough in bloody characters on the sheets" (166). The body writes up a text that at the same time functions as empirical proof for the classifier to write up a classificatory text. At the same time the actual organs that distinguish gender are in fact seen as the names "man" and "woman." In this way the male organ is the "label of manhood" (196) or "the male stamp" (188), while the female bears "the mark of the sex" (48), "that mysterious mark, the cloven stamp of female distinction" (98). Another way of putting this is to realize that, since we are named by our distinguishing organ, we can take a compound name such as "man-machine" (194), and each half of such a name is able to name us. The name of the distinguishing organ, then, while never literally spelled out, becomes equal to, and thereby sounded in, the key name in *Fanny Hill*, the gender name. The mechanical repetition of the same stale metaphors for the male and female organs is superseded in these "natural" names. With such "natural" names we approach Cleland's later etymological work, in which he searches after the primitive, universal language of nature. The etymologist's natural language is pared down, in the hands of the erotic novelist, to two names: "man" and "woman." The crucial names in *Fanny Hill*, then, are always verifiable, unlike the hidden name of personal identity that so persistently threads its way through the traditional novel.

The employment of this "natural" naming system conflicts with the comprehensive classification of every novel species of erotic act. Like *Lolita*, then, *Fanny Hill* explores the coexistence of competing systems of naming. If one makes "man" and "woman" the entirely natural point of origin, those erotic acts that were until this point legitimated by the enterprise of classification suddenly become stigmatized. *Fanny Hill* illustrates the way in which, at the moment we hierarchize a name, the neutral and scientific task of classification becomes "moralized"; the list whereby each act is simply placed beside another is disrupted by a cultural ideology. From the point of view of the classification "man/woman," the sodomists in *Fanny Hill* are stigmatized, bearing the grotesque variation of the stamp or mark that legitimizes persons according to gender: "there was a plague-spot visibly imprinted on all that are tainted with it, in this nation at least; for that among numbers of that stamp whom she had known, or at least was universally under the scandalous suspicion of it, she could not name an exception hardly of one of them whose character was not in all other respects the most worthless and despicable that could be, stripped of all the manly virtues of their own sex, and filled up with the worst vices and follies of ours" (189). In such words Mrs. Cole, Fanny's mentor, cannot "name" a single sodomist who escapes this "monstrous inconsistence," and hence they must all be classed as "unsexed male misses" (189). In such a case you are not allowed to be named by the body you are equal to (through the "natural" system of naming); instead, you are named by the "unnatural" act you perform. Cleland shrewdly makes Mrs. Cole, and not Fanny, responsible for the disruption of the neutral classification of erotic acts. Nonetheless, *Fanny Hill* instructs us in the ways in which persons are ostracized by being classified by the kind of name that explodes the community's system. We have already seen how the values of this culture are grounded in the difference between man and woman in *Clarissa* (where Anna Howe mocks the transgression of the *"man-woman"*),[29] while perhaps the most well-known exploration of this transgression occurs in Proust's *A la recherche* under the heading *"hommes-femmes."*

The other cultural capitulation in the otherwise subversive text of *Fanny Hill* comes with its ending, where it yields to a traditional novelistic climax: the return of Fanny's true lover, Charles, and her happy marriage to him. Cleland's innovation in *Fanny Hill* was to take the traditional erotic forms that he knew from the Continent—the erotic dialogue between a young virgin and an experienced woman, and the erotic picture-book with illustrative engravings—and to fuse it with the novel. *Fanny Hill* is "the first original English prose pornography, and the first pornography to use the form of the novel."[30] When we realize that Cleland's models took the form of the catalogue or list—a description with pictures, say, of thirty-five postures[31]—we can understand why narrative in *Fanny Hill* plays such a minimal role. One could even say that precisely because there is no novelistic love plot in *Fanny Hill* there is no narrative; in other words, because Fanny feels no love for any of the men or women she encounters in her adventures, she can become the scientific observer, the classifier. Fanny brings science to the realm of the erotic because her heart is not engaged. It is only insofar as Cleland frames the apparently unending catalogue of erotic acts with Fanny's love for and marriage to Charles that he gives to *Fanny Hill* the semblance of novelistic form. What are the implications of this framing narrative?

First, one can see how the text at one level divides itself between the antithesis of novelistic narrative and erotic classification, and at another level negotiates the compromise between these two forms. At the first level Fanny can argue, even with her maidenhead gone, that she is still a virgin intact when her husband-to-be returns at the end of the novel. It is a sentimental rendering in line with the traditional novel's choice of field, the heart as opposed to the organs of gender. Charles becomes "the possessor of my virgin heart" (213), and all the experiences she has recorded, she tells us, have not made a "pin's point impression on a heart impenetrable" (207). From this angle, the anatomy of the body (or the person) in *Fanny Hill* takes the form of a specific compartmentalization. The virgin heart of the romantic love plot of the novel seems sealed off from the "vale" or "mine" or "avenue" that we have seen penetrated time and again in the classification of the erotic. But when the text adds one further figure of the impression, it allows both forms of experience, for while no other man made an impression on her heart, the extraordinary detailing of each erotic adventure is made possible only by still another kind of impression: "this minute detail of things, that dwelt so strongly upon my memory, after so deep an impression" (107), makes of the memory an organ that comprehends both the impression on the heart (love) and the impression on the female organ (pleasure).

Novelistic form looks as if it is going to triumph at the end when Fanny reinstates the domain of the individual, instead of the general, in the person of Charles. While every man comes to Fanny simply as another man to a woman, her husband-to-be comes as Charles, with his own proper identity meeting hers (in true novelistic fashion): "affecting me infinitely more with my distinction of the person than of the sex, . . . [he] brought my heart deliciously into play" (214). For this reason even the recording of his proper name has a special urgency in what I am calling the novelistic portions of the text: "Charles, the dear familiar name I must take the liberty henceforward to distinguish my Adonis by" (57). Charles, it must be added, comes not to break the reign of pleasure, but to fulfill it. Suddenly Fanny is "in touch, at once, with the instrument of pleasure, and the great seal of love" (215). It is significant that the reader is not prevented from viewing the lovemaking of Fanny and Charles; "once more" Fanny draws open "the curtains" (213), in a final unveiling. This has its narratological reason: we must see and note what ends the system of classification, what transcends it, what in fact causes the classifier to record, "my pen drops from me" (216).

But at the same time, by replacing the plot that translates "maiden" into "woman" with the plot that translates "woman" into "wife," *Fanny Hill* underscores the way in which the conventional marriage plot is simply another form of classification. One could even argue that the natural names of erotic classification, "man" and "woman," are simply exchanged for the cultural names (and norms) of the traditional novel, "man and wife" (213) (whereby "the title to womanhood" becomes erased). Like *Lolita*, *Fanny Hill* exposes the novelistic plot that seems to confer proper identity as no more than a plot that ultimately classifies; at the same time, again like *Lolita*, *Fanny Hill* offers no successful model for the naming of persons. In fact, both novels reenact the failures of philosophy and science.

Proust and the erotics of naming

For Proust, the earliest epoch of memory is the one in which the power of the name is undiminished as yet. This is the epoch in which the child believes in the magic power of names; it is "the age in which one believes one gives a thing real existence by giving it a name" (I.97–98).[32] The mature man reinvents this epoch in the form of a fantasy in which the name has power over the transformations of identity: it is "the moment when our name rings out on the lips of the person introducing us, . . . that sacramental moment, as when in a fairy tale the magician commands a person suddenly to become someone else" (I.932). I wish to explore the development of the Proustian consciousness—to discover the power of name magic in childhood, and its transformations in the mature man, especially when it becomes transformed into an erotics of naming and an aesthetics of language. For the child's belief in the magic of naming is an early stage in what will become Proust's mature conception of the lover's belief in names and the writer's belief in words. Such a history actually coincides with one of Proust's early plans to organize his novel around three successive epochs: "the Age of Names," "the Age of Words," and finally "the Age of Things."[33] In the final text of Proust's novel, the idea behind the Age of Names has left its most visible signs in such chapter titles as "Place-Names: The Name," "Place-Names: The Place," and "Names of People: The Duchesse de Guermantes," all of which appear in the first three volumes.

"Place-Names: The Name" is perhaps Proust's most discursive drawing out of the way in which the child lives in a world of names rather than things. In a special Eden, the child gives substance to an invented world through a series of real names that nonetheless have a magical function for him: "I need only, to make them reappear, pronounce the names Balbec, Venice, Florence, within whose syllables had gradually accumulated the longing inspired in me by the places for which they stood" (I.420). For the child, places are names, and the name is a place where the accumulated longing of many years turns into an invented pleasure that can be let loose simply by utterance. Because Balbec and Venice and Florence actually exist, the child expects to see the pleasure of the name some day realized in the place. The child thinks of "names not as an inaccessible ideal but as a real and enveloping atmosphere into which I was about to plunge, the life not yet lived, the life, intact and pure, which I enclosed in them" (I.423). Names seal up the world of pleasure, and hold it secure for the child, until he is ready to experience it. They bestow the power of acquisition upon the child who in fact is not empowered to travel, to visit such places for himself. But when, in later years, Marcel actually arrives at Balbec, he experiences the trauma of an explosion which he himself inadvertently seems to set off:

> as for Balbec, no sooner had I set foot in it than it was as though I had broken open a name which ought to have been kept hermetically closed, and into which, seizing at once the opportunity that I had imprudently given

them, expelling all the images that had lived in it until then, a tramway, a café, people crossing the square, the branch of the savings bank, irresistibly propelled by some external pressure, by a pneumatic force, had come surging into the interior of those two syllables which, closing over them, now let them frame the porch of the Persian church and would henceforth never cease to contain them. (I.710)

The plunge into the dream world that the safe custody of names has until now protected produces unexpected consequences. The substance that the mind gives to names makes them all the more vulnerable, as if they can suffer a mortal wounding, as Hardy's epigraph to *Tess* suggests: "Poor wounded name . . ." Marcel learns the limits of his magic and the consequences of mistaking its power. The magic name is like an envelope that holds the life of the imagination intact through a delicate membrane that, once broken, can never be entirely repaired. Like the violation of the virgin body, the wounding of the name suggests the fall from innocence, the loss of the pure envelope within which the child has until now safely dreamed; it is the breaking of the spell of childhood.

The apparently simple dichotomy between the actuality of the object and the fantasy of the name finds its most significant elaboration in the naming of persons, especially in the naming of the beloved. *Swann's Way* asks, in what way is the child's fantastic appropriation of Balbec through naming analogous to the child's fantastic appropriation of Gilberte through naming? And in practicing his name magic on persons, must the child be wary of the named object breaking open the envelope of private pleasure otherwise held intact by the name?

The initial power shared by the names of places and the names of persons stems entirely from the fact that both are proper names. The epoch of childhood in this way reinstates the conventional belief that it is the proper name, the name that designates an individual object, that is the instrument of name magic. For Proust, the names of places take their value from being like the names of people: "How much more individual still was the character they assumed from being designated by names, names that were for themselves alone, proper names such as people have!" It is precisely the fact that places are given proper names that "accustom[s] us to regard [them] as individual, as unique, like persons" (I.420–21). Such passages make us see why the name of Gilberte gives her a special value for Marcel by giving her a proper identity. Her name is the sign of that individual and foreign life (like "Balbec" or "Venice") which entices the narrator, making him seek the secret place of entrance, sounded always—as we saw in *Lolita*—in the special pronunciation of the syllables of the name. "Thus was wafted to my ears the name of

Gilberte, bestowed on me like a talisman which might, perhaps, enable me some day to rediscover her whom its syllables had just endowed with an identity, whereas the moment before she had been merely an uncertain image. So it came to me . . . with the mystery of the life of her whom its syllables designated, . . . with the unknown world of her existence into which I should never penetrate" (I.154–55). The name's ultimate value becomes the gift of time; its fullest essence develops over a period of time, and only then might it allow the narrator to rediscover Gilberte, in fact to know her for the first time. Names in this way constitute the secret power of *la recherche du temps perdu*; instead of giving Marcel immediate access to an object, the name carries the identity of the object over time. Names rise above the power of time by succeeding through time. The name is the boundary that keeps pleasure locked up and intact, always there for the child to savor anew. He can carry the name away with him, and enjoy it at will, in after times, because he can envelop it the way in which he never can envelop the object, whether place or person. The name holds within it the deepest pleasure, while its power to excite is never exhausted. Through it one possesses the mystery of life without fear of dissipating that mystery.

Once the talisman of the name has bestowed personhood on Gilberte, she takes up her full position in the narrator's mind through the power of her name. But the irony is clear: this personhood that the name confers is entirely fictional. With the magician as his model, the boy makes the name the means by which he commands the person named to become someone else, to serve his own erotic desire. In short, the name becomes the impetus to fantasy, and the boy loses no time in trying to work the magic of names. What is the power of the talisman he possesses? While the child endlessly repeats the name "Gilberte Swann" to himself, the power of the name once again seems to depend on openly uttering it. But even this practice takes a special form that requires at another level a form of secrecy: an obsessive attempt to make his family use the name "Swann," a name the family has often used before, but which now has acquired (unknown to them) a special significance. The name "Swann" becomes a complicated locus of diverse meanings, for while the family has attributed to the name an entirely eccentric meaning that holds only within the bounds of the family itself, the child now recodes the same name with his own peculiar meaning:

> I went out of my way to find occasions for my parents to pronounce Swann's name. In my own mind, of course, I never ceased to murmur it. . . . Moreover, the name Swann, with which I had for so long been familiar, had now become for me (as happens with certain aphasiacs in the case of the

most ordinary words) a new name. It was for ever present in my mind, which could not, however, grow accustomed to it. I analysed it, I spelt it: its orthography came to me as a surprise. (I.447)

Once again the name possesses the power of the eternally virgin: it allows the maximum of play, surprise, and excitement, without becoming used up. The name is the envelope of pleasure that the boy is able to enter without breaking. While the name magic the boy practices is meant "at last [to] have the effect of making Gilberte suddenly burst into the room, come to live with us for ever" (I.448), we understand that the power of "Gilberte Swann" depends on Gilberte Swann's being absent.

I have said that the child encodes the name; I mean that he makes it erotic. The constant repetition of the name assumes in the child's mind the status of a crime because it is his access to the secret world of sexual pleasure. He sometimes even enjoys this pleasure in front of his parents, but at the same time safely hidden from them because they do not have the key by which to decode the name "Swann":

> The name Swann had for me become almost mythological, and when I talked with my family I would grow sick with longing to hear them utter it; I dared not pronounce it myself, but I would draw them into the discussion of matters which led naturally to Gilberte and her family . . . ; and I would suddenly force my father . . . [to say] "*Swann.*" And then I would be obliged to catch my breath, so suffocating was the pressure, upon that part of me where it was for ever inscribed, of that name which, at the moment when I heard it, seemed to me fuller, more portentous than any other, because it was heavy with the weight of all the occasions on which I had secretly uttered it in my mind. It caused me a pleasure which I was ashamed to have dared to demand from my parents. . . . All the singular seductions with which I had invested the name Swann came back to me as soon as they uttered it. (I.157–58)

The name of the beloved teaches the child the pleasure of the erotic—and, more dangerously, initiates the child into the ways in which one can enjoy this pleasure singly, without the beloved present. In this way the constant repetition of the name is like masturbation; it is a form of self-seduction. The erotic name takes the child's breath away with the pleasure it causes, and relocates the erogenous zone as the place where he inscribes the name of the beloved. While the child hopes the name will some day allow him to penetrate the foreign world named Gilberte, the interior repetition of the name is a self-penetration, with the child inscribing himself on the inside, or at least on that part of the body that goes unnamed precisely because it is the center of pleasure. Such self-seductions end with the child's guilty projection. The child moves from knowing that his parents do not have the key to this private meaning to imagining that they experience "Swann" in the same way he does: "and I was as wretched as though I had ravished and corrupted the innocence of their hearts" (I.158). The erotic power of the name is so overwhelming that he imagines he has sullied his parents through tempting them into those conversations that use the name. In this way the child begins to learn what it means not simply to use his name magic, but to experience it at work beyond his control.

The corollary to Marcel's possession of Gilberte through her name is Gilberte's possession of Marcel through his name:

> "You know, you may call me 'Gilberte.' In any case, I'm going to call you by your first name. It's too silly not to." Yet she continued for a while to address me by the more formal "*vous*," and when I drew her attention to this, she smiled and, composing, constructing a phrase like those that are put into the grammar-books of foreign languages with no other object than to teach us to make use of a new word, ended it with my Christian name. (I.437)

When Gilberte uses Marcel's name for the first time, he imagines her having to change the rules of the language community to which she belongs. The addition of the proper name to one's vocabulary is a critical moment that changes one's entire system of language. It is once again the acquisition of the foreign. When she finally uses Marcel's proper name, the mere utterance of that name becomes an erotic experience, at least for him:

> Recalling, some time later, what I had felt at the time, I distinguished the impression of having been held for a moment in her mouth, myself, naked, without any of the social attributes which belonged equally to her other playmates and, when she used my surname, to my parents, accessories of which her lips—by the effort she made, a little after her father's manner, to articulate the words to which she wished to give a special emphasis—had the air of stripping, of divesting me, like the skin from a fruit of which one can swallow only the pulp. (I.437)

As in the opening paragraph of *Lolita*, speaking the proper name is having it inside oneself, within one's mouth. But in Proust's text this becomes an act that the author projects onto another, and yet he himself remains the beneficiary of the pleasure. In this way the boy turns to his own erotic advantage the utterance of both names—the name of the beloved and his own name. To have Gilberte use his name is to discover a secret access to her body and her inner life—and to control her body so that it absorbs him. The child's fantasy of consubstantiation with Gilberte through his name recalls the famous passage describing his mother's bedtime kiss. In both cases the erotic act takes its form from the

Christian method of appropriating the divine body. When his mother bent her face to him, she "held it out to me like a host for an act of peace-giving communion in which my lips might imbibe her real presence" (I.14). When Gilberte pronounces his name, she consumes him as if he were a Host, as if his name and body were the divine name and body upon which further life depended. And he himself is made new again, by having her find his *real* presence by stripping him of his exterior. This is another entrance into the mysterious envelope, but while Gilberte seems to perform the magic this time, it is the boy's proper name that holds the magical power, and it is he who once again enters her through the magic power of a name. The name draws on two parallel traditions: the name is the "talisman" of magic and the "sacrament" of Christianity.

Like Balbec and "Balbec," Gilberte cannot support the illusion of "Gilberte," and we see the way in which the movement from love to love is a movement from name to name. Just as the miracle of a journey is best explained "not so much because it covered a certain distance as because it united two distinct individualities of the world, took us from one name to another name" (I.693), the miracle of love takes Marcel from "Gilberte" to "Albertine." The question becomes, does a new "individuality" reside under the name "Albertine," or has the narrator made no journey at all in the erotic transfer from "Gilberte" to "Albertine"?

I would like to begin to answer this question by way of *Lolita*. Gilberte is for the narrator of *A la recherche* what Annabel Leigh is for the narrator of *Lolita*: each plays the role of an "initial girl-child" (11). Humbert's compulsion to repeat, while good textbook Freudianism, has its literary analogue in Proust's novel. It is a parody of the Proustian idea that all our later history depends on some initial, fixating experience that we repeat over and over again. Perhaps the simplest way to see that Proust's Albertine plays the role of Nabokov's Lolita—both are belated fixations, copies of a more original love—is to recall that, when Lolita disappears, Humbert thinks of naming his text "*Dolorès Disparue*" (255), evoking Proust's title *Albertine Disparue*. When Proust's narrator says, "I could almost believe that the obscure personality, the sensuality, the wilful, cunning nature of Gilberte had returned to tempt me, incarnate this time in Albertine's body" (III.512), he prepares the way for Humbert's saying, "I broke her [Annabel's] spell by incarnating her in another [Lolita]" (17). One could even argue that Annabel Leigh necessitates Lolita because Gilberte necessitates Albertine. Formulated in this way, parody is built upon the special necessity called literature. Parody itself becomes a form of obsession, a compulsion to rewrite. The idea of the "precursor" (11) in love doubles back in *Lolita* to the idea of the precursor in art, to "the Proustian intonations" (79) that Nabokov cannot shake. "My fancy was both Proustianized and Procrusteanized" (266) is a kind of lament, a confession of conformity that the writer cannot escape.

In the initial experience of love, it is difficult to separate person and name. One could argue that Humbert falls in love with Annabel Leigh only because he has already loved "Annabel Lee," and that Marcel does not fall in love with Gilberte Swann but with "Gilberte Swann." In the love that follows these initial experiences, the name plays an even more powerful role, so much so that the beloved object seems a belated appendage to the erotic name; the name precedes the person by making her possible as the beloved. "Annabel Lee" makes possible (or requires) "Lo-lee-ta," while Marcel actually falls in love with the name "Albertine" before he falls in love with the person who bears the name. This may be so because "Albertine" secretly repeats "Gilberte" (just as "Dolores," via "Lo-lee-ta," repeats "Leigh" and "Lee"). In the midst of Marcel's pleasure over Gilberte's signature on a letter that she has written him, "Francoise refused to recognize Gilberte's name because the elaborate capital 'G' leaning against the undotted 'i' looked more like an 'A' ["*Gi*lberte" on the way to becoming "*A*lbertine"], while the final syllable was indefinitely prolonged by a waving flourish [as if the "te" in "Gilber*te*" were being elongated into the "tine" of "Alber*tine*"]" (I.541). The heart of the two names ("bert") is the same. The servant who is noted for her inadvertent, comical name changings (like a character in a novel by Dickens) here offers the clue to the structure of the first two volumes of *A la recherche*. Francoise's "reading" occurs in the first chapter of *Within a Budding Grove*, precisely at the midpoint between *Swann's Way* and the second and final chapter of *Within a Budding Grove*—in other words, between the magical name "Balbec" and the actual place Balbec, and between the trip from "Gilberte" to "Albertine."

The young man's initial magical possession of the name Albertine Simonet recapitulates the boy's possession of the name Gilberte Swann, with one significant difference: the name is entirely disembodied because he does not yet know whom it names. It is in this sense that he falls in love with the name before the person, a name that he accidentally overhears and proceeds to invest with magic:

> Once again I fashioned such a being, utilising for the purpose the name Simonet and the memory of the harmony that had reigned between the young bodies which I had seen deployed on the beach. . . . I did not know which of these girls was Mlle Simonet, if indeed any of them was so named, but I did know that I was loved by Mlle Simonet, and that with Saint-Loup's help I was going to try to get to know her. (I.865)

The narrator's recollection of his first hearing of the name, and of the subsequent meaning it develops for him, suggests that once Albertine arrives on the scene willing to take up and embody the name Simonet, appearing as the proper person so denominated, she succeeds Gilberte in what turns out to be perhaps an even deeper inscription of the name on the narrator (as if the copy, as in Lolita's case, assumes a value the original can never attain).

> I have often since then sought to recall how it first sounded to me there on the beach, that name of Simonet, still uncertain in its form, which I had not clearly distinguished, and also in its significance, its designation of such and such a person as opposed to another; instinct, in short, with that vagueness and novelty which we find so moving in the sequel, when a name whose letters are every moment engraved more deeply on our hearts by our incessant thought of them has become . . . the first coherent sound that comes to our lips, whether on waking from sleep or on recovering from a fainting fit, even before the idea of what time it is or of where we are, almost before the word "I," as though the person whom it names were more "us" than we are ourselves, and as though after a brief spell of unconsciousness the phase that is the first to dissolve were that in which we were not thinking of her. I do not know why I said to myself from the first that the name Simonet must be that of one of the band of girls. . . . (I.858–59)

The moment depicted here repeats what may be the most primitive moment in the text, when the narrator describes in the first pages of *Swann's Way* awakening with the feeling that "I could not even be sure at first who I was" (I.5). In love, he awakens to know who he is by reading the name of his beloved engraved upon his body. "Albertine Simonet" becomes the name with which the narrator inscribes himself after "Gilberte Swann." In the quest for the beloved, one seems to transform oneself into the beloved, bearing her name. The narrator who remains nameless through so much of the *Recherche* takes his name, so to speak, from the names of others—from Gilberte, from Albertine, from Bergotte (in whose books, for example, he finds the better part of himself), and so on. It is in this sense that the narrative of one's life is inscribed through the names of others, through the qualification and partial eclipse of "I"— a narrative paradigm I have explored from *Clarissa* through *Tess* (with its parodic exaggeration in *Lolita*).

Here in Proust's novel, however, the paradigm is realized not through self-sacrifice, but through the theme of erotic self-seduction, through the lover's loss of his own name in the names of the beloved. For this reason the paradigm functions in Proust's text by pairing self-negation with self-magnification. In the world of Proust, there seem to be only two alternatives: either I take my name from my beloved, inscribing my body with her name, or I give my name to my beloved, inscribing her body with my name. This second alternative is symbolically represented when the narrator uses a famous sculpture of the Virgin for his fantasy: "if I had chosen to scribble my name upon that stone, it was she . . . who would have displayed—powerless to rid herself of them—to all the admiring strangers come there to gaze upon her, the marks of my piece of chalk and the letters of my name" (I.710). In this light, the erasure of "I" in Proust, the rewriting of his own name in another's, always has its limit in the fantasy of his own name taking possession of another, making another powerless to escape him—the kind of name magic that we have seen the philosopher–lover work upon the female from *Clarissa* through *Lolita* in one form or another. The mark the man leaves on the female body is equal to his name. And in either of the two Proustian alternatives, as I have been noting from the start, the erotic pleasure seems to remain entirely Marcel's own.

The erotic name in Proust's and Nabokov's texts functions to allow the fantasy by which the lover knows and possesses the as yet unknown and unpossessed beloved. But after a period of time, when the beloved abandons the (name) lover, the name suddenly becomes not the means to erotic pleasure and power, but to obsession and impotence. For Marcel, having nothing but the name of the beloved realizes for him all the more that she leads an unknown life, that even in the possession of her body he has failed to assimilate her, that he has failed to make her his own. We are at that point in love when the "person itself counts for little or nothing" (III.439); the lover wishes only to hold the beloved object captive. But she escapes out of the envelope of the magical name and leaves it empty. The lover returns to the name, pathetically. It is a return that makes of repetition an almost insane compulsion, an ironic exaggeration of remembrance that makes us forget everything but the name itself.

As for Albertine herself, she scarcely existed in me save under the form of her name, which, but for certain rare moments of respite when I awoke, came and engraved itself upon my brain and continued incessantly to do so. If I had thought aloud, I should have kept on repeating it, and my speech would have been as monotonous, as limited, as if I had been transformed into a bird, a bird like the one in the fable whose song repeated incessantly the name of her whom it had loved when a man. One says the name to oneself, and since one remains silent it is as though one were inscribing it inside oneself, as though it were leaving its trace on one's brain, which must end up, like a wall on which somebody has amused himself scribbling, by being entirely covered with the name, written a thousand times over, of the woman one loves. (III.439)

In such a passage the lover has lost the power of name magic. He is not the magician erotically inscribing his own body with a name; the name acts upon him, for it has become his master. Earlier, the inscription of the name of the beloved seemed to hold out the possible joy of transforming him into her; now it threatens a grotesque transformation of him into a parrotlike creature. Once the magician in the fairy tale, the lover now is held captive in a beast's body in which he seems even to lose the power of language itself, able to repeat only a single name. This name dries up all other words; it erases from his memory every word but itself. But then speech itself is only imagined: "If I had thought aloud . . ." Saying the name to himself, the narrator inscribes the wall of his own consciousness. The lover who seeks to make the beloved his captive becomes a prisoner himself, locked within the claustrophobic prison of the name. Finally the repetition of the name wears him out: "And one feels a constantly recurring need to repeat this name which brings one nothing more than what one already knows, until, in the course of time, it wearies us" (III.439). Uttering the name becomes, like the exhausted erotic act itself, a joyless and mechanical repetition that no longer can fulfill one.

Perhaps the lover whose name magic backfires, so that it imprisons him (and not the beloved), can find his escape by moving from the proper name to the general name. If Albertine is a repetition of Gilberte, perhaps there is a more general name by which the lover can name and enjoy the series of his loves. Such an idea marks the birth of "collective love" (I.1007) in Proust's text. And Albertine begins this epoch not simply by being a repetition of Gilberte but, more importantly, by being one member of a band of *jeunes filles*. If the power of name magic becomes exhausted, demystified, perhaps it can be exchanged for the scientific power of classification. In both Proust's and Nabokov's texts, such a moment arrives when the beloved object is conceived as multiple in nature—that is, in need of not a proper name but a class name. In *Lolita* this multiplication of the beloved takes the parodic form of designating Lolita and her handmaidens by the class name "nymphet." Humbert's parody, I must add immediately, is not as exaggerated as we might expect, because in *Within a Budding Grove*, especially in the second chapter on the *jeunes filles*, the science of classification begins to reshape the text of Proust's novel by moving us from the Age of the Proper Name to the Age of the Class Name. Marcel goes out to discover the bearer of the evocative name "Simonet" like the natural scientist who sets out to seek in the flesh the creature about whom he has read, the creature to which he can pin the tantalizing name. Marcel sets out with "that same curiosity as a human naturalist . . . to become acquainted with a new variety of feminine beauty" (I.865). Inspecting the *jeunes filles "en fleurs"* (of the second volume's title), he enjoys "a botanist's satisfaction, that it was not possible to find gathered together rarer specimens than these young flowers" (I.856). The metaphor that transforms the girls into flowers dehumanizes them in order to study them, to discover a general truth. As in *Lolita*, the lens of science is consistently used to unname and rename the young girls. The *jeunes filles* remind Marcel of "those primitive organisms in which the individual barely exists by itself, is constituted by the polypary rather than by each of the polyps that compose it" (I.881–82). In a passage that anticipates *Lolita*, the narrator confesses "that one comes to like only the very youngest girls, those in whom the flesh, like a precious leaven, is still at work" (I.966). The very attraction of young girls, then, is that they have no proper identity; they are the raw material by which the lover–scientist can constitute his idea of the beloved. They remind one of Angel's search for "untraditional newness," for the "novel" and "fresh,"[34] and the way in which Tess's history (where her ancient family history *is* her "impure" sexual history) makes her unsuitable for Angel's fantasy. In a similar vein, Albertine is classified as a *jeune fille*—the class name that Humbert alters to "nymphet" in *Lolita*.

The multiplication of the beloved image across space (so that the young boy loves the entire band of young girls at Balbec) becomes, for the mature man, a reflection that we love the same beloved image across time. So, while Albertine repeats Gilberte, she at the same time comes to function as a significant difference by instituting a new epoch in the lover's life: "when I gave up Gilberte and knew that I might love another woman some day, I hardly dared entertain a doubt as to whether, at any rate as regards the past, I could have loved anyone else but Gilberte. Whereas in the case of Albertine I no longer even had any doubt, I was sure that it might well not have been her that I loved, that it might have been someone else" (III.511). With such knowledge comes the final demystification of the proper name: "when we love, we sense that our love does not bear a name, that it may spring up again in the future, could have sprung up already in the past, for another person rather than this one" (I.658). From the period in which we love a name and not a person, we move to the period in which we love a type but still not a person; this is the contour of the plot by which Marcel moves from the proper name to the class name. One could also say that the beloved, the female, moves from being designated by a highly charged proper name which has projected onto it the fantasies of the lover ("Albertine" or

"Lolita") to being designated by being unnamed, disallowed any name but a class name, so that again the lover's fantasy is allowed full rein (as in "*jeunes filles*" or "nymphet").

In such ways Proust's text recalls a crucial use to which the class name is put: to stigmatize through naming. In *Within a Budding Grove* there is a disturbing parallel between the tribe of *jeunes filles* and the tribe of Jews. The classification "Jew" reminds us of the way in which, in the realm of the human, the proper name is the sign of authentication. The Israel family at Balbec loses its proper name to a class name: "Israel—at least that is the name these people go by, though it seems to me a generic, an ethnic term rather than a proper name. One cannot tell; possibly people of that sort do not have names, and are designated only by the collective title of the tribe to which they belong" (I.820).

In addition, when used about the human being as specimen, the science of classification not only dehumanizes; it produces a corpse. I recall here the troubling scene in which the narrator seems sexually to possess Albertine while she is asleep, a crucial source for Humbert's fantasy of "operating only in the stealth of night, only upon a completely anesthetized little nude" (126)—a scene that goes back to *Clarissa*, when Lovelace finds his only access to the body of Clarissa while she is drugged and corpselike, and to *Tess*, when Angel Clare, with a rapturous kiss and hard breathing, lays what he takes to be the dead body of Tess in a tomb on their wedding night. In Proust, such a scene explains the way in which the erotic becomes invested with the language of scientific mastery. The dead body makes no resistance to whatever (science) fiction the lover wishes to impose upon it. In sleep "she [Albertine] was animated now only by the unconscious life of plants, of trees" (III.64); "I felt at such moments that I had possessed her more completely, like an unconscious and unresisting object of dumb nature" (III.67). Proper identity dies at once in the primitive tissue of the *jeunes filles* and in the corpse of the mature woman. When the scene is replayed, later in the same volume, what is implicit in it—namely, the view of Albertine as a dead woman—becomes explicit: "It was indeed a dead woman that I saw when, presently, I entered her room. She had fallen asleep as soon as she lay down; her sheets, wrapped round her body like a shroud, had assumed, with their elegant folds, the rigidity of stone" (III.366).

We have seen the way in which the class name stigmatizes; but even when the class name is supposed to serve the dignified purposes of allegory, it gives us a bloodless abstraction: "that twisted body, that allegorical figure" (III.367) of the dead woman shows the contorted shape which the allegorical fancy of the lover imposes on her. The allegorical figure of woman in this way writes up the sign of death. What Humbert sees, when he finds Lolita in the dead of sleep, is that "her lightly veiled body and bare limbs formed a Z" (130). The allegorical female body contains within it the omega sign of mortality; in fact, that body has been made into no more than a linguistic sign, a rhetorical figure, the allegory of Death itself. Similarly, when Marcel walks through the allegorical Garden of Woman, he finds it peopled by the specters of all the real women upon whom the idea Woman parasitically feeds. The allegorical quest for the essence of the female produces a series of literal corpses—Clarissa, Tess, Albertine, Lolita.

In both philosophy and fiction, the issue of the particular versus the general is played out through the dilemma of the proper name versus the general name. Fiction flirts with allegory but finally rejects it because, I think, fiction rejects the class name, whether it puts the beloved within our hands (as in the scientific classification "nymphet") or beyond our grasp (as in the allegorical classification "Woman," which produces a corpse). And yet the proper name can make the writer parrotlike, able only to repeat the beloved name and unable to recall all other words, as we have seen. Proust contemplates this dilemma from different angles throughout his text: "To be quite accurate, I ought to give a different name to each of the selves who subsequently thought about Albertine; I ought still more to give a different name to each of the Albertines who appeared before me, never the same, like those seas—called by me simply and for the sake of convenience 'the sea'—that succeeded one another and against which, a nymph likewise, she was silhouetted" (I.1010). In such a passage we see the way in which the entire question of naming becomes part of the text's narrative, or at least part of its subject matter. The narrator in Proust's text keeps redirecting the procedures of naming, and keeps contemplating these procedures openly, as part of the narrative. Here, once the class name has become valorized in *Within a Budding Grove*, its weaknesses are realized, so that the writer must move back to the proper name. In this particular passage, the narrator must contemplate moving as far as possible in the opposite direction from the class name. Instead of colorless class names or allegorical class names that distort multiplicity through simplification, a series of different proper names could be used to designate the multiple self that replaces the philosophic subject in fiction. In this light, the proper name itself is insufficient, unless it gets divided and multiplied, refracted into a series of other proper names. Without such division, it is no more than a false class name because it denies the multiplicity of the person or object named. These are the antipodes between which the text of the *Recherche* swings—whether to assign the proper name or the class name, whether to move toward a proliferating series of proper names or toward a concentration upon the allegorical name.

Before I explore Proust's attempt to solve this problem, I wish to make clear the way in which the same dilemma overtakes Humbert's text. Humbert puts into action the hypothesis by which one names the multiple self by multiple names, so that in *Lolita* we have Humbert the Bel, Humbert the Hoarse, Humbert the Wounded Spider, Humbert the Hound, Humbert the Cubus, Humbert the Terrible, Jean-Jacques Humbert, and so on. Such names make us see how the use of multiple names merely attaches to the self a meaning, or a series of meanings, by which we classify, or allegorize, the person so named. When Lolita is named "*die Kleine*" (137), or "My Frigid Princess" (168), or "My Love" (210), or "my golden pet" (236), or "my spoiled slave-child" (190), or "Lollikins" (225), she is still being classified. In *Lolita* the proliferation of names threatens narrative by becoming a shorthand—and replacement—for narrative. The story of persons is told by a series of classifications. It is in this sense that the "story" of *Lolita* could be encapsulated in a list of names. In Proust's text, on the other hand, the lengthily elaborated sentence—itself a sign of narrative elaboration—with its complicated series of subordinations, places the name inside a larger structure. In Proust's text we have a proliferation not of names, but of words (and thereby a proliferation of the sentence), delineating the multiplication of selves that constitutes Proustian identity. In *Lolita* the name which puts an end to narrative is not simply contemplated (as in Proust's text), but is enacted, in those name sentences I have already analyzed ("Lolita."), and in that chapter that becomes nothing more than the repetition of the name Lolita, as if Humbert becomes the parrotlike lover that Proust imagines, robbed of all other words: "Lolita, Lolita, Lolita, Lolita, Lolita, Lolita, Lolita, Lolita, Lolita" (111). In this way the Proustian sentence, the apotheosis of time, is the antithesis of the Nabokovian list (of which the proliferation of the proper name is a special case), the apotheosis of space. The lengthy Proustian sentence, which designates the multiplicity of the self by placing the self in a labyrinth of time, eschews the single proper name at the same time that it does not yield to the simplification of allegory. The lengthy Nabokovian list, which designates the multiplicity of the self by naming the self over and over again, always ends with the list of "Lolita." It is as if Nabokov chooses as his narrator the Proustian lover who is fixed on the name of the beloved, the lover for whom the Proustian attempt at "retrievable time" (263) is narrowed to recapturing the bliss of uttering the beloved name. Perhaps the simplest way to understand these differences between the two texts is to realize that in the comparatively short text of *Lolita* the narrator names himself countless times, while in the extraordinary length of *A la recherche du temps perdu* the narrator never names himself.[35] The shifting "I" of Proust's text is the best vehicle for that recovery of the self which always continues to embed the self in time, in the time of the suspended sentence that names the self by not allowing it a name. In this way one could say that the entire narrative project of *A la recherche du temps perdu* is constructed against the childish fantasy that seeks the essence of personality within the narrow envelope of the name.

I have been trying to present a picture of the problems that lie behind a critical point in the Proustian consciousness: the moment of the birth of writing. For Proust, writing is born the moment we escape the mastery of the name, when, for example, the obsessive repetition of the proper name Albertine gives way to the act of narration that inscribes a life story. The obsessive repetition of the name Albertine, we remember, does just the opposite: the name silences us by robbing us of all our other words. It is in this sense that writing—narrative writing across time—is opposed to the repeated scribbling of the same name on the wall of consciousness. The naming plot of Proust's text, then, attempts to describe the means by which the lover obsessed with proper names becomes cancelled in the writer who writes the narrative of his life. Writing in this light puts to use a common language by making words public and available—the exact opposite of the private obsession with the magical proper name, whereby such names as Gilberte and Albertine (or Lolita) function as part of a private sign system.

> But since we live at a great distance from other human beings, since even our strongest feelings—and in this class had been my love for my grandmother and for Albertine—at the end of a few years have vanished from our hearts and become for us merely a word which we do not understand, since we can talk casually of these dead people with fashionable acquaintances whose houses we still visit with pleasure though all that we loved has died, surely then, if there exists a method by which we can learn to understand these forgotten words once more, is it not our duty to make use of it, even if this means transcribing them first into a language which is universal but which for that very reason will at least be permanent, a language which may make out of those who are no more, in their truest essence, a lasting acquisition for the minds of all mankind? (III.940–41)

The lover's private attempt to assimilate the beloved through a secretive magical name evolves, at the end, into the novelist's public attempt to write a universal language by which the people he has loved can be assimilated by all. The writer seeks the Age of Words and the art of narrative—at the same time that the transcription of the dead into the living requires that he reimagine the power which the names of those now dead once held for him.

9

Epilogue

For magic consists in this, the right naming of a thing.
URSULA LE GUIN

By the advantage of *names* it is that we are capable of *science*.
THOMAS HOBBES

Naming as ordinary magic

It has been my primary goal in the body of this book to assemble a group of novels considered more or less canonical, and to document the ways in which acts of naming lie at the heart of the plots and other fictional strategies of these novels. In short, I have attempted to reformulate a tradition by reading fiction through the idea of naming. I now wish to extend this goal by moving temporarily into the foreground a group of texts that exist on the margin of the novelistic canon and that push fictionality to its limits: contemporary children's fantasy. Here we find preserved in our own time the magic of naming in its most archaic forms. For this reason, contemporary children's fantasy allows me to reimagine the dialogue between fiction and philosophy by turning to two related, perhaps purer forms of discourse that have emerged in the course of my argument: magic and science.

As forms of knowing, magic and science intersect at the point at which both accord power to names. And while in the history of Western civilization (especially from the Enlightenment on) science has superseded magic as an acceptable theory of knowledge, the magical view still persists, whether parodied (along with the scientific view) in *Lolita* or rejuvenated in such contemporary children's fantasies as Ursula Le Guin's *Earthsea Trilogy* and Madeleine L'Engle's *A Wind in the Door.* Such persistence makes me ask whether the battle between these two different views of naming has in fact ended, or whether one might more accurately understand the story of naming as the persistently renewed (and resisted) attempt to demystify names in the name of science. In other words, the convergence of magic and science in the idea of naming remains highly suspect, highly suggestive; these two enemies share the deepest bonds, and perhaps it would be wiser to read their relationship not as a simple antithesis, but as a complicated historical interplay of antithesis *and* conjunction which even in our own day has not ended. After all, I have argued that the novelistic tradition (at least in the modern period) often exposes the magic *in* science, so that science is another name and another procedure for controlling and appropriating the world through naming. And so I return, by way of contemporary children's fantasy, to my introductory chapter, to inquire into the reason behind the long persistence of the debate over naming that arises in Western culture in the form of a dialogue between Cratylus and Hermogenes, a debate which I am now designating as the dialogue between magic and science.

Lolita and *A Wind in the Door* dramatize especially well the ways in which different fictional forms of the same period collect the traditions of naming—*Lolita* in order to refashion them into a modern parody, and *A Wind in the Door* to make of them a modern fable. What Nabokov wants to ironize (and undermine), L'Engle wants to legitimate (and preserve). Both texts are modern fictions precisely insofar as they call attention to themselves as palimpsests, determined to make us recognize within them a layering of traditional discourses based on well-known theories of naming. L'Engle has in mind nothing less than the preservation of the most basic structures of Western civilization, structures that are informed by a serious belief in the magic of naming. In *A Wind in the Door*, whose title is taken from Malory's *Le Morte d'Arthur*, the traditional medieval quest is thinly disguised as a series of trials in the practices of naming: the Miltonic "war in heaven" (98)[1] is translated into a war between the forces of Naming (which uphold creation) and of "un-Naming" (98) (which threaten to extinguish all creation); the traditional *Bildungsroman* is refashioned as a coming of age through mastering a series of lessons in naming; and the otherworldly leader of the heroic quest declares, "if I care more about Naming than anything else, then maybe I have to give myself away, if it's the only way to show my love" (101), so that the traditional figural cancellation of Adam in Christ functions here to make Christ a kind of Adamic namer, whereby the act of sacrificing oneself to redeem another rests on the act of Naming. One can recognize in such a list both the oldest structures of Western discourse and the modern designs and plots of the realistic bourgeois novel. The influence of the latter is especially recognizable in the denouement toward which L'Engle's tale is directed: saving (or reclaiming) a dying child through naming. The restoration of the patriarchal name and order (in such ancient texts as the *Odyssey* and the Old Testament) is revised by an emphasis on what I have been stressing in the tradition of the novel: the child's place in the chain of signifying names (as in *Oliver Twist*). In L'Engle's tale the power of restoring order through (re)naming rests with the daughter—with Meg, who by successfully completing the trials of Naming, saves her brother Charles Wallace (in a fabled version of *The Mill on the Floss* that plucks the tragedy out of Eliot's story). In L'Engle's hands, then, modern fantasy reinscribes the ancient secular and sacred texts of a culture, and reveals Naming at their center.[2]

Part of the sophistication of *A Wind in the Door* is the self-consciousness with which it suggests that these various structures of naming and discourse—whether competing or cooperating—form part of a single, complex network of myths, which I wish to call the mythologies of naming in Western culture. Fantasy, then, is a form of retelling, or renaming, sometimes no more than a return home. The "war in heaven" has, Meg is told, what "your mythology would call . . . fallen angels" (97) (which are here called Echthroi), and even contemporary psychoanalytic terminology gets rewritten (or reinscribed through a more ancient name): "Perhaps in your world today such a phenomenon would be called schizophrenia. I prefer the old idea of possession" (125). Schizophrenia enters the text as an updated or scientific explanation of the ancient magical belief in the possession of persons. Mr. Jenkins is (the three Mr. Jenkinses are) in need of healing through the master cure of Naming. For Naming in this text restores persons to their proper identity, to their unique and proper place in the scheme of things. The answer to "what *is* a Namer?" is put this way: "A Namer has to know who people are, and who they are meant to be" (97). Behind *A Wind in the Door*, then, stands the myth of the transparency of persons. By knowing Mr. Jenkins (better than he knows himself), Meg is able to Name him and thereby to restore him to himself. She performs for him the act that the divine Creator performs at the beginning for all creation.

The restorative power that *A Wind in the Door* reveals in the magic of naming throws into relief the entire tradition of realistic fiction. In *A Wind in the Door* the tragic split in personhood gets healed in precisely the way in which it gets evoked as tragic cause in the tradition of realistic fiction: through naming. Contemporary children's fantasy reveals the way in which name magic leaves its traces everywhere in the novelistic tradition. In fact, the magic of naming is the unwritten text over which the tradition of realistic fiction gets written. In L'Engle's tale Naming (where the capital letter signifies the transcendent nature of the act) is no more than an idealized version of that naming (and unnaming and renaming) which directs the plots of tragedy (in a novel like *Clarissa*) and comedy (in a novel like *Oliver Twist*). That we find ourselves in our names and lose ourselves when we lose our names; that we can control another by knowing his or her name and escape another by hiding our own name—these are the mythologies of naming in Western culture, and we discover some version of them in the realistic novel and children's fantasy. *A Wind in the Door* simply returns us to one form of their expression, and thereby makes us realize all the more sharply the way in which Clarissa and Tess are tragic heroines who seek but fail to find (in their fallen world of the realistic novel) the Name within which they can live whole. Perhaps the novel of demystified bourgeois reality, where property and appropriation make the selling of daughters the final valuation (and devaluation) of the proper name, yearns for the magical Name (just as the novel often yearns for the epic, especially in George Eliot's novels). In this light children's fantasy and realistic fiction spin off each other, like two threads from one spool, just as magic and science do.[3]

A Wind in the Door is meant for children in a special sense, then. It is the child's repossession of a cultural inheritance, a return to those naming structures which are discoverable in different forms from the Greek epic and the Old and New Testaments to the bourgeois novel.[4] But we still need to understand the relationship between the magic of naming and the realm of the ordinary, whether represented in realistic fiction, science, or philosophy (as in "ordinary language philosophy"). The *Alice* books suggest a way of negotiating these two apparently disparate realms. Doesn't the deep undertone of sadness in the *Alice* books stem from the ordinariness of the fantasy—that is, from our realization that the child is *ordinarily* at the mercy of the magic of naming in those institutions (familial, pedagogical, theological, legal) which regulate every day of her real life? In such a statement, how can we understand "the magic of naming"? And in what sense can we recover the traces of name magic in the realistic novel, and perhaps in other forms of discourse?

From the outset, it is important to recognize the ways in which contemporary children's fantasies share with other forms of discourse a picture of the child learning the power of naming. In relation to the realistic novel, for example, one could read contemporary children's fantasies as magical *Bildungsromane*. Le Guin's *Wizard of Earthsea*, for example, mythologizes the ordinary picture of the child discovering how to be a part of the world, and even to control it, by learning the names of things. In this way the magic of naming functions as, say, a mythic description of Piaget's account of the child learning language or of Cassirer's account of the development of symbolic thinking (made especially clear when first hindered but finally mastered, at the dramatic moment when Laura Bridgman and Helen Keller discover the "magical" power of naming).[5] The turning point in the life of Ged, the hero of Le Guin's trilogy, occurs when "he hungered to know more such names,"[6] names that make objects and other creatures do the bidding of the young child. At this point the hero of fantasy becomes an illustration of what Cassirer calls the "hunger for names": "All observers agree in describing the almost insatiable hunger for names which seizes the child at this point; he wants to know the name of every new impression. For a time, some writers have pointed out, this desire to name things becomes a kind of mania."[7] This ordinary hunger becomes mania for Cassirer and myth for Le Guin. In both cases it is an account of the role naming plays in the development of the child (as we saw in the history of consciousness that Proust delineates, the first stage of which he calls the Age of Names). The activity of naming functions as a rite of passage, whether for Le Guin, Piaget, Cassirer, Proust—or Augustine, for whom the passage from helpless infancy to the growing power of early childhood occurs, in the first book of *The Confessions*, through learning the practices of naming.

The learning of names, then, plays a crucial role in a wide variety of discourses—in fantasy, in psychology, in philosophy, in fiction, in confession. It is described as a magical or manic moment, an initiation into what Augustine calls "the stormy life of human society,"[8] and as such it functions to mythologize the ordinary course of a person's biography. It is itself a moment set apart, an epoch named, and hence it rises above the course of everyday events. How can we identify in which contexts and discourses the magical view of naming becomes valid or invalid, useful or useless, in understanding the activity of naming?

Such a question allows us to investigate the ways in which discourses prized for their rationality nonetheless employ the magic of naming; in other words, the question frees us to discover how the magic of naming is recuperated in forms of discourse where we least expect to find it, and thereby invites us to speculate on the usefulness of the magic of naming in a variety of discourses. I have in mind here, for example, Wittgenstein's exposure of the magic in traditional philosophical practices of naming. While the standard history of Western thought tells us that science's most decisive (even ultimate) victory over magic takes place during the seventeenth and eighteenth centuries, we find Wittgenstein still fighting the battle at the beginning of the twentieth century—and with philosophy, the parent of modern science, as his central target:

> This is concerned with the conception of naming as, so to speak, an occult process. Naming appears as a *queer* connexion of a word and object.—And you really get such a queer connexion when the philosopher tries to bring out *the* relation between name and thing by staring at an object in front of him and repeating a name or even the word "this" innumerable times. For philosophical problems arise when language *goes on holiday*. And *here* we may indeed fancy naming to be some remarkable act of mind, as it were a baptism of an object.[9]

In this passage Wittgenstein seems to redraw the boundaries of discourse: traditional philosophy, in the guise of rationalism, is no more than a masked form of the magic of naming, a disguised version of the contemporary children's fantasies that we have been looking at. In part, I wish to use Wittgenstein against himself by saying that he substantiates for us once again the fact of the persistence of the magical view (a view whose truth claims he wants to debunk) and how that view occupies discourses in which we least expect to find it. Wittgenstein returns us, then, to the question of the validity of the magic of naming, and its capacity to shift its home from one discourse to another and thereby to be represented differently (perhaps even in disguise) in different discourses. Naming as an occult process, when not disguised as philosophy, speaks openly the magic that spells creation in *A Wind in the Door*: "I Name you, Echthroi. I Name you Meg. I Name you Calvin. I Name you Mr. Jenkins. I Name you Proginoskes. I fill you with Naming. Be!" (203) One could write the story of modern philosophy (and Wittgenstein's role in that story) as the attempt to dislodge philosophical thinking from this idea that naming (or language generally, or even philosophy itself) takes us to the center of being. Perhaps one could begin to write the story of modern discourses as a transfer of settings, or as a reshuffling of (occupied) territories, whereby the magic of naming shifts its ground, or sphere of influence, from philosophy to contemporary children's fantasy (and perhaps to other forms of discourse). Nonetheless, by understanding that both philosophy and fantasy have served as a home for name magic, we see all the more clearly how, even in the modern period, philosophy functions as a cover for fantasy and vice versa, especially when representing how we learn to use words and names. The *Alice* books, for example, function at one level as philosophical compendia cast in the form of fantasy (in which, say, the debate in the *Cratylus* is put in the mouths of Humpty Dumpty and Alice), while philosophy relies on its well-known "Supposes" which, in the modern period at least, populate the philosophic universe with automata, imaginary exotic islanders, and extraterrestrial beings.[10]

I have referred to Wittgenstein here not simply because he problematizes philosophic discourse by exposing the magic of naming at its heart; he also occupies an as yet unacknowledged but unique place in the argument I am making about naming. While I will argue that his disqualification of naming as an occult process needs revising, first I must adjust the claim (in my Introduction) that philosophy neglects the naming of persons for the naming of things. Wittgenstein represents, inside philosophy, an attack on the same philosophic practices of naming that fiction does. The *Philosophical Investigations* is an attack on philosophy's obsession with the naming of things. I cannot say that Wittgenstein moves the activity of naming from things to persons in the same way that fiction does, but I wish for the moment to explore the qualifications within which such a statement might be made. In order to open up immediately the question of names and things—a deeply ingrained foundation of philosophic thinking that survives, in one form or another, until the present—Wittgenstein takes as his point of departure the passage from the *Confessions* to which I have already referred, where Augustine seems to suggest that learning a language is no more than learning the names of things. If one sees the *Investigations* as an attempt to dislodge the association name/thing from the center of philosophic discourse, specifically by way of adding the alternative of describing, say, states of consciousness, one could argue that Wittgenstein brings naming into the arena of the human in a significant way. I do not mean simply that Wittgenstein conceives of the human by describing those linguistic conventions within which human life is constituted (though he does in fact do this). I mean as well that in investigating how we describe human states of consciousness (perhaps the celebrated example of "pain" is most useful here), he explores the way in which persons represent themselves to each other.

But while Wittgenstein brings philosophy an important step closer to naming what is human, he still does not set himself the task of inquiring into the naming of humans. He does not ask what it means to be a person who bears a name, or a complex cluster of names. One could put the distinction even more sharply: while Wittgenstein demystifies the naming of things, he neglects the way in which the naming of persons may in fact function as an occult process. So, while Wittgenstein banishes from the kingdom of philosophy the occult process of baptizing things, the novelist reveals the conditions under which baptism—the procedure whereby human beings (not things) are named—does in fact function as an occult

process. Wittgenstein's attack on the name/thing association that dominates philosophy ends in a view of language as a system within which
names play a much more limited role than had usually been thought. In
this way Wittgenstein's project overlaps with other modern philosophical
systems in devaluing proper names. When modern philosophy finally
does approach the names of persons, it does so only by formulating first a
linguistic category—"the proper name"—and then a series of linguistic
puzzles which reside under the purview of logic.[11] In short, the "science"
of personal names neglects—or insidiously banishes by neglect—the complex human circumstances under which the naming of persons becomes
charged with meaning and power.

I have returned to the distinction between philosophy and fiction with
which I began this study, to complicate it in two important ways: first, to
qualify the distinction by including Wittgenstein's crucial role in undermining philosophy's naming of things; and second, to sharpen the distinction by arguing that Wittgenstein fails to understand the ways in
which the occult process of naming (persons) does in fact constitute not a
strange set of philosophic questions, but a form of life within which we
ordinarily live.[12] By "ordinarily" here (and elsewhere in this chapter) I
mean to recall what modern language philosophy takes to be the revolution by which it purges philosophic discourse, or what I am calling the
fantasy in philosophy; but I am suggesting that this ordinariness has its
own fantastic blind spots. Philosophy is haunted by the progeny it has
produced; it cannot escape science. The absorption of the issue of naming
within ordinary language philosophy, or logic, or semantics too quickly
dispenses with the idea of name magic, an ancient form of thought which
predates both the acts of naming that Wittgenstein (too locally) diag-
noses as the central symptom of philosophy's illness and the acts of
naming that I have uncovered at the heart of the strategies of fiction. The
tradition of fiction makes it possible to record a history of naming in
which the magic of naming is neither masked (traditional philosophy)
nor banished (modern philosophy). In short, the discourse of the novel
defines the ordinary conditions under which naming functions as an
occult process.

But to understand this we cannot dispense with philosophy, for at its
heart lies a naming plot that occultly names—and unnames—persons.
Philosophy traditionally masks this naming plot in a theory of knowledge, in keeping with the characteristic gesture by which philosophy
establishes itself as the final arbiter of knowledge.[13] We can discover the
naming plot of philosophy by recalling the moment (reborn time and
again, from Descartes on) when philosophy formulates the issue of

human identity as a question in knowledge—that is, as the problem of knowing other persons. When philosophy takes over as its own domain our knowledge of each other, it does so by instituting a naming plot whose consequences we still feel today. I wish to show how the philosophic act of knowing is from the beginning a form of naming, and why philosophy tries to hide this truth from us.

The critical moment in the philosophy of personal identity occurs when the philosopher declares that we can only *infer* our knowledge of other persons. At this moment the knowing of persons becomes indistinguishable from a potent act of (un)naming. Other persons, like things, are cast out, placed on the other side of a border where they await, like the creatures in Eden, the time when they can be known and named—that is, when they can become human once more. I am describing here a magical or fantastic moment in the history of philosophy. This magical moment comes into being with the birth of the (Cartesian) philosophic subject, or master namer, who draws up the boundary between self and other and thereby activates (by granting to himself) the powers of unnaming and renaming. In the novelistic tradition this figure is ironized as the lover-rapist (Lovelace, Alec d'Urberville, Angel Clare, Humbert Humbert) who assumes his power most often by copying the role of the patriarch within the family plot, the father who is himself made in the image of that patriarchal Adam, the arch philosopher. In this way the naming plot in fiction exposes and ironizes the naming plot in philosophy. From the moment the philosophic problem of self and other arises, born full-blown from the head of this Adam, the problem of the other never ceases to carry with it the question of the humanness of the other. Fiction underscores this moment by showing the circumstances in which the question "Who are you?" is cancelled in "What are you?" In my reading of the naming plot of philosophy, the formulation of the problem of the other is from the start a masked version of knowing by naming—that is, of working a system, which can be sustained or suspended at will, whereby other persons come into one's ken, or into one's power, by the names one (dis)allows them. The positioning of the knowing of other persons within the domain of philosophy is a highly influential moment in Western culture, a moment whose power depends on masking the way in which *the practice of naming* intrudes from the first upon *the theory of knowing*. In other words, under the cover of theory, philosophy exerts its authority through a discourse that fails to acknowledge the practical consequences of withholding the name of another person and thereby withholding the value and human status of another person.

The practice of naming (which philosophy tries to hide, even to erase, inside the theory of knowing) comes to the surface in any number of "practical" discourses which philosophy is in charge of speaking for, or describing, monitoring, and regulating. Philosophy obfuscates its own role in naming when it puts before us, and evaluates from an apparently neutral position, the practice of naming in another discourse—in the discourse of law, for example. It is especially relevant for our purposes to recall that the relationship between law and philosophy surfaces in the seminal text on naming in Western culture, the text with which I began this study. It is in the *Cratylus* that Socrates approvingly calls "the legislator" the "maker of names": "ought not our legislator also to know how to put the true natural name of each thing into sounds and syllables, and to make and give all names with a view to the ideal name, if he is to be a namer in any true sense?" (389d). In such a passage we see the origin of the fantasy of the ideal namer we met in *A Wind in the Door*, only in our day making the legislator the ideal namer would resign such an idea to the realm of parody (which is where it does in fact resurface in *Lolita*).

But while the legislator is christened the ideal namer, he always has behind him, waiting in the wings, the philosopher who judges the names the legislator gives. In the *Cratylus*, the philosopher plays this role in the guise of the dialectician: "the work of the legislator is to give names, and the dialectician must be his director if the names are to be rightly given" (390d). But the actual names the legislator gives are confounded in philosophical (that is, theoretical) arguments that in fact neglect to evaluate the legal practices of naming, especially the legal practices of naming persons. For example, the way in which personal names actually function under the law enters the *Cratylus* only by the back door, when Hermogenes advances his argument for the conventionality of names by reminding Socrates that "we frequently change the names of our slaves, and the newly imposed name is as good as the old" (384d). Philosophy's complicity in the practices of naming is characterized best by those moments when, to maintain its own legitimacy, it retires from the world of praxis but nonetheless contributes (silently, apparently without intention) to a practical discourse like the law, and even licenses, unwittingly, the brutality of the law. In philosophy, the theoretical conventionality of names can be proven in the "successful" practice of arbitrarily changing the names of slaves.

In such an example, philosophy fails to examine the system, legal *and* philosophical, by which certain persons are named and unnamed—that is, the system by which human communities are founded and expunged. When a state attempts to eradicate an entire race by controlling the names people bear, doesn't it set in motion at a practical level the magic whereby philosophy makes people disappear (or things appear, to use Wittgenstein's example) by withholding from them the name "human," or by placing them in that philosophic limbo where they must wait until their names are known? The history of the creation of states could be written by recording a (magical) formula for naming in each case. I am thinking especially of the way in which naming functioned at the heart of the enterprise of Nazi Germany, or America, or ancient Greece and Rome. Nazi Germany, for example, depended upon those decrees in which Jews were required to take names from one list and Aryans from another,[14] so that the law became a grotesque variation on the philosophic distinction between self and other. Such names functioned as a way of "knowing," even as a correction to "false" appearances (to prevent Jews from appearing as Aryans, and vice versa). In short, the Nazi name decrees were a dark and brutal fantasy by which the German state hoped to return to that magical time when essences were known by name (and mass-murdered). In America too the "purification" of the citizenship— that is, the eradication of certain races—depended on the instrument of naming. A text like Mark Twain's *Pudd'nhead Wilson* explores the relationship between naming and racial identity by focusing on a cultural system that withholds value by withholding names, as Roxy makes clear to her son when she instructs him, "you ain't *got* no fambly name, beca'se niggers don't *have* em."[15] Ralph Ellison explains the sense in which all black Americans are misnamed: "we bear, as Negroes, names originally possessed by those who owned our enslaved grandparents"—a fact that assumes all the more significance in light of Ellison's remark about the magic of naming: "For in the dim beginnings, . . . there was my own name, and there was, doubtless, a certain magic in it."[16] Perhaps less well known is the way in which American Army officials in the 1870's named the native Indian population in Arizona through serial numbers, and the Indian Service renamed that population through names arbitrarily picked out of the pages of the New York City telephone book.[17] We cannot separate such modern attempts at genocide from the system of so-called rational government whereby, in ancient Greece and Rome, for example, the populace was divided between the nameless (the slaves) and the named (the citizens), a division that is not without its profound connections to ancient philosophy. In short, the discourses of law and philosophy share a continuum over time: knowing, naming, mastering, banishing, annihilating. In such cases naming has the effect of an occult process, and may be fueled by an occult desire.

My exploration of the symbiotic relationship between philosophy and law is a way of exposing the complicated and underground negotiations

between two apparently different, even separate, spheres: philosophy/
theory/knowing and law/practice/naming. And I am arguing that in the
tradition of the novel we discover most palpably those acts of naming
which function as, and thereby specify and expose, the (dangerous and
worldly) power of knowing, and which locate the contexts within which
naming functions with the force of an occult process. Perhaps this is why
fiction makes a more or less direct attack on the procedures of knowing
and naming in philosophy and law. This is what makes it possible to read
the naming plot in the story of fiction as a parallel and ironized version of
the naming plot in the story of philosophy. And this is what makes it
possible to read Humbert's joke about "*Know Your Own Daughter*" as a
reference to the system of knowing as naming as raping that the novelistic
tradition exposes from its beginnings. And finally, this is what makes it
possible to read the entire enterprise of fiction as a critique of the law,
both insofar as fiction ironizes the theme of the law (most prominently in
such novels as *The Scarlet Letter*, *Bleak House*, *The Mill on the Floss*,
and *Lolita*) and shapes its own means and ends—its own function as an
act of naming—in counterpoint to the concept of the letter of the law.

   How can we identify those acts in fiction which reveal to us the
ordinary contexts within which naming functions with the force of an
occult process? I will begin to answer this question by recalling the
practices of name magic with which I introduced *Lolita*, and the forms
such magic takes in the novelistic tradition. For example, in light of the
magical practice of changing a name to disguise and thereby to protect a
person (even against disease and death), I recall Huck Finn's mock death
and his reemergence for a life of adventures made possible by working a
system of name changing; or Roger Chillingworth's creation of a new
identity through the invention of a name, and Hester's advice to Dimmesdale that he do the same; or Mrs. Compson's changing Maury's name to
Benjy, as if to cure him of idiocy (and to protect her brother Maury from
contamination), and Dilsey's attempt to demystify such a plan: "Name
aint going to help him. Hurt him, neither. Folks dont have no luck,
changing names."[18] I recall as well the feverish, almost mystical protection of people by secreting their names: Tess's refusal to speak Angel's
name, and Esther's refusal to speak her mother's name. The well-known
prohibition against speaking the names of the dead for fear of bringing
them alive is reversed in *Oliver Twist* in a plot that resurrects the dead
mother by publishing her name. And in a text like *The Turn of the Screw*
we see a narrative directed toward the "supreme surrender of the
name,"[19] by which the governess thinks she exorcises the child of the evil
spirit that possesses him (while reducing him to a corpse in her arms).

And the intention to kill, or at least banish, a person by prohibiting the utterance of his or her name occurs everywhere in fiction: in the prohibitions against speaking the name of Clarissa, or of Caddy in *The Sound and the Fury*, or of Oliver Twist: "Never let me hear the boy's name again."[20]

With such a list as a brief reference back to my entire study, I hope to justify my claim that the documents of fiction restore to the history of naming the efficacy of name magic by presenting it in an ordinary setting. Fiction presses not the ontological validity of the magic of naming, not its claim to truth, but its power in the significant and signifying realm of human intention and belief: naming as (fictitious) knowing, naming as ordinary (as opposed to philosophic or transcendent) knowing.[21] I am arguing that the despotic acts of unnaming and renaming are licensed by the claim (whether explicit or implicit) that the namer knows another person—that is, that naming is knowing, and vice versa—say, when Humbert proves that he knows his daughter by naming her "Lolita" and "nymphet," or when the mother claims that Pearl is not her child, or when Lovelace claims that Clarissa is (Mrs.) Lovelace, or when Proust's narrator claims that Charlus is a woman (just as Charlus claims that the young men around him are nothing but women). Even when such acts of naming (as knowing) are literally true, they can function as untruths, with an insidious power to unname and scandalize, as in the case of Lovelace's attempt to prove that Clarissa is a woman (with the special meanings he attaches to that class name). The knowing of other persons is a means of specifying how to master them, to make them present or absent, to eroticize them, to slander them—in short, to use them by naming them, a hint that the practical philosopher Alice gives us when the Gnat asks her, "What's the use of their having names . . . ?": "'No use to *them*,' said Alice; 'but it's useful to the people that name them.'"[22] It is precisely this usefulness that takes the form of name magic. While Wittgenstein seeks, as economically and directly as possible, to cut short what he calls language's "holiday" by returning philosophy to a language that is ordinary, fiction dwells on those acts of naming in which such a holiday produces the most profound effects in ordinary circumstances. Fiction studies the abuses of naming and sees their tragic consequences; understands the power with which names are endowed and the magical effects which are the consequences of such power; acknowledges how these extraordinary effects constitute the ordinary forms of life within which we live. In this light the realistic novel does not so much domesticate the magic of naming (if we mean by this tame or disenchant it) as provide another setting for it.

I began my study with the observation that philosophy neglects the naming of persons for the naming of things. Now I wish to suggest that we need to revise the philosophic concept of knowing other persons because philosophy neglects, or pretends to neglect, or obfuscates, the naming of persons. I wish to argue that the magic of naming implicitly revises the major formulation that grounds the philosophic interpretation of personal identity. In philosophic discourse, the body/soul formulation is a way of posing questions about verifying the existence of other persons, and assigning to them their epistemological and/or ontological status. Within the context of my claim that knowing is always a way of naming, I wish to ask in what way the name shares with the body the function of bringing another person into existence and assigning that person's status.

The novelistic tradition suggests that the name not only shares but often supersedes the role of the body here. The body is often in the service of the name, and has its significance insofar as it bears a name. Fiction repeatedly shows us this profound transaction between body and name, in bodies that function to perpetuate a name, bodies that are sacrificed to a name, bodies on which one writes one's own or another's name, bodies on which one reads one's own or another's name, even bodies whose clearest meaning is cancelled by having a name attached to them (when, for example, Proust's narrator names Charlus a woman). While the body often remains an obscure medium, difficult to interpret, the name is readability itself, so that the body is made readable by carrying a sign. Sometimes the name functions as the explicit illumination of the body, and hence a clarification of essence. Humpty Dumpty tells Alice, "My name means the shape I am." While Wittgenstein claims that "The human body is the best picture of the human soul,"[23] the human name is often seen as the best picture of the human body. I can represent the mediating role of the name by deliberately situating it in the middle of the (often unoccupied and nebulous) space between body and soul: body/name/soul.[24] To understand the source of such a formulation, one can turn to the ancient tradition that I hear (unconsciously?) sounded when Stanley Cavell glosses Wittgenstein's body/soul claim in the following way: "I have penetrated the veil of the other by taking his body as an omen, in this case a good omen, of a soul."[25] In ancient literature it is the name that functions as the omen of the soul in a well-known apothegm that gets reworked at least until the time of the Renaissance: "*Nomen atque omen*" suggests an omen in the name.[26] This is why the body serves the function of carrying the very name which philosophical skepticism calls into question. When Dante reads "OMO" on the human countenance (*Purg.*, XXIII, 32), it is the human name (which the body serves to carry) that is the omen of the human soul. What Cavell suggestively calls "the veil of the other" reminds me of the veil as a hermeneutic figure that stands in the way of a full reading, and hence suggests the superior function typically granted to the name in mastering people by claiming to know them. The name, because it is a readable linguistic sign, appears to give us the most direct access to the other.[27] When Othello asks, "Was this fair paper, this most goodly book, / Made to write 'whore' upon?" he figures Desdemona's body as the *tabula rasa* on which he writes the name that is the terrible lesson he thinks he has learned.[28] The great warrior puts down his sword to become the scholar engaged in the activities of knowing, naming, and writing: Othello becomes the philosopher–king. In a play haunted by the threats and dangers of black magic and by the racial slurs that make Othello the manipulator of this magic, the cruelest irony discovers Othello caught in the trap of using the name magic that the rationalist philosopher employs. The attempt to textualize identity, to make it readable by assigning it a name, is exposed in Othello's slander of Desdemona, in his mistaken claim to know her. In this way we see how the name is empowered with the magic to mediate the space between body and soul, and how this "ordinary" act of naming sets the scene for the murder of body *and* soul—lest we forget that "Good name in man and woman, dear my lord, / Is the immediate jewel of their souls."[29]

The novel as naming plot

My attempt in this chapter to remystify the naming of persons requires that I reimagine the complicated ways in which the enterprise of fiction both grants and limits the power of naming. This will allow me to make clear why it has been necessary to cast the particular parts of my book in dialectical form, and why it is necessary to continue to see the naming plots of fiction in dialectical relationship, both to each other and to the historical and cultural values such plots at once reflect and constitute. With the prominent examples of fantasy and philosophy in mind, we begin to understand the ways in which naming is embedded in a wide variety of discourses. It remains to be shown how the novel, or at least the traditional reading of the novel, has masked the ways in which naming lies at the center of a wide variety of plots we do not at first recognize as naming plots. The idea of naming can help us reformulate the traditions of the novel by making us reconsider the ways in which the central plots of fiction represent family, gender, nation, and race.

ONE. The attempt to demystify acts of naming always runs up against the same obstacle, and the structure of Part One of my book is meant to illuminate the nature of this obstacle. The dialectic of losing a name (chapter 1) and finding a name (chapter 2) discovers a means neither of synthesis nor of transcendence (chapter 3). The deepest irony of *Pierre* proves the intransigence of the naming plot, its inescapability, which the lives of both Pierre and Isabel (from different angles) prove. The idea that we can demystify the power of naming by simply escaping names altogether, *Pierre* makes us see as only one more mythology of naming, and the one that has the least efficacy, the least practicability. This is why it is always cast in the form of fantasy, often with political (in this case, Utopian) overtones. In *Pierre*, for example, such an idea functions within the purview of the myth of American revolution, while in a recent story by Ursula Le Guin it is used to launch a feminist attack on what I have been describing as one of the centers of patriarchal power. "She Unnames Them" reimagines Eden with an unnamed Eve ("she") empowered to unname the creatures and thereby free them (and by extension to free herself, woman as other/creature).[30] And Le Guin's fantasy certainly has in mind something like the wood without names in *Through the Looking-Glass*, where both the faun and the human child find temporary refuge from the divisive power of names. In the end, this (Utopian) idea of namelessness restores the dialectic of losing and finding a name at another level. It underwrites (by idealization) the plot of losing one's name, in the same way that the ideal proper name underwrites the plot of finding one's name.

Pierre's exposure of the American plot as a naming plot, then, limits the demystification of naming by returning the possibilities of fictional plots to the two prominent (British) forms such plots characteristically take. At the same time *Pierre* opens up the question of naming as a significant problem in literary history, especially within the domain of national literatures. In calling *Pierre* an American naming plot, we need to recognize that such a plot has a complicated and important history whose origins lie in Cooper's novels. Cooper situates his novels at that moment, more mythic than historical, when the "unchristened sheet" (119)[31] or *tabula rasa* known as America is about to be inscribed (and violated) by names: "If [the King's people have not] begun to blaze their trees, and set up their compasses, and line off their maps, it's likely they've not bethought them to disturb natur' with a name" (36). Natty suggests that only the Indians are able to give "reasonable and resembling" (37) names, and the primary naming plot of *The Deerslayer* works out this idea through focusing on that series of acts whereby Natty, on his first warpath, earns the name Hawkeye. Earning one's name, instead of inheriting it, is the core of the democratic American plot. One could argue that in *The Deerslayer* the American plot that shows us Natty earning his name runs parallel to the ironic, or British, subplot that shows Judith Hutter losing her name. When the Hutter family secret is discovered, and the true name of the bastard daughter is unrecoverable (in a set of documents where the names have been erased and cut out), we learn the advantage of the American system: when you earn your name yourself, you bear a "natural" name, while in the British system your name is merely nominal and depends entirely on your family. When it is discovered that "Thomas Hutter wasn't Thomas Hutter," Judith echoes the cry by which we recognize the daughter of the British naming plot from *Clarissa* to *Tess*: "I scarce know by what name to call myself now!" (403).

It would be possible to write a history of American fiction by charting the ways in which such a text—what one might call the ur-text of American naming plots—gets repeated, complicated, ironized, and parodied within the tradition of American fiction. I have in mind not simply Hawthorne, Melville, and Nabokov (all of whom I have already used more or less with this purpose in mind), but also such writers as James and Faulkner. One could initiate such a study with Ralph Ellison's remark, "As Henry James suggested, being an American is an arduous task, and for most of us, I suspect, the difficulty begins with the name."[32] And I would like to take up briefly what undoubtedly would be one especially useful text in such a history: Twain's *Huckleberry Finn*.

Like the Hutter subplot in *The Deerslayer*, the subplot of the Duke and King in *Huck Finn* could be used to describe the peculiarly American attempt to escape the (British) naming plot. When the "Duke" reveals himself as "the lineal descendant of that infant—I am the rightful Duke of Bridgewater," and when the "King" reveals himself as "the pore disappeared Dauphin, Looy the Seventeen, son of Looy the Sixteen and Marry Antonette" (100–101),[33] *Huck Finn* debunks the British or Continental naming plot—the plot in which the entire story turns on the discovery of a noble name—and clarifies its own American plot, the story of an orphan child and black slave who nonetheless sustain a story of dignity, where the end rewards us with no further revelation than the signature of sincerity, "YOURS TRULY, HUCK FINN." One could read *Huck Finn* as an American myth in which we see the protagonist successfully live beyond names (the goal of Deerslayer and Pierre), as if the child's successful series of impersonations, each carrying a fictitious name as its sign, is a literal acting out of the series of masks by which one is apparently named and known in the world. Huck outsmarts the false world of names by going to land armed with a name and family plot—what everyone who meets him expects of him—and by returning to the freedom of the raft and the river. In this way Huck connives to live the innocent American dream of namelessness. The series of impersonations, or reincarnations in the name of someone else, constitutes the naming plot, apart from which *Huck Finn* is merely a poetic idyll where the ego is stripped naked, suspended between life and death, until Huck must take up another mask, another name.

But the naming plot succeeds in catching up with Huck when he assumes a real name, the name of "Tom Sawyer," the power of which seems to unravel Huck's newfound wisdom. Trying to beat the system by using the system has its dangers, and even American ingenuity has its limits. It is at such a point that the power of naming—to constrain, and even to enslave—is most potent. And when I say that Huck is enslaved in a name, I wish to evoke a particular moment in Jim's story that catalyzes the other crucial irony in the naming plot of the novel. This moment occurs during Tom's restoration of the British or Continental plot—"the custom in Europe" (189)—as the basis of the tale: "Why, hain't you ever read any books at all?—Baron Trenck, nor Casanova, nor Benvenuto Chelleeny, nor Henri IV, nor none of them heroes?" (188). Jim is made to impersonate a prisoner after the manner of "The Iron Mask" (190), with a coat of arms and noble ancestry. When Jim tires of the plot, Tom chastises him for neglecting "more gaudier chances than a prisoner ever had in the world to make a name for himself" (207). We understand at once the extraordinary loophole in America's democratic system of namelessness which, in practical terms, translates into being able to make a name for yourself. The slave who is allowed no name of his own (and who is stigmatized as "nigger") can pretend to make a name for himself only in an elaborate game based on the Old World social hierarchy of blue blood and noble name. Jim's namelessness is the social and thereby ironic counterpart of the idyllic namelessness to which Huck aspires on the river, or to which Deerslayer aspires in the wilderness. And Jim's inability to make a name for himself in America is the realistic counterpart of the mythic plot in which Deerslayer periodically makes a name for himself—a tradition whose roots lie in the native American system of naming, and not in the European naming practices which overlay and immediately expunge the native system.

TWO. In Part Two I reimagine the problem of escaping or transcending names, the need for which problematizes at the outset the comic plot of finding a name—the plot that is comic only when it is fantastic, when it reveals through the chinks of its realistic setting the fantasy of finding the ideal proper name. I do this by exploring the way in which both British and American novels contemplate another form of namelessness—not namelessness in the American wilderness, not namelessness that encourages earning a name through courage or boldness (reminding us that American "solutions" to the naming plot are male plots), but namelessness based on the Christian paradigm of selflessness and thereby in antithesis to the male naming plot. But it is precisely the patent feminization of such an idea in a text like *Tess of the d'Urbervilles* that undermines the tradition's exploration and exploitation of the daughter in her role as the child who charitably takes for herself the name of no one, or the name of anyone, or perhaps even the name of everyone—what, by the time we reach the twentieth century, becomes so clear that Faulkner names this figure precisely by unnaming her: she has her being in the final self-effacement that unnames her, making her "the eternal female, the eternal Who-suffers."[34] It is in this sense that I use *Tess* as a dialectical limit by which to reexamine the ways in which Hawthorne contemplates resolving questions of naming and confession and fiction in *The Scarlet Letter*. Like *Pierre*, then, *Tess* is a climactic moment in my argument insofar as it undermines a mode of escaping the threatening power of names, of demystifying the occult power of naming systems. And as in the case of *Pierre*, this allows *Tess* to open up an entire tradition of fiction by revision. *Tess* invites us to reconfigure the naming plots of fiction neither along purely structural lines (losing a name, finding a name) nor along purely national lines (British plots, American plots), but along the lines of gender, and in so doing requires that I redraw some of the boundaries within which we have been working.

In *Tess* Hardy manages to reveal that the plots of losing a name and finding a name are, in some profound sense, gender plots. He does this by radically reconfiguring the two plots as the same plot. These two plots are recognizable as the two best-known plots of fiction when I call them by more conventional names. The plot of seduction (what I call losing one's name, in *Clarissa*) and the plot of inheritance (what I call finding one's name, in *Oliver Twist*) are, in my formulation of the tradition, both naming plots. *Tess* takes the comic plot that is traditionally reserved for the male (for Tom Jones and Humphry Clinker and Oliver Twist) and awards it to the female in a profoundly ironic move, by making it serve the plot of seduction—Tess seduced in the name of the family. In this way *Tess* undermines the comic plot of finding a name by exposing the family plot, the plot in which one is named in the name of the family, as a plot of seduction. *Tess* makes us realize how a novel like *Clarissa* also combines the two plots. Reducing Clarissa to namelessness means disinheriting her, which is after all the deepest motive of her brother and sister; both wish to push her out of the family, just as Lovelace wishes to remake her so that she is no longer a Harlowe. In this way the plot of seduction is revealed as the plot of disinheritance, the plot of losing a name. *Clarissa*'s subversive strategy shows how the comic male plot of inheritance gets turned around in the female plot of seduction, or what we now can call the plot of disinheritance and unnaming, while *Tess* takes an even more radical step by showing how the comic inheritance plot turns tragic, as if in our culture the daughter's story cannot sustain it, though *Tess*'s point may be broader still, in exposing the inheritance plot universally as a plot of family violation by naming.

In a similar way, the feminization of the plot of namelessness undermines the apparently democratic plot of *The Deerslayer*. Once we recharacterize the American and British plots in Cooper's novel as male and female plots, we discover a crucial flaw in the myth of America. One could rewrite the plot in which Deerslayer earns a name ("Hawkeye") and Judith loses a name ("Hutter") in the following manner: Hawkeye wins the name "man," and Judith plays her role as woman insofar as she loses her "good name." Perhaps the worst stigmatizing name in *Deerslayer* is "woman" ("you are not even a woman" [281]), so that when Natty is scandalized by that name ("He is a Delaware woman, dressed in the skin of a Yengeese!" [477]), the plot recenters itself on his regaining his name of honor, his name as man: "Rivenoak now told his people that the paleface had proved himself to be a man" (486). Judith, on the other hand, seems to validate the stigma in the name "woman" by losing her "good name": "Young women's good names are a pleasant matter of discourse with some that wouldn't dare to be so open-mouthed if there was a brother in the way" (86; also see 194, 262). The tale hints that Judith confirms Harry's prejudicial insinuations when, at the end of the novel, we read: "None knew her—even her person was no longer remembered. Other officers had again and again succeeded the Warleys and Craigs and Grahams, though an old sergeant of the garrison, who had lately come from England, was enabled to tell our hero that Sir Robert Warley lived on his paternal estates and that there was a lady of rare beauty in the lodge who had great influence over him, *though she did not bear his name*. Whether this was Judith, relapsed into her early failing, or some other victim of the soldier's, Hawkeye never knew" (emphasis added, 534). The woman's plot, then, offers only two alternatives: she is either renamed in the marriage plot (see Judith's touching and finally

humiliating attempt to win the name "Bumppo"), or she loses her name—
her good name and her family name—in the seduction plot (which once
again can be viewed as a plot of disinheritance, whereby the daughter
loses her family name). The plot that democratically allows Deerslayer to
earn his name offers Judith no such chance, and in fact reveals the name
of "woman" as a stigmatizing class name. Finally, we realize that namelessness in America in fact carries with it not simply the freedom to earn a
name, but a stigma that is most readily attached to Indians and women,
dehumanizing both by classifying both as no more than bodies (in a
telling revision of the formulation body/name/soul): while Harry can
speak of Indians as "them that have neither souls nor names" (391), the
text shows us that women are typically stigmatized as soulless and
nameless. Such ironies undermine Deerslayer's lofty remark, the slo-
gan of the American naming plot: "I put no great dependence . . . on
names" (58).

Another way of specifying this difference between the gender plots of
fiction is to say that the man escapes naming insofar as he is able to
escape the family plot, something that the woman traditionally is never
able to do, in America or Britain. I mean here that Deerslayer is a new
kind of orphan. The wilderness is precisely the setting in which he can
escape the naming system of the family (and the lack of freedom that the
inheritance plot entails) by continually cancelling his family name in the
sobriquets he earns. But when Judith says, "I am Judith, and Judith
only, . . . until the law gives me a right to another name" (403), she
explains her inability to escape a naming system that is designed to make
women take up their names only inside the family plot, first as daughters
(known by the names of their fathers) and then as wives (known by the
names of their husbands). Even in America, the naming of women takes
place under the old law; the new or natural law of the wilderness is
reserved for men.

One could continue to investigate the attempt at escaping the family
plot and its system of naming by turning to texts such as Conrad's
political novels, which reach out well beyond the bourgeois family for
their plots. But even a novel like *Under Western Eyes* craftily positions
the family plot at the center of the story of revolution. I take my cue from
the narrator when he tells us, "The thought that the real drama of
autocracy is not played on the great stage of politics came to me as, fated
to be a spectator, I had this other glimpse behind the scenes, something
more profound than the words and gestures of the public play. I had the
certitude that this mother refused in her heart to give her son up after all"
(253).[35] Conrad unsentimentalizes the narrator's hint about the family

plot at the heart of this political novel by focusing not on the mother's lost son (Victor Haldin), but on another son's lost family—namely, on Razumoz as bastard and orphan. In this way Razumov takes up his place as an English hero, as "nobody's child" (8),[36] and it is perhaps for this reason that he is so consistently dubbed "a regular Englishman" (24). True to form, the story of nobody's child becomes the search for the name ("I have no name" [159]), but in this revolutionary plot—as in the American democratic plot—the search is not for the bastard's name (or the father's name), but for the name he can earn for himself: if "The word Razumov was the mere label of a solitary individuality" (16), "Distinction would convert the label Razumov into an honoured name" (18); and again, "The field of influence was great . . . once one had conquered a name" (60). I would read the bourgeois plot in which the hero seeks to make a name for himself against the radical plot in which the revolutionaries uphold their namelessness. As Tekla puts it, "I have no use for a name, and I have almost forgotten it myself. . . . That is the lot of all us Russians, nameless Russians. There is nothing else for us, and no hope anywhere, unless . . . all these people with names are done away with" (179–80). The series of subtle ironies that make up the texture of *Under Western Eyes* depend on Conrad's extraordinary positioning of a characteristic English plot (with a characteristic Englishman who happens to be Russian) inside revolutionary Russia where the goal is equality through namelessness. For instance, Razumov does in fact win a famous name, but unexpectedly among the revolutionaries ("Your name is a sort of legacy" [147]); he wins a name for aiding Haldin when in fact he has betrayed him. In this way *Under Western Eyes* ironically reconfigures the plot in which one successfully earns a name: "He was nothing but a name, you will say! Exactly! A name! And what's more, the only name" (129). With the discovery of Razumov's betrayal of Haldin, the narrator's hyperbole is exploded, and we discover that Razumov is in fact only a name, an empty name.

By undermining the plot of earning a name, Conrad exposes the emptiness at the heart of the traditional hero's self-aggrandizement: "I am become a name."[37] Razumov has one further strategy left open to him: in an attempt to free himself from the false name he has earned, he confesses. In fact, he uses a strategy we have already looked at in some detail, especially in the context of Dimmesdale's confession in *The Scarlet Letter*: Razumov confesses in the third person. Whether confession occurs in the first person (as in *Tess*), in the third person (as in *The Scarlet Letter*, *Under Western Eyes*, and *Crime and Punishment*), or in both (as in *Lolita*, where Humbert uses both "I" and "he" to confess), it adds to the plots of inheritance and seduction one further well-known plot: the plot of crime and punishment. And I wish to argue that the plot of crime and punishment, insofar as it functions as a search for what Hawthorne calls "the guilty name," is a specific kind of naming plot. In a novel like *Tess* all three well-known plots converge as naming plots: Tess confesses her crime, and is punished, under the same sign that represents her seduction and her family inheritance; the guilty name is the family name. When Tess confesses that she is the criminal (the female seduced), Angel Clare punishes her by reassigning to his wife (legally "Mrs. Angel Clare") the family name of "d'Urberville."

While confession in the first person names the subject as the criminal, confession in the third person—it is interesting that the main exemplars here are male—problematizes the issue of moral responsibility, and in fact displaces the crime onto an unspecifiable "he." For instance, Raskolnikov in *Crime and Punishment* (like Dimmesdale in *The Scarlet Letter*) uses the form of confession as if it were fiction, telling Sonya the story of the murder in the third person as if he were a novelist with privileged information of an event about which no one else knows: "He did not want to . . . kill Lizaveta. He . . . killed her by accident. . . . He meant to kill the old woman . . . when she was alone . . . and he went there. . . . But Lizaveta came in. . . . He was there . . . and he killed her" (393).[38] One could say that such a passage questions the role of the subject in syntactic propositions. But to question this grammatical structure inside the form of the confession is to undermine the idea of the subject in the language of morals and the law—that is, in the discourse of crime and punishment. In short, confession in the third person presses us to ask the central question of *Crime and Punishment* in the most profound and open way: "The whole question is: am I a monster or am I myself a victim?" (269)—the same question, posed in the same terms, in such texts as *Frankenstein* and *Pierre*.

But the third-person confessions in both *Crime and Punishment* and *Under Western Eyes* do not come as the climax to the naming plots, as does Dimmesdale's confession. Whereas Dimmesdale conveniently dies before the nature of his confession can be fully understood or acted upon (so that the equivocal confession that names him as a mediate self is never unravelled), Raskolnikov and Razumov go on to suffer their punishment precisely insofar as their "fictional" confessions in the third person are finally understood as a form of self-naming—that is, insofar as "he" becomes understood as "I."[39] And *Under Western Eyes* ironizes the plot of *Crime and Punishment*. First, upon understanding Razumov's confession, Natalia (unlike Sonya in *Crime and Punishment*) deserts the confessor, and buries her own selfhood in the revolutionary cause: "There was no longer any Natalia Haldin, because she had completely ceased to think of herself—a characteristic Russian exploit in self-suppression" (279) (an exploit in unnaming that we recognize from female naming plots in general). Second, the revolutionaries puncture Razumov's eardrums in a grotesquely willed conversion of the traitor into a nameless revolutionary, for now when Tekla calls him by name the deaf man cannot hear. The label which Razumov hoped to transform into a distinguished name first becomes a false sign, and now becomes a dead sign, with Razumov unable to hear his own name spoken by another, or even spoken by himself. An unwilling and ironic copy of the nameless revolutionaries, Razumov becomes the man barred from recognizing himself in his own name. In sum, *Under Western Eyes* succeeds in undermining two radical or revolutionary plots: the plot of earning one's name (instead of inheriting it) and the plot of being nameless (instead of being named).

THREE. With *Tess* and *Lolita* as tragic and ironic variations (respectively) on the comic English naming plot (in which the unknown and misnamed son inherits his true name in the end), my argument proceeds from Part Two to Part Three. My argument can proceed without rupture because both *Tess* and *Lolita* employ naming plots in which the daughter is seduced in the name of the family. I wish to reimagine this development by focusing now on the idea of personal duplication and its consequences for naming plots—in light of 'Liza-Lu's replacement of Tess, for example, or Lolita's replacement of Annabel Leigh, or Natalia's ironic replacement of her brother in *Under Western Eyes*, so that she begins by naming herself as her brother (when she first meets Razumov, she inadvertently introduces herself as "Victor Haldin") and ends by losing herself in her brother's cause. A history of fiction could be written by charting the role such duplications play in naming plots in both the traditional and the modern novel.

Humbert's crazy fantasy of the three Lolitas (from "Lolita the First" to "Lolita the Third") has as its model a novel in which the same girl is in fact reincarnated over three generations. In Hardy's *The Well-Beloved* (which Nabokov would have known at least through Proust's discussion of it in *A la recherche*), the protagonist falls in love with his cousin Avice, then twenty years later with her daughter (Avice the Second), and then twenty years later with the granddaughter of the first Avice (Avice the Third). Hardy's "nymph" (93)[40] shares with Nabokov's "nymphet" a similar list of literary ancestors: Laura, Lilith, Eve, and so on. And, as in *Lolita*, Hardy's allegory depends on the failure of the "specimen" (141) flesh to satisfy the protagonist's ideal desire: "The Beloved of this one man, then, has had many incarnations—too many to describe in detail. Each shape, or embodiment, has been a temporary residence only. . . . [T]he first embodiment of her occurred, so nearly as I can recollect, when I was about the age of nine. Her vehicle was a little blue-eyed girl of eight or so, one of a family of eleven, with flaxen hair above her shoulders" (51)—Humbert's Annabel Leigh. In this light, one could argue that what I have taken to be the origin of the idea of erotic fixation in *Lolita*—Proust's *A la recherche*—is itself a belated edition of *The Well-Beloved*. When the protagonist of *The Well-Beloved* speaks of "a gigantic satire upon the mutations of his nymph" (93), he inadvertently designates the entire form of the novel of which he is the hero and anticipates by half a century our best-known satire upon nympholepsy, *Lolita*.

In its picture of the self duplicated in body, soul, and name, *The Well-Beloved* calls to mind two crucial plots in the history of the novel. The first we find everywhere in the tradition, and the second is a modern commentary on the ubiquitous earlier form. The traditional form of this plot I wish to designate as a "species" naming plot; its central sign is the birth of the namesake. I have in mind such examples as Clarissa (the Second), born to Anna and Hickman; Esther (the Second), born to Caddy and Prince; Maggie (the Second), born to Bob Jenkins and his wife; Pip (the Second), born to Joe and Biddy; and Ursula (the Second), born to the parents on the barge in *The Rainbow*. The birth of the namesake always occurs at a crucial moment in the narrative, and often at the end, where it serves the purpose of resolving at least one strand of the plot. The introduction of the namesake into the naming plot may well be the most magical moment in these texts and in realistic fiction generally. It is a moment that crystallizes perhaps the most important problem of personal naming in Western culture: the properness of the proper name. Such a moment characteristically plays a Utopian function in the plot. It suggests, for example, the way in which Anna Howe gets back her beloved Clarissa (at the same time that it ironically suggests the power that Anna now has over "Clarissa," with the friend suddenly playing the authoritarian role of parent). The birth of the namesake in *Great Expectations* comes with the Utopian reassurance that the new Pip will not fall into the blinding selfishness of the old Pip. In fact, the birth of the new Pip in some sense is no more than the literalization of the second Pip who has been present everywhere in the "double" narrative of Pip recreating his former self; the double consciousness of Pip, which propels the entire project of *Great Expectations*, ends with the splitting off of the two Pips, so that the birth of the namesake signals the climax of the narrative. Such a pattern is the backbone of many of Dickens's plots: at the end of *Bleak House*, for example, Richard (the Second) restores Rick to Ada, but with the hopeful expectation that this second Richard will not grow up to become the man devoured by Chancery. It is the only way that the original Rick (or any of these characters) can in fact "begin the world again" (to use Rick's favorite phrase).

I call such plots "species" naming plots in order to suggest their function as experiments in Darwinism. They remap the individual as a species in a history in which the fittest survive in order to ensure the continuity of what I have been calling the family plot. Tess hands over 'Liza-Lu to Angel Clare as the unblemished copy of herself. Will they reproduce Tess—Tess the Second? In such an example we begin to see that the science of classification and the novelistic plot are cross-fertilizing forms; the novel borrows the notion of species from science, just as scientific classification is a masked version of the novelistic family plot, as Darwin himself suggests: "all true classification is genealogical; . . . community of descent is the hidden bond which naturalists have been unconsciously seeking, and not some unknown plan of creation, or the enunciation of general propositions, and the mere putting together and separating objects more or less alike."[41] But in fiction the Utopian wish for the repetition of a particular person questions the very basis of novelistic form—the history of the individual—and a culture whose oldest values and oldest stories depend on the individual securing his right to his proper name. The "species" naming plot, then, forces us to ask what we mean by an individual and the proper name that so designates him or her: how many Pips or Clarissas are possible?

It is precisely by raising such a question, especially in the form of tragic (*Tess*) or ironic (*Lolita*) plots, that the modern novel reflects back on an earlier tradition. The modern novel often functions to expose the fantasy in the "species" naming plot, especially by portraying the protagonist as the man who tries to replot (or control) his history, with the woman regularly cast in the serviceable role of duplicate. After all, when Tess gives Angel Clare an unstained copy of herself, doesn't she hope finally to succeed in satisfying his original desire? And doesn't Angel become the symbolic father–scientist who now is given another chance to make and to produce Tess in what amounts to an experiment on an "interesting specimen of womankind"?[42] In *The Well-Beloved*, Pierston tries to use the second and third Avices to assuage his guilt: he desires "to make reparation to the original woman by wedding and enriching the copy" (113). Humbert uses his fantasy of the three generations of Lolita to satisfy his original desire for Annabel Leigh (and his unappeasable appetite for nymphets), and in this way *Lolita* parodies the ostensibly moral motive of Hardy's hero. In every one of these examples the family plot insinuates its way into the heart of the erotic plot, where the male lover attempts to control the community of descent (of the beloved) after the fashion of the patriarchal family. This is why Hardy can characterize the hero's desire for the three Avices as "genealogical passion" (160). The lover's attempt to (re)produce the female copy that perpetuates his dream and eternalizes his passion is a version of the perpetuity the patriarch achieves through his name—that is, through sons who perpetuate his name and daughters who are sacrificed for his name.

The gender subtext of genealogical classification has perhaps its most complicated but nonetheless telling example when Proust speaks the language of Darwin in plotting the community of descent of Charlus, the man who the narrator tells us not only "looked like a woman: he was one!" (II.637): "In this respect the race of inverts . . . might be traced back further still, to those experimental epochs in which there existed neither dioecious plants nor monosexual animals, to that initial her-maphroditism of which certain rudiments of male organs in the anatomy of women and of female organs in that of men seem still to preserve the trace" (II.653). Does the classification of Charlus take up its place beside the narrator's classification of "Woman," or "*jeunes filles*," because Char-lus is a *woman*? One could read this classification of Charlus as a complicated fantasy in which the author wins his maleness in two ways, both in his role as Adamic classifier and in his classification of "invert" as woman or hermaphrodite. I recall, for example, Lovelace's claim that his manhood depends on the success of his attempt to classify Clarissa as woman; perhaps the narrator's (and author's) manhood in *A la recherche* depends on the success of his attempt to classify Charlus as woman. Such examples remind us that the namer earns a name in the very act of naming another. In any case, true to form, Charlus becomes known in the text through the generalization and pluralization of his proper name—that is, as "*un Charlus*," "*les Charlus*," and "*les messieurs de Charlus*"—just as Lolita becomes "Lolitas" (or "nymphet" to Charlus's "invert"). And I am claiming that such experiments in reconstituting the individual as a species develop logically from the "species" naming plot in the traditional novel—from the plot, for example, in which Lovelace's transformation of Clarissa into "a Clarissa" (that is, "Clarissa" is a repeatable idea, not an individual person) takes its final form when Clarissa (the Second) in fact materializes.

Wuthering Heights could be read as the kind of traditional model that is ironically undercut in such novels as *The Well-Beloved* and *Lolita*. I am recalling the way in which Lockwood is initiated into the intricacies of the Heights and the Grange by reading a mystifyingly repeated name whose variations only the plot of the entire novel can unfold and explain. Toward the beginning of the novel Lockwood secures himself in a large oak case in which he hopes to take refuge from Heathcliff, but where he finds himself prey to the mysteriously powerful name "Catherine," finding the "name repeated in all kinds of characters, large and small— *Catherine Earnshaw*, here and there varied to *Catherine Heathcliff*, and then again to *Catherine Linton*. In vapid listlessness I leant my head against the window, and continued spelling over Catherine Earnshaw— Heathcliff—Linton, till my eyes closed; but they had not rested five minutes when a glare of white letters started from the dark, as vivid as spectres—the air swarmed with Catherines."[43] The "obtrusive name" that will not let him rest and that penetrates his refuge is the harbinger of the complicated family plot to which he will yield during the next many months; in fact, it is the harbinger of Catherine herself, who will violate his refuge further by coming alive and pleading to let her come in at the broken window pane (in a variation on the magical idea of the name raising the dead). The obtrusive name ensnares Lockwood, then, and initiates the telling and retelling of the tale of the different Catherines. The name is the most potent sign of the labyrinthine genealogy which ensnares all the characters of *Wuthering Heights*, where *Catherine Linton* is at once *Catherine Earnshaw* (made over, or married) and the daughter or namesake of Catherine Linton (nee Earnshaw), and where *Catherine Heathcliff* is a fantasy (or a redundancy, if we remember Cathy's claim that she *is* Heathcliff), and where proper names function as surnames ("Heathcliff") and surnames function as proper names ("Linton"). A study of family genealogies in *Wuthering Heights* reveals the novel as a Darwinian battle, sustained through several generations, among three classifications of essence: "Earnshaw," "Heathcliff," and "Linton." I read the three Avices in *The Well-Beloved* and the fantasy of the three Lolitas in *Lolita* as parodic variations on the three Catherines in *Wuthering Heights*, that archetypal family plot of radical duplication and otherness. In this light *Wuthering Heights* begins to make us see the usefulness of Hardy's term, "genealogical passion," for characterizing the moving force behind "species" naming plots in general.

The repetition of the name "Catherine" at the beginning of *Wuthering Heights* suggests a specific kind of plot in which a palpable narrowing or collapsing of names occurs, both within its own pages (so that not only "Catherine" but also "Heathcliff" and "Linton" do double and triple duty in the plot) and within the tradition of the novel generally. Hardy, for example, produces this kind of naming plot by choosing to set the action of *The Well-Beloved* on an island (like the isolated Heights) where there are "only half-a-dozen surnames" (120). For this reason the naming plot keeps doubling back on itself, producing ironic copies of itself as sub-plots, as in the case of the second Avice marrying a man with the same surname as the protagonist's. Pierston in this case witnesses Avice won in name only, in the name of "Pierston"—an ironic variation on his quest to secure the beloved in *her* name. The limited number of surnames becomes the sign of the sameness of body or family types—that is, species types—in the controlled environment of the novel. The island setting limits the population of the novel to a small number of "species," so that once again we imagine the main action taking place in a kind of hall of mirrors: "the type of feature was almost uniform from parent to child through generations; so that, till quite latterly, to have seen one native man and woman was to have seen the whole population of that isolated rock" (150). *The Well-Beloved*, then, is an experiment not unlike Proust's researches into the species "invert" or Nabokov's researches into the species "nymphet." Moreover, as a controlled experiment in the family plot, *The Well-Beloved* parodies the traditional "species" naming plot by laying bare the consequences, and perhaps motives, of "genealogical passion": self-duplication.

The Sound and the Fury suggests another way in which the modern novel ironizes the obsessive functioning of the traditional family plot as a "species" naming plot, especially through the arresting and pathetic undercutting of the name of the beloved (as sister). Once again, the plot is signalled by the intentional repetition of a few highly charged names and by the consequent restriction of the variety of names its central characters bear. One of the first confusions we encounter in reading the text occurs when we fail to realize that there are two Jasons (and sometimes one is dead and one is alive), or that there are two Quentins (and one is male and one is female), or even that there are two Caddys. I refer here to the pain that Benjy experiences at hearing "Here, caddie"—what I would call the initiating moment of the naming plot—on the first page of the novel. "Here, caddie," we realize only in retrospect, is the teasing pun that undercuts the proper name in the cruelest way possible. For Benjy, it is the call to presence (in his innocent belief in the full power of the name) that takes him back to the time before his pasture was turned into a golf course, and before his beloved sister Caddy was turned into a "caddie"— the only version of his sister's name to survive, since "Caddy" is not allowed to be spoken in the Compson household. In this way "caddie," on the first page of the novel, introduces the idea of the debased copy that informs the histories of Jason (the Second) and Quentin (the Second). Such names ironically undercut the idea of the Utopian namesake, and "caddie" is at once the most ironic version of such an idea and the one that contains implicit in it the deepest tragedy of the novel precisely because it is the name that contains for all three brothers their most potent (and impotent) fantasies. In other words, as the name of the sister duplicated in a debased form, "caddie" spells the failure of the family in general to duplicate itself. So, while novels like *The Well-Beloved* and *Lolita* ironize the "species" naming plot by laying bare the fantasy behind it—that is, the (male) Utopian desire to play out, and even correct, one's destiny by controlling a system of personal (female) duplicates—a novel like *The Sound and the Fury* uses the ironic distance between the original and the copy (both of which bear the same so-called proper name) to predict the end of the family line.

Such examples underscore the dialectic that informs Part Three of my study by calling into question whether or not the act of narrative can demystify the talisman of the name. Modern texts such as *The Well-Beloved*, *The Sound and the Fury*, and *Lolita* become reflections back on traditional forms by emphasizing the classifying power inherent in narrative, as if all narrative, no matter how it tries to function as realistic history, is a form of allegory. We realize that the mere names of Tom Jones and Oliver Twist and Clarissa Harlowe call to mind for us the character as "example"[44]—that is, the character as specimen—and thereby the novel as science. We begin to recognize the ways in which a name can absorb an entire narrative.

But we need not depend on the modern novel to make such ironies clear for us. Indeed, I have attempted to show that the entire tradition of the novel exposes the way in which personal names function not as neutral referents but as labels of meaning—for the other characters in the text, who use naming to establish the meaning and value and use of a person, and for the reader, who inevitably uses the name to recall the meaning (the allegory) of the life story that the text inscribes. It is precisely my intent, by moving the family plot into the foreground of my study and by demonstrating its function as a naming plot, to make clear the way in which the proper name, when assigned a meaning, loses the function that it is ideally supposed to have in Western culture—to refer to an individual without assigning any use to him or her. The study of personal naming reveals the ways in which we use persons to construct our own allegories of meaning. Personal names are the central tool we use in constructing such allegories, and fiction is the name of the discourse that exposes this enterprise.

Notes

Introduction

1. Florence Emily Hardy, *The Life of Thomas Hardy 1840–1928* (London: Macmillan and Co., 1962), p. 217.

2. Stephen K. Land, *From Signs to Propositions: The Concept of Form in Eighteenth-Century Semantic Theory* (London: Longman, 1974), p. 6.

3. John Locke, *An Essay Concerning Human Understanding*, ed. Peter H. Nidditch (Oxford: Oxford University Press, 1975), p. 406.

4. Thomas Hobbes, *Leviathan Parts I and II* (New York: Liberal Arts Press, 1958), p. 39.

5. Hobbes, *Leviathan*, p. 41; *The English Works of Thomas Hobbes* (London: John Bohn, 1839), IV.21.

6. Locke, *An Essay Concerning Human Understanding*, p. 404.

7. *The Dialogues of Plato*, trans. B. Jowett (Oxford: Oxford University Press, 1968, 4 vols.), III.71 (410b), III.54 (395a). Quotations from the *Cratylus* refer to this edition of Plato's works.

8. Ian Watt astutely characterizes a feature of the realism of the novel in the following way: "the early novelists . . . made an extremely significant break with tradition, and named their characters in such a way as to suggest that they were to be regarded as particular individuals in the contemporary social environment" (*The Rise of the Novel: Studies in Defoe, Richardson and Fielding*, Berkeley and Los Angeles: University of California Press, 1957, p. 19.) But for Watt the use of proper names in fiction is an essentially minor example of the overall harmony between Enlightenment philosophy and eighteenth-century fiction. I am arguing the opposite by claiming that the crucial matter of human naming uncovers the division between two different kinds of discourse: philosophy and fiction. I will go on to suggest the ways in which Enlightenment systems of philosophic classification, within the plots of novels from *Clarissa* to *Lolita*, work to undermine what Watt rightly sees as the novel's attention to the proper name. Finally, it seems less important to me that eighteenth-century novels begin to use individual proper names (as opposed to names from myth, say) than that the names in these novels are consistently problematic. I wish to position, alongside Enlightenment philosophy's search for the general names of things, what I wish to call a series of mistakes in the naming of persons in

the eighteenth-century novel—as if, as in the example of Hardy, the novel begins by acknowledging that we do not know how to name persons. Defoe's title characters typically are incorrectly named; and the "real" name of the hero in Fielding's novels is unveiled only toward the end; and much of the comedy of *Tristram Shandy* depends on what Mr. Shandy takes to be a critical mistake in naming; while much of the tragedy of *Clarissa* depends on a series of manipulative acts in which others mistake the name of Clarissa.

9. See Lawrence Stone, *The Family, Sex, and Marriage in England, 1500–1800* (London: Weidenfeld and Nicolson, 1977), p. 409; and Joseph E. Illick, "Child-Rearing in Seventeenth-Century England and America," in *The History of Childhood*, ed. Lloyd de Mause (New York: Psychohistory Press, 1974), p. 324.

10. Perhaps the child's new status as individual in the eighteenth century provokes a new and insidious form of parental power: "The child was no longer so full of dangerous projections, and rather than just examine its insides with an enema, the parents approached even closer and attempted to conquer its mind, in order to control its insides, its anger, its needs, its masturbation, its very will." Lloyd de Mause, "The Evolution of Childhood," in *The History of Childhood*, ed. de Mause, p. 52.

11. Joseph E. Illick, "Child-Rearing in Seventeenth-Century England and America," in *The History of Childhood*, ed. de Mause, p. 324. Also see David Leverenz, *The Language of Puritan Feeling* (New Brunswick, N.J.: Rutgers University Press, 1980), p. 118, for a similar list of Puritan names: "More Fruit, Faint Not, The Lord is Near, Joy Again, More Trials, Sufficient."

12. Rudolf Schnackenburg, *Baptism in the Thought of St. Paul*, trans. G. R. Beasley-Murray (New York: Herder and Herder, 1964), p. 20. The title of another book on baptism, *Made, Not Born* (Notre Dame: University of Notre Dame Press, 1976), produced by the Murphy Center for Liturgical Research, suggests how profoundly the act of naming in baptism is an act of making.

13. Claude Lévi-Strauss, *The Savage Mind* (Chicago: University of Chicago Press, 1968), p. 195.

14. See Ernst Robert Curtius, *European Literature and the Latin Middle Ages*, trans. Willard R. Trask (Princeton, N.J.: Princeton University Press, 1973), for a rich sampling of examples of "Etymology as a Category of Thought," pp. 495–500.

15. See, for example, *Totem and Taboo*, especially pp. 56–58 and 110–13, in *The Standard Edition of the Complete Psychological Works of Sigmund Freud*, trans. James Strachey (London: Hogarth Press, 1968), vol. xiii; and James George Frazer, *The Golden Bough* (New York: Macmillan, 1963), chapter 23 ("Tabooed Words," especially the section called "Personal Names Tabooed"). Also see Ludwig Wittgenstein, *Philosophical Investigations*, trans. G. E. Anscombe (New York: Macmillan, 1973), p. 19^e.

16. *The Collected Works of C. G. Jung*, ed. Herbert Read, Michael Fordham, and Gerard Adler (New York: Pantheon, 1966), 8.427.

17. Laurence Sterne, *Tristram Shandy*, ed. Howard Anderson (New York: W. W. Norton, 1980), pp. 36, 39. See Sigurd Burckhardt's brilliant exploration of the opposition between Walter's faith in names and Toby's faith in things, and his analysis of Tristram's ironic failure to own for himself "the saving name": "As Toby seeks innocence in things, so Tristram, farcically improving on the learned doctors, seeks it in names. If the sacrament of name-giving can follow immediately upon that of marriage, before man has paid tribute to his fallen estate in the sexual act and has thereby perpetuated the sin of Adam, the gap is closed." ("*Tristram Shandy*'s Law of Gravity," in *Tristram Shandy*, ed. Howard Anderson, p. 600.) I have forborne writing on *Tristram Shandy* at least in part because Burckhardt has already given us a profound version of what I would call the novel's naming plot.

18. Herman Melville, *Pierre or The Ambiguities*, ed. Harrison Hayford, Hershel Parker, G. Thomas Tanselle (Evanston and Chicago: Northwestern University Press and Newberry Library, 1971), p. 286.

19. William Faulkner, *The Sound and the Fury* (New York: Random House, 1956), pp. 128, 225, 247, 109.

20. John F. Walzer, "A Period of Ambivalence: Eighteenth-Century American Child-hood," in *The History of Childhood*, ed. de Mause, p. 364.

21. Roger Shattuck, *The Forbidden Experiment: The Story of the Wild Boy of Aveyron* (New York: Farrar Straus Giroux, 1980), p. 42. See Shattuck's description of the uses to which the child has been put, especially during the Enlightenment, pp. 44–45.

22. Locke, *Essay*, p. 454.

23. Locke, *Essay*, pp. 414–15.

24. James Fenimore Cooper's Leatherstocking Tales are a novelistic account of this topic as the key moment in the colonization of America. *The Deerslayer*, for example, shows Natty Bumppo consistently arguing against the idea that Indians are only "half human" (p. 41), "only a slight degree removed from the wild beasts" (p. 309) (New York: New American Library, 1980). The series of names red man/savage/half-human/beast is part of an inquiry into the politics of naming where "man" is a name worthy of empirical proof—Natty "proved himself to be a man" (p. 486)—and where "boy" (p. 307) and "woman"—"you are not even a woman" (p. 281)—are slurs perhaps more scandalous than "savage."

Lévi-Strauss explains that the colonization of America had behind it the view that "'It would be better for the Indians to become human slaves than to remain free animals'" (p. 75). One could interpret this use of class names alongside the later passage (in "On the Line") on the tabooed use of proper names (*Tristes Tropiques*, trans. John and Doreen Weightman, New York: Atheneum, 1981).

In our own day, the special naming of Jews in Nazi Germany is a powerful example of ruling—and dehumanizing—by naming (or unnaming and renaming). See Robert M. Rennick, "The Nazi Name Decrees of the Nineteen Thirties," *Names*, vol. 18, no. 1 (March 1970), 65–88.

25. Shattuck, *The Forbidden Experiment*, p. 137.

26. See Charles Dickens, *Oliver Twist*, ed. Kathleen Tillotson (Oxford: Oxford University Press, 1966), p. 223, where Harry speaks of being "unworthy . . . of the name of man." A great number of characters in fiction are referred to by the name "monster." Lovelace and Sikes are notable examples, and Pierre is addressed at one point as "Mr. Monster," while Humbert calls his narrative in *Lolita* the confession of "a pentapod monster."

27. Nathaniel Hawthorne, *The Scarlet Letter*, ed. Sculley Bradley, Richmond Croom Beatty, E. Hudson Long, and Seymour Gross (New York: W. W. Norton, 1978), p. 69; William Faulkner, *Absalom, Absalom!* (New York: Random House, 1964), p. 196.

28. Mary Shelley, *Frankenstein* (New York: New American Library, 1965), pp. 115, 123.

29. Charles Dickens, *Bleak House*, ed. George Ford and Sylvere Monod (New York: W. W. Norton, 1977), p. 565.

30. The page references to the *Alice* books in the next three paragraphs are from Lewis Carroll, *Alice in Wonderland*, ed. Donald J. Gray (New York: W. W. Norton, 1971).

31. Samuel Richardson, *Clarissa or, The History of a Young Lady* (New York: Dent, reprinted 1978, 4 vols.), 3.206, 3.427.

Chapter 1. *Clarissa*

1. Samuel Richardson, *Clarissa or, The History of a Young Lady* (New York: Dent, reprinted 1978, 4 vols.). References to this edition are given parenthetically in the text and indicate volume and page number.

2. For a fine account of Hume's position, see James T. King, "The Place of the Language of Morals in Hume's Second *Enquiry*," pp. 343–61, in *Hume: A Re-Evaluation*, ed. Donald W. Lingston and James T. King (New York: Fordham University Press, 1976).

3. John Locke, *An Essay Concerning Human Understanding*, ed. Peter H. Nidditch (Oxford: Oxford University Press, 1975), p. 408: "And every Man has so inviolable a Liberty, to make Words stand for what Ideas he pleases, that no one hath the Power to make others have the same Ideas in their Minds, that he has, when they use the same Words, that he does."

4. See Richardson's letter to Lady Bradshaigh, 14 Feb. 1754, in *Selected Letters of Samuel Richardson*, ed. John Carroll (Oxford: Clarendon Press, 1964), p. 286.

Chapter 2. *Oliver Twist*

1. Charles Dickens, *Oliver Twist*, ed. Kathleen Tillotson (Oxford: Oxford University Press, 1966). References to this edition are given parenthetically in the text and indicate page number.

2. Nathaniel Hawthorne, *The Scarlet Letter*, ed. Sculley Bradley, Richmond Croom Beatty, E. Hudson Long, and Seymour Gross (New York: W. W. Norton, 1978), p. 67.

3. There is, in fact, historical support for such a double function. See Ruth Mellinkoff, *The Mark of Cain* (Berkeley: University of California Press, 1981), who explains that "the historically ubiquitous practice of human branding" (p. 23) has functioned as a sign of punishment and humiliation (on criminals, heretics, vagabonds, deserters, Jews) and of ownership (American runaway slaves were branded at least until the American Revolution), as well as a sign of community (to represent a cult, for example). On this latter use, see Emile Durkheim, *The Elementary Forms of the Religious Life*, trans. Joseph Ward Swain (Glencoe, Ill.: Free Press, 1947), who explains how in certain tribes each clan represents itself by body markings of the clan totem (pp. 113–19). Durkheim uses such information to make the point that "the totem is not merely a name; it is an emblem, a veritable coat-of-arms" (p. 113), hence drawing the association between name and body mark that I am investigating.

4. Hawthorne, *The Scarlet Letter*, pp. 147, 152.

5. There is a long tradition of the inscribed body, perhaps the most notable examples being the engraved soul in the *Phaedrus* and the fleshy tables of the heart in II Corinthians. Ernst Robert Curtius, in chapter 16 ("The Book as Symbol") of *European Literature and the Latin Middle Ages*, trans. Willard R. Trask (Princeton, N.J.: Princeton University Press, 1973), mentions numerous examples from the ancients through the Renaissance.

6. In "The Name of Odysseus," reprinted in *The Odyssey*, trans. Albert Cook (New York: Norton, 1967), G. E. Dimock reminds us of this association between mark and name in Homer: "For the scar which the boar gave him is in particular the mark of Odysseus as Trouble" (p. 422), so that the scar or mark functions as a name. Dimock in effect reads *The Odyssey* through what I am calling a naming plot: "Odysseus killed a boar to win his name; he went to Troy to enlarge it; in order to keep it, he will presently kill the suitors" (p. 410).

Another ancient example of this association between the bodily mark and the name functions in the custom of circumcision. See Guy Rosolato, *Essais sur le symbolique* (Paris: Gallimard, 1969), pp. 63–82, who connects God's change of Abram's name to Abraham as a sign of his nomination, and God's establishment of circumcision as a readable sign of the covenant between God and Abraham's people. By circumcising the son, the father bestows on him a mark of recognition that is like the bestowal of the paternal name.

7. Lewis Carroll, *Through the Looking-Glass*, in *Alice in Wonderland*, ed. Donald J. Gray (New York: W. W. Norton, 1971), p. 159. I take Wittgenstein's remark, "I feel as if the name 'Schubert' fitted Schubert's works and Schubert's face," to be at least in part a gloss on the profound and ancient association between name and face (*Philosophical Investigations*, trans. G. E. Anscombe, New York: Macmillan, 1973, p. 215e). In note 11, I take up this association in the context of the Old and New Testaments. The association is especially apt for my purposes when the face, because it is inscribed, resembles the name, so that both face and name are linguistic signs of identity, as in the following passage: "These features of the face were moreover sufficient in themselves to charm the eye, since, having merely the conventional value of a specimen of handwriting, they gave one to read a famous and impressive name" (*Remembrance of Things Past*, trans. C. K. Scott Moncrieff and Terence Kilmartin, New York: Random House, vol. II, p. 37). In Proust's work generally, the face is a text to be read, and in the narrator's reading of the faces of the *jeunes filles*, he reads the

same message as the plot of *Oliver Twist* finds inscribed on Oliver's face: "the word 'innocence' . . . I had read . . . upon their faces" (*Remembrance*, vol. I, p. 1012).

8. See, for example, Locke's remark, "The use then of Words, is to be sensible Marks of Ideas," *An Essay Concerning Human Understanding*, ed. Peter H. Nidditch (Oxford: Oxford University Press, 1975), p. 405; or Hobbes's remark, "So that the first use of names is to serve for *marks* or *notes* of remembrance" (*Leviathan Parts I and II*, New York: Liberal Arts Press, 1958, p. 38). I also recall the definition of *mark* as "a character made with a pen, usually a cross, used by illiterate persons in place of a signature," as in this example from Melville: "Dost thou sign thy name or make thy mark?" (*O.E.D.*).

9. Thomas Hardy, *Tess of the d'Urbervilles*, ed. Scott Elledge (New York: W. W. Norton, 1979), p. 33.

10. Dickens represents the loss of Mary Hogarth as "a blank" (see Edgar Johnson's *Charles Dickens: His Tragedy and Triumph*, New York: Simon and Schuster, 1952, vol. 1, p. 196). I am suggesting that the figure of the blank (which gets reified in the June issue of *Bentley's Miscellany*, when a brief notice of mourning replaces the expected installment of *Oliver Twist*) represents death as an absence of discourse, just as the death of Agnes is represented by a blank (the missing engraved locket, the erased name), and just as the death (symbolic and literal) of Nancy is represented by an obliterated or defaced text, or "one loathsome blank" (164), as we will see.

11. I am thinking of those occasions on which the divine name is withheld in the Old Testament (Gen. 32:29, Judg. 13:18), and the way in which Jesus makes the Lord manifest through the name: "And I have declared unto them thy name" (John 17:26). In a similar vein, I recall Ex. 33:20, where God tells Moses, "Thou canst not see my face; for there shall no man see me, and live," and the way in which the glory of God is made manifest in the face of Jesus: "For God, who commanded the light to shine out of darkness, hath shone in our hearts, to give the light of the knowledge of the glory of God in the face of Jesus Christ" (II Cor. 4:6).

Chapter 3. *Pierre*

1. Herman Melville, *Pierre or The Ambiguities*, ed. Harrison Hayford, Hershel Parker, G. Thomas Tanselle (Evanston and Chicago: Northwestern University Press and Newberry Library, 1971). References to this edition are given parenthetically in the text and indicate page number.

2. I explain in chapter 9 the way in which American naming plots have their origins in Cooper's novels.

3. Compare Helen Keller's remark, "I left the well-house eager to learn. Everything had a name, and each name gave birth to a new thought," and her teacher's remark, "Helen got up this morning like a radiant fairy. She has flitted from object to object, asking the name of everything and kissing me for very gladness," in Helen Keller, *The Story of My Life* (New York: Doubleday, 1954), pp. 36 and 257. Ernst Cassirer uses the example of Keller time and again to mark the moment of the child's symbolic appropriation of the world through naming. See, for example, his discussion of Keller and the child's "hunger for names" in *An Essay on Man* (Garden City, N.Y.: Doubleday, 1953), pp. 170–71.

4. George Eliot, *Daniel Deronda* (Gloucester, Mass.: Peter Smith, 1973), p. 586.

5. There exist various versions of what George Meredith, in *The Ordeal of Richard Feverel* (New York: Holt, Rinehart, and Winston, 1964), calls the "progenitorial blot" (p. 145) or what Nathaniel Hawthorne, in *The Scarlet Letter* (ed. Sculley Bradley, Richmond Croom Beatty, E. Hudson Long, and Seymour Gross, New York: W. W. Norton, 1978), calls "the natal spot" (p. 12) (which I take to be not simply the geographical locale of the child's birth, but his inheritance of the stain of the family—that spot or stain or mark that is ever present in Hawthorne's text). See, for example, the following description of

Razumov: "Yes, as a threatened man may look fearfully at his own face in the glass, formulating to himself reassuring excuses for his appearance marked by the taint of some insidious hereditary disease" (*Under Western Eyes*, London: Pan, 1975, p. 164). In chapter 9 I explain how *Under Western Eyes* reformulates the story of the nameless orphan ("I have no name, I have no . . . ," p. 160) within the political framework of Russian politics.

6. See Henry Murray's pioneering "Introduction to *Pierre*," reprinted in *Endeavors in Psychology: Selections from the Personology of Henry A. Murray*, ed. Edwin S. Schneidman (New York: Harper and Row, 1981), pp. 419–20.

Chapter 4. *The Scarlet Letter*

1. Nathaniel Hawthorne, *The Scarlet Letter*, ed. Sculley Bradley, Richmond Croom Beatty, E. Hudson Long, and Seymour Gross (New York: W. W. Norton, 1978). References to this edition are given parenthetically in the text and indicate chapter and page number.

2. See Aristotle's *Poetics* in *On Poetry and Style*, trans. G. M. A. Grube (New York: Bobbs-Merrill, 1958), p. 21. The editor points out that "bond of love" means specifically "'dear ones,' by virtue of blood ties," and thereby that recognition involves the discovery that the other is kindred or that someone thought to be kindred is an enemy. The definition is significant, for we will see that Hawthorne collapses the antithesis between kindred and enemy.

3. The kind of linguistic identity that I will argue for both Pearl and Dimmesdale, Larzer Ziff claims generally for the Puritan, who "must always be as good as his word . . . because he had only his word as his identity" (*Puritanism in America*, New York: Viking, 1973, p. 16). My emphasis on the speech acts of Hawthorne's characters can be established in correspondence with the picture given by cultural historians of Puritan New England. Ziff explains Puritanism as a language revolution that elevates the pulpit over the altar (p. 6), and Perry Miller describes the central position of the spoken word in the Puritan world (*The New England Mind: The Seventeenth Century*, New York: Macmillan, 1939, p. 295). My suggestion that speech (especially the act of naming) is depicted as an act of potency sees its corollary in the Puritan view of obscene speeches (of the kind Dimmesdale contemplates making to the Puritan children on his return from the forest): "the frequent use of obscene speeches seemeth to be more hurtful to piety, than the simple act of fornication" (William Ames, quoted by Ziff, p. 15).

My own emphasis will be on language as the crucial moral and psychological element within the domain of the family—or on what I call family discourse. Frederick Crews's *The Sins of the Fathers: Hawthorne's Psychological Themes* (New York: Oxford University Press, 1966) turned the tide of Hawthorne criticism, making us see how the family (and especially its unconscious urges toward incest and patricide) is the central subject of Hawthorne's fiction. But Crews's convincing and revolutionary approach to the tales stops short at *The Scarlet Letter*, as he seems to admit, with his unexplained reticence on the question of familial relations in Hawthorne's masterpiece (see pp. 268–69).

4. While critics have not spoken of Dimmesdale as his own child's double—a pattern I take to be as significant as it is specific—they have underscored Hawthorne's descriptions of Dimmesdale as childlike. See, for example, Leslie Fiedler's *Love and Death in the American Novel* (New York: Stein and Day, 1966, p. 237) for a fine discussion of Dimmesdale as "the eternal son."

5. See Roman Jakobson's influential essay, "Shifters, Verbal Categories, and the Russian Verb," in *Selected Writings* (The Hague: Mouton, 1971, 4 vols.), vol. 2, pp. 130–47. R. D. Laing, without using the term *shifter*, suggests how familial roles rename a single member of the family in a dizzying way—as, for example, "granddaughter, daughter, sister, wife, mother, grandmother, niece, cousin, etc. etc." (*The Politics of the Family and Other Essays*, New York: Vintage, 1972, p. 54).

6. While the Pauline description of writing on the "fleshy tables of the heart" (II Corr. 3:3) stands most clearly behind the letter printed on Hester's and Dimmesdale's hearts, I suspect Hawthorne's image is as well an ironic rendering of Socrates's claim that "the true way of writing" is "graven in the soul," "the word which he finds in his own bosom" (*Phaedrus*, 278, a–b).

7. *Hawthorne's Lost Notebook 1835–1841* (University Park: Pennsylvania State University Press, 1978), p. 19.

8. The association between author and father is suggestively discussed by Edward W. Said in *Beginnings: Intention and Method* (Baltimore: Johns Hopkins University Press, 1975), pp. 83–85.

9. *The American Notebooks*, ed. Randall Stewart (New Haven, Conn.: Yale University Press, 1932), p. 101.

10. My emphasis on the third-person pronoun as a way of naming stems from my wish to situate Hawthorne's text, and fiction generally, somewhere between Puritan spiritual autobiography and Freudian psychoanalysis—two modes of discourse that seem especially relevant both to Hawthorne's psychological tale set in Puritan New England, and to the novel as a genre that grows out of the inwardness of Puritan self-consciousness while successively treating psychological experience more and more insistently. Fiction avoids two extremes: on the one hand, Puritan autobiography, where a form of self-disclosure has as its goal the cancellation of the self, and on the other hand, Freudian case history, where the positing of an "I" occurs through the discourse of another.

On the first issue, see Sacvan Bercovitch's discussion of "the dilemma of Puritan identity" in *The Puritan Origins of the American Self* (New Haven, Conn.: Yale University Press, 1975), p. 18, where he cites numerous examples of the mirror as the Puritan tool used to reject individuality by reflecting not the self, but the image of the Lord (p. 14). My point is that in Hawthorne's text the mirror (of fiction) that shows the self in terrifying self-division finally shows it lost in neither simple narcissistic solipsism nor complete otherness. On the second issue, one could argue that the Puritan war against "I, or ihood, or iness" (p. 18) is precisely the illness that psychoanalysis tries to cure by reestablishing the "I"—stated most succinctly in Freud's famous formula, "Wo es war soll Ich werden." But as a form of self-disclosure, the case history (like the Puritan autobiography) has its own internal contradictions. As a specialized scientific discourse, for example, it discloses the subject's most intimate and private life in those words of another ("projection," "primal scene," "anal phase") that are themselves alienated from the subject. See Freud's acknowledgment of the problem of "the betrayal" of his patients' secrets, in the Prefatory Remarks to "Fragment of an Analysis of a Case of Hysteria" (*Standard Edition of the Complete Psychological Works*, trans. and ed. James Strachey, London: Hogarth Press, 1964, vol. 7), where he insists that "the organs and functions of sexual life will be called by their proper names" (pp. 8–9), but that the subject herself will be called by a pseudonym; where the subject's loss of voice is a symptom of the case history itself, in which Freud speaks for the subject; and where the subject may meet herself in what must be a disturbing chance encounter with someone who seems at once herself and another—for if she accidentally comes across her case history, "she will learn nothing from it that she does not already know; and she may ask herself who besides her could discover from it that she is the subject of this paper" (p. 9). The case history hides her while exposing her. Her first anxiety, as she talks to herself about herself in Freud's paper, is whether anyone will know her. In this light one could argue that what one learns from all three kinds of discourse—Puritan autobiography, the psychoanalytic case history, and fiction—is that there is no such thing as the pure language of the self or the pure language of the other, but that discourse by its nature is mixed and that fiction capitalizes on this fact, deliberately representing the self as "he," under which sign self-defense and self-disclosure occur simultaneously.

Of course, certain uses of "I" reveal an understanding of how the first-person pronoun can be empowered with another's meaning, as in Hawthorne's use of "I" in "The Custom-House"; or in fiction narrated in the first person; or in those moments when a reader wants to express the reemergence of his or her own identity through that of a character or author (see Georges Poulet's remark, "An identical *I* had to operate within the author and the critic," in "The Self and the Other in Critical Consciousness," *Diacritics* 2, Spring 1972, p. 49). Such examples make me recall Otto Jespersen's examples of the child speaking of himself in the first person, the second person, and the third person, and speaking of another in the first person (*Language: Its Nature, Development and Origin*, London: George Allen and Unwin, 1949, p. 124). While the child is eventually taught to fix pronominal terms, his confusion dramatizes the genuine nature of selfhood. Hence Jespersen pokes fun at "the great psychologists" who insist that "The child uses no pronouns; it speaks of itself in the third person, because it has no idea of its 'I' (Ego) nor of its 'Not-I'" (p. 123).

11. My explanation of Hawthorne's reticence here is a reaction against what I take to be a general misunderstanding of critics who speak of Hawthorne's own brand of Puritanism. Fiedler's brilliant reading is marred time and again by his jibes at Hawthorne: "little children of the seventeenth century . . . are franker than the adults of the nineteenth" (Fiedler, *Love and Death*, p. 228). The intermittently jeering tone of twentieth-century critics (characterizing Hawthorne, for example, as "improbable in the marriage bed," p. 239) convinces me all the more of the value of a certain kind of reticence, and of Hawthorne's wise defense of himself and his characters. For Fiedler, Hawthorne's text is "sterilized" (p. 228), "dispassionate" (p. 229), "abstract" (p. 228), and "pussyfooting" (p. 236). For me, its irony is balanced by its mercy, its quietude by its sympathy, its aesthetic distance by its sharp autobiographical nature and painful psychic revelations.

12. *Love Letters of Nathaniel Hawthorne 1839–1863* (Chicago: Society of Dofobs, 1907; reprinted Washington, D.C.: NCR Microcard Editions, 1972), vol. I, pp. 243–44.

Chapter 5. *Bleak House*

1. Charles Dickens, *Bleak House*, ed. George Ford and Sylvere Monod (New York: W. W. Norton, 1977). References to this edition are given parenthetically in the text and indicate chapter and page number.

2. The question of names in Dickens's novels, a popular critical subject, usually leads to the critic's explanation of the appropriateness of characters' names. The most suggestive treatment of the subject I have seen is contained in J. Hillis Miller's brilliant introduction to the Penguin edition of *Bleak House* (Harmondsworth: Penguin Books, 1976), pp. 11–34. Miller emphasizes that Dickens "seems to remain in that realm of fiction where names truly correspond to the essence of what they name" (p. 23), and briefly explains how Dickens's characters become linguistic fictions. Also see, on *Our Mutual Friend*, the following useful studies: G. W. Kennedy's "Naming and Language in *Our Mutual Friend*," *NCF* 28 (1973): 165–78; and U. C. Knoepflmacher's *Laughter and Despair: Readings in Ten Novels of the Victorian Era* (Berkeley and Los Angeles: University of California Press, 1971), pp. 143–50.

3. Critics have been quick to acknowledge the symbolic appropriateness of the name Summerson. See, for example, Joseph I. Fradin's "Will and Society in *Bleak House*," *PMLA* 81 (1966): 107; and Norman Friedman's "The Shadow and the Sun: Notes Toward a Reading of *Bleak House*," *Boston University Studies in English* 3 (1957): 154. Even while my argument accepts such a reading, I am suggesting that the novel impels the reader, as it does Esther, to look behind this name and all the nicknames she is given. In the very appropriateness of symbolic names we begin to suspect that the self or place so named is only a fiction, a mere linguistic trick.

4. "For who would bear . . . / . . . the law's delay/When he himself might his quietus make/With a bare bodkin?" *Hamlet*, III, i, 70–76.

5. By taking the name of "No one," Esther's father repeats the strategy of the most well-known missing father, Odysseus. I refer to the celebrated passage in the ninth book of *The Odyssey* in which, when the Cyclops asks for the name of the escaping criminal who has put out his eye, Odysseus answers "No one." For two excellent readings of this passage, see

G. E. Dimmock, "The Name of Odysseus," p. 410, reprinted in *The Odyssey*, trans. Albert Cook (New York: W. W. Norton, 1967); and Max Horkheimer and Theodor W. Adorno, *Dialectic of Enlightenment* (New York: Seabury Press, 1972), p. 60.

I wish to add that "the son of nobody" actually became a technical term in English law: "The rights are very few, being only such as he [the bastard] can acquire; for he can inherit nothing, being looked upon as the son of nobody; and sometimes called *filius nullius*," Sir William Blackstone, *Commentaries on the Laws of England*, quoted by Grace Abbot, *The Child and the State* (Chicago: University of Chicago Press, 1938, 2 vols.), II.508. See, for example, Henry Fielding, *Tom Jones*, ed. Sheridan Baker (New York: W. W. Norton, 1973), p. 60: "Tho' the law did not positively allow the destroying of such base-born children, yet it held them to be the Children of No-body."

6. See the fascinating analogue from Oriental poetry, quoted by Ernst Robert Curtius, *European Literature and the Latin Middle Ages*, trans. Willard R. Trask (Princeton, N.J.: Princeton University Press, 1973), p. 342: "Does all this white signify all thy marks of favor, and are these black dots signs of thy unyieldingness?—She answered me: My father is scribe to kings, and when I approached him to show him my filial love, he feared that I might learn the secret of what he had written, he shook his pen, and the ink spotted my face."

7. See D. W. Winnicott's suggestive essay in which, referring to Lacan's "Le Stade du Miroir," he compares the child's looking into the face of the mother with the child's looking into a mirror. He speaks of a case in which the patient has "the task of getting the mirror to notice and approve" (I recall Esther's talks with herself in her mirror), and finally has "to be her own mother." "Mirror-role of Mother and Family in Child Development," in *The Predicament of the Family*, ed. Peter Lomas (London: Hogarth Press, 1967), p. 29.

8. The relationship between the law and the Gospel, especially when represented through the idea of a symbolic patrimony, underlines this aspect of Esther's role in *Bleak House*: "the relation of God's promise to Abraham and the Mosaic legislation . . . Paul works out by using the analogies of a will and a codicil and of a minor's coming of age." R. M. Grant, *The Letter and the Spirit* (London: S.P.C.K., 1957), p. 49.

9. Considerations of Esther's role in the novel have largely been given over to justification or condemnation of her character. See, for example, William Axton, "The Trouble with Esther," *Modern Language Quarterly*, 26 (1965): 545–57; or Alex Zwerdling, "Esther Summerson Rehabilitated," *PMLA* 88 (1973): 429–39. Such essays, and even that large group of critical essays on the dual point of view in the novel, have neglected Esther's actual role as a writer. Judith Wilt's article, "Confusion and Consciousness in Dickens's Esther," *NCF* 32 (1977): 285–309, is an admirable exception, opening with a few pages on the actual style—the use of dashes and parentheses in what Wilt calls "the grammar of suspension" (p. 288)—of Esther's writing.

Chapter 6. *The Mill on the Floss*

1. George Eliot, *The Mill on the Floss*, ed. Gordon S. Haight (Oxford: Oxford University Press, 1980). References to this edition are given parenthetically in the text and indicate page number.

2. The well-known phrase comes from Ludwig Feuerbach's 1862 work, *Die Geheimniss des Opfers oder der Mensch ist was er isst.*

3. See George Eliot's translation of Feuerbach's *The Essence of Christianity* (New York: Harper and Brothers, 1957), p. 2.

4. See Gordon S. Haight, *George Eliot* (New York: Oxford University Press, 1968); and Ruby V. Redinger, *George Eliot: The Emergent Self* (New York: Alfred A. Knopf, 1975).

5. When Ruby Redinger opens her biography by telling us that "George Eliot came into being on 4 February 1857, already a mature woman of thirty-seven," and proceeds to tell us that the pseudonym "evolved into another self, her writing self, which arched over the not always harmonious selves of Mary Ann Evans, Marian Evans, Marian Lewes, and even

Mrs. John W. Cross" (p. 3), I cannot help thinking of each of those fictional daughters who bears a similarly long list of names: Clarissa, Pearl, Esther, Tess, and Lolita. Redinger does a brilliant job in making us see the consequences of the fact that "both the masculine name of 'George Eliot' and the feminine one of 'Mrs. Lewes' were unfounded in reality" (p. 335); that is, both were fictions.

For another biographer especially astute on this question of the novelist's names, see Frederick R. Karl, *Joseph Conrad: The Three Lives* (New York: Farrar, Straus and Giroux, 1979): "It all began with naming. Even after he anglicized Konrad, he thought enough of it to keep it as his pen name. He was rarely known as Joseph to his closest English friends; he was 'Conrad,' so that we see him turning his surname into a Christian name, matching the 'Konrad' of the Mickiewicz poems. The 'Konrad' of Christian name and surname firmly embedded in him the idea of Poland. . . . Even as he signed his novels and stories Joseph Conrad, he was writing to Polish friends and relatives as Korzeniowski, but with unusual variations" (pp. 12–20). Karl goes on to note eleven such variations.

The entire issue of novelists' names is a fascinating one. Names such as "Boz" and "Mark Twain" come immediately to mind, but there are also some little-known peculiarities of name changing in the lives of novelists, such as Hawthorne's insertion of the *w* in the family name Hathorne, and Hardy's desire to return his family's name to the earlier version "le Hardy." Is it because the relationship between meaning and author stands in an unusually indeterminate position in fiction (among all the kinds of discourse) that the name of the novelist is especially questionable? A useful study could be made of self-naming among fiction writers by analyzing the periods during which the writer's work appeared anonymously, pseudonymously, and/or under his or her "true" name.

6. See J. W. Cross, *George Eliot's Life* (New York: Harper and Brothers, 1885), 3.221.

7. See chapter 18 of "Janet's Repentance" in George Eliot, *Scenes of Clerical Life*, ed. Thomas A. Noble (Oxford: Oxford University Press, 1985).

8. Cross, *George Eliot's Life*, 3.306.

Chapter 7. *Tess of the d'Urbervilles*

1. Florence Emily Hardy, *The Life of Thomas Hardy 1840–1928* (London: Macmillan, 1962), p. 240.

2. Thomas Hardy, *Tess of the d'Urbervilles*, ed. Scott Elledge (New York: W. W. Norton, 1979). References to this edition are given parenthetically in the text and indicate page number.

3. *The Collected Letters of Thomas Hardy*, ed. Richard Little Purdy and Michael Millgate (Oxford: Oxford University Press, 1978), vol. I, p. 250.

4. Hardy's contemporaries drew attention to Tess's kinship with Clarissa and Maggie. See Andrew Lang's remark, "Poor Tess, a most poetical, if not a very credible character, is a rural Clarissa Harlowe," and Lionel Johnson's remark, "like Maggie Tulliver, Tess might have gone to Thomas a Kempis. . . . She went through fire and water, and made no use of them: she is pitiable, but not admirable" (both reprinted in *Tess*, pp. 385 and 397).

5. Florence Emily Hardy, *The Life*, p. 177.

6. Thomas Hardy, *The Well-Beloved*, introduction by J. Hillis Miller (London: Macmillan, 1976), pp. 97, 150, 104. I am suggesting that Tess's tragic role in the long descent of the name "d'Urberville" is ironized in the story of the Beloved reincarnated every twenty years under the name "Avice." It is no surprise, then, that Avice sounds the same note as Tess's "I am one of a long row": "Ah!—mother says I am only one of many!" (p. 33). Hardy emphasizes the *textual* basis of identity in *The Well-Beloved* not only by listing the literary ancestors of Avice (a strategy Nabokov will use in *Lolita*) but also in using the term *edition* for the different copies of the original text: the "modernized, up to date edition of the two Avices" (p. 142), for example, or the "terribly belated edition of the Beloved" (p. 150). For other examples of the son or daughter as the belated edition of a more original text, see the

reference to "refined editions of the family types" (p. 122) in George Eliot's *Daniel Deronda* (Gloucester, Mass.: Peter Smith, 1973), or the daughter as "a second edition of the mother" (p. 164) in Emily Brontë's *Wuthering Heights* (New York: Holt, Rinehart and Winston, 1966).

7. *The Literary Notes of Thomas Hardy*, ed. Lennart A. Bjork (Gotebord, Sweden: Acta Universitatis Gothoburgensis), vol. I, p. 131.

8. *Hawthorne's Lost Notebook 1835-1841* (University Park: Pennsylvania State University Press, 1978), p. 85.

9. *The Literary Notes of Thomas Hardy*, vol. I, p. 193.

10. *Totem and Taboo*, in *The Standard Edition*, trans. James Strachey (London: Hogarth Press, 1968), vol. xiii, pp. 143 and 59.

11. *Jude the Obscure*, ed. F. R. Southerington (New York: Bobbs-Merrill, 1972), p. 196. Hardy expresses the same unnatural wish in "To a Motherless Child": "I wish that thou couldst be/ But One's alone!" *The Collected Poems of Thomas Hardy* (London: Macmillan, 1965), p. 58.

12. See the opening sentences of Robert Gittings's *Young Thomas Hardy* (Boston: Little, Brown, 1967): "Thomas Hardy determined to set up a barrier against biography. Angered by biographical speculations in books published in his own lifetime, and always abnormally sensitive about any reference to his private life, he devised a scheme by which he hoped to silence future writers. . . . He wrote his own life, or what he cared to tell of it, in the third person, to be passed off as a biography written by her [his second wife]," p. 1.

13. Robert Gittings, *The Older Hardy* (London: Heinemann, 1978), p. 93.

14. See *The Personal Notebooks of Thomas Hardy*, ed. Richard H. Taylor (New York: Columbia University Press, 1979), which reprints Hardy's notes to himself. In a sentence like "Put in *my will* that *I* have written no autobiography but that *my* wife has notes sufficient for a memoir" (p. 101), the italicized words are the editor's decipherment of the most eccentric symbols.

15. Florence Emily Hardy, *The Life*, p. 280.

16. See Gittings, *Young Thomas Hardy*, p. 217, and F. R. Southerington's Introduction to *Jude the Obscure*, p. xxiv.

17. Florence Emily Hardy, *The Life*, p. 239.

18. Gittings, *The Older Hardy*, p. 55.

19. J. T. Laird, *The Shaping of Tess of the d'Urbervilles* (Oxford: Oxford University Press, 1975), p. 5.

20. The words "manipulations" and "pervert" appear in Hardy's Preface to the fifth and later editions of the novel. In the *Life*, under the heading "A Novel's Dismemberment," Hardy discusses destroying the "mutilated" novel that once had been "intact" (pp. 213–22).

21. *The Literary Notes*, vol. I, p. 4.

22. Gittings, *Young Thomas Hardy*, p. 1.

23. The title of the last poem in *The Collected Poems*.

Chapter 8. *Lolita*

1. Vladimir Nabokov, *Lolita* (New York: G. P. Putnam's Sons, 1955). References to this edition are given parenthetically in the text and indicate page number.

2. Ernst Cassirer, *Language and Myth*, trans. Susanne K. Langer (New York: Dover, 1946), p. 54.

3. Ernst Cassirer, *The Philosophy of Symbolic Forms*, trans. Ralph Manheim (New Haven, Conn.: Yale University Press, 1955, 3 vols.), II.41.

4. Cassirer, *Language and Myth*, p. 48.

5. Cassirer, *Language and Myth*, p. 48. James George Frazer, *The Golden Bough* (New York: Macmillan, 1963), p. 303, also records the well-known Egyptian story.

6. Cassirer, *Language and Myth*, p. 50.

7. Frazer, *The Golden Bough*, p. 284.

8. Samuel Richardson, *Clarissa*, 4.525.

9. See Vladimir Nabokov, *Speak, Memory* (New York: G. P. Putnam's Sons, 1966), p. 133, where Nabokov records being scandalized in youth by being referred to as one of those "schoolboys who keep naming minute varieties of the Poplar Nymph!"

10. Nabokov, *Speak, Memory*, p. 136.

11. Perhaps by giving the name John Ray to the man who introduces the text to us, Nabokov intends a subtle clue about the ways in which *Lolita* is a descendant of the science of classification. I take Nabokov's John Ray, Ph.D., as a comic modern-day version of the celebrated naturalist of the Enlightenment, the John Ray who has been called the father of natural history in England, and who, as a pioneer in the science of classification, made possible the work of Linnaeus. John Ray's preface to *Lolita* is filled with inflated examples of classification; see, for example, his anatomy of the characters ("the wayward child, the egotistic mother, the panting maniac" [p. 7]). When Humbert describes himself as "Ray-like" (p. 52), I suggest he is at once the predatory spider whose silken rays reach out to trap Lolita, and the classifier who names her "nymphet" (p. 52)—that is, the classifier as predator.

12. The relationship between the more or less "scientific" attempts to found a technical nomenclature in the middle of the seventeenth century and the mystical tradition of the cabalist belief in the power of names is a complicated and controversial subject. Recent scholarship has revealed that, while the philosophical languages of the mid-seventeenth century often worked in reaction against cabalist methods, the works of such writers as Dalgarno and Wilkins share significant features with the work of Ramon Lull and cabalist methods generally. For a fine discussion of this problem, see James Knowlson, *Universal Language Schemes in England and France 1600–1800* (Toronto: University of Toronto Press, 1975), pp. 82–87.

13. See Michel Foucault, *The Order of Things* (New York: Random House, 1973), p. 97, but more generally chapters 4 ("Speaking") and 5 ("Classifying"). I am indebted to Foucault's suggestion that "it is the Name that organizes all Classical discourse" (p. 117).

14. See Mowbray's remark to Lovelace, "she [Clarissa] is gone away with thy marks," *Clarissa*, 3.307.

15. Hans Aarsleff, *From Locke to Saussure* (Minneapolis: University of Minnesota Press, 1982), pp. 9–10.

16. From a sermon preached by Robert South, Locke's old school-friend, quoted in Aarsleff, *From Locke to Saussure*, p. 59. For examples of sixteenth- and seventeenth-century commentaries on Adam as a namer, see Arnold Williams, *The Common Expositor: An Account of the Commentaries on Genesis 1527–1633* (Chapel Hill: University of North Carolina, 1958).

17. From Besnier, "Discours sur la Science des Etymologies," quoted in Aarsleff, *From Locke to Saussure*, p. 59.

18. *The Way to Things by Words* (Menston, England: Scolar Press, 1968), no. 122 in the series *English Linguistics 1500–1800*, p. iii.

19. See Foucault, *The Order of Things*, pp. 129–30.

20. Thomas Hardy, *Tess of the d'Urbervilles*, p. 107.

21. That the erotic *name* confers value on the *person* is suggested when the name comes into existence as a tantalizing presence before the person herself—in *Lolita* (in Lo-*lee*-ta), in Proust's *Remembrance* (as we will see most clearly in the case of Albertine), and in Nabokov's *Speak, Memory*, where we have a curious "autobiographical" rendering of the kind of naming I am examining in *Lolita*: "When I first met Tamara—to give her a name concolorous with her real one—she was fifteen, and I was a year older. . . . During the beginning of that summer and all through the previous one, Tamara's name had kept cropping up (with the feigned naiveté so typical of Fate, when meaning business) here and there on our estate (Entry Forbidden) and on my uncle's land (Entry Strictly Forbidden) on the opposite bank of the Oredezh. I would find it written with a stick on the reddish sand of

a park avenue, or penciled on a whitewashed wicket, or freshly carved (but not completed) in the wood of some ancient bench, as if Mother Nature were giving me mysterious advances of Tamara's existence" (p. 229). Such a passage makes clear that not simply in writing *Lolita*, but in writing his "autobiography," Nabokov put into practice what he learned from Proust.

22. Cleland, *The Way to Things by Words*, pp. 31, 49, 52, 53, 84, respectively.

23. Cleland, *The Way to Things by Words*, p. 76.

24. *Allegory: The Theory of a Symbolic Mode* (Ithaca, N.Y.: Cornell University Press, 1970), p. 39.

25. Fletcher, *Allegory*, p. 65.

26. See chapter 9 of this book for an explanation of Cooper's role in this tradition. Is the reference to "a Dr. Cooper" (15, 17) who interrupts Humbert and Annabel's lovemaking a sly allusion to James Fenimore?

27. John Cleland, *Memoirs of Fanny Hill* (New York: New American Library, 1965). References to this edition are given parenthetically in the text and indicate page number.

28. The *O.E.D.* defines person not simply as "an individual human being," but also as "the living body of a human being."

29. Richardson, *Clarissa*, 2.118.

30. David Foxon, *Libertine Literature in England 1660–1745* (New Hyde Park: University Books, 1965), p. 45.

31. *La Puttana Errante*, for example, described in Foxon, *Libertine Literature*, p. 23.

32. Marcel Proust, *Remembrance of Things Past*, trans. C. K. Moncrieff and Terence Kilmartin (New York: Random House, 1981, 3 vols.). References to this edition are given parenthetically in the text and indicate volume and page number.

33. See André Maurois, *A la recherche de Marcel Proust* (Paris: Hachette, 1949), p. 270.

34. Hardy, *Tess of the d'Urbervilles*, p. 109.

35. The narrator is named "Marcel" only twice in the entirety of the *Recherche*, both times by Albertine in *The Captive*. But even in the naming of him, there is a kind of suspended syntax that postpones the name, and comes close to eliding the name and problematizing its meaning: "Then she would find her tongue and say: 'My——' or 'My darling——' followed by my Christian name, which, if we give the narrator the same name as the author of this book, would be 'My Marcel,' or 'My darling Marcel'" (III.69). The reader should consult this remarkable passage in French: "*Elle retrouvait la parole, elle disait: 'Mon' ou 'Mon chéri', suivis l'un ou l'autre de mon nom de baptême, ce qui, en donnant au narrateur le même prénom qu'à l'auteur de ce livre, eût fait: 'Mon Marcel', 'Mon chéri Marcel'*" (*A la recherche du temps perdu*, Paris: Pléiade, 1954, III.75). The question of the Proustian "I" is a longstanding topic of discussion; for an especially interesting recent account, which takes up the topic through a discussion of fiction and autobiography, see David R. Ellison, *The Reading of Proust* (Baltimore: Johns Hopkins University Press, 1984).

Chapter 9. Epilogue

1. Madeleine L'Engle, *A Wind in the Door* (New York: Dell, 1973). References to this edition are given parenthetically in the text and indicate page number.

2. The religious tone of *A Wind in the Door* especially recalls the Jewish mystical tradition of naming, a highly influential sacred version of the rational search for the name that we saw in the *Cratylus*. On the mystical value of the name in Jewish thought, see Gershom G. Scholem, *Major Trends in Jewish Mysticism* (New York: Schocken Books, 1961): "For this is the real and, if I may say so, the peculiarly Jewish object of mystical contemplation: The Name of God, which is something absolute, because it reflects the hidden meaning and totality of existence; the Name through which everything else acquires its meaning" (p. 132). One should keep in mind that such a tradition is not simply an

ancient one. Scholem documents the mystical search for the name in the Middle Ages; I have already referred to the influence of the cabala on philosophical (naming) systems in the seventeenth and eighteenth centuries; and it would be possible to demonstrate the ramifications of this tradition for such diverse modern texts as *Lolita* and *A Wind in the Door*.

3. One could in fact pair realistic novels with their counterparts in contemporary children's fantasy. For example, the second volume of Ursula Le Guin's *Earthsea Trilogy*, entitled *The Tombs of Atuan* (New York: Bantam Books, 1974), begins where *Tess of the d'Urbervilles* leaves off, with the daughter sacrificed to the eternal cycle of birth and death by having her proper name taken from her: "O let the Nameless Ones behold the girl given to them, who is verily the one born ever nameless. . . . Let her be eaten!" (5). And unlike Angel Clare, who simply furthers Tess's dissolution in the d'Urberville name, the hero of Le Guin's trilogy arrives to restore the daughter's proper name.

4. An important link in such a tradition is the folk tale, upon which both contemporary children's fantasy and realistic fiction draw. The most well-known example of a magical naming plot in folk-tale literature in Western culture is the story of Rumpelstiltskin, but for numerous variations on the theme of naming, see the entries under "Name" in Stith Thompson, *Motif-Index of Folk-Literature* (Bloomington: Indiana University Press, 1958).

5. See above chapter 3, note 3, for an example of Cassirer's use of the story of Helen Keller; also see pages 53–57 in *An Essay on Man* (Garden City, N.Y.: Doubleday, 1953) for Cassirer's use of Laura Bridgman's story.

6. Ursula Le Guin, *A Wizard of Earthsea* (New York: Bantam Books, 1984), p. 5.

7. Ernst Cassirer, *The Philosophy of Symbolic Forms*, trans. Ralph Manheim (New Haven, Conn.: Yale University Press, 1957), vol. iii, p. 121.

8. St. Augustine, *Confessions*, trans. R. S. Pine-Coffin (Harmondsworth, England: Penguin Books, 1966), Book I, sec. 8, p. 29.

9. Ludwig Wittgenstein, *Philosophical Investigations*, trans. G. E. Anscombe (New York: Macmillan, 1973), p. 19e.

10. See, for example, A. J. Ayer's *The Concept of a Person and Other Essays* (London: Macmillan, 1963), pp. 56–57, where a series of philosophical "supposes" begin to support a piece of "science fiction" that the philosopher finds especially useful; or pp. 44 ff., where the philosopher makes his point by requiring that we "Imagine a Robinson Crusoe left alone on his island while still an infant, having not yet learned to speak"; or pp. 106 ff., where the construction of "a rather artificial example" leads into a useful fiction about a child who is kept from having any contact with other human beings but is surrounded by a number of automata. Lest we think Ayer has a monopoly on such strategies, we should realize that he probably borrows the example of the automata from Wittgenstein's *Philosophical Investigations* (p. 178e).

11. See such famous examples as Bertrand Russell's "On Denoting" and Gottlob Frege's "On Sense and Nominatum," in *Contemporary Readings in Logical Theory*, ed. Irving M. Copi and James A. Gould (New York: Macmillan, 1967). The kinds of linguistic puzzles I have in mind include the celebrated arguments over such names as "the morning star" and "the evening star," or "Cicero" and "Tully." To understand how such arguments proceed (where there are two proper names for the same object or person), see, for example, Alvin Plantinga, *The Nature of Necessity* (Oxford: Oxford University Press, 1974), pp. 81–87 (on "Hesperus" and "Phosphorus").

12. I deliberately call to mind here Wittgenstein's well-known term *Lebensform*, or form of life, to suggest that the occult practice of naming can be seen as functioning within the parameters of Wittgenstein's useful notion.

13. See Richard Rorty, *Philosophy and the Mirror of Nature* (Princeton, N.J.: Princeton University Press, 1979), for an excellent account of the historical origins of this idea.

14. See Robert M. Rennick, "The Nazi Name Decrees of the Nineteen Thirties," *Names* 18, no. 1 (March 1970): 65–88.

15. *Pudd'nhead Wilson* in *Author's National Edition, The Writings of Mark Twain, vol. xiv* (New York: Harper and Brothers, 1899), p. 84.

16. See Ralph Ellison's essay "Hidden Name and Complex Fate," in *Shadow and Act* (New York: Random House, 1964), pp. 148, 166.

17. See Byrd Howell Granger, "Naming: in Customs, Beliefs, and Folk Tales," *Western Folklore* 20 (1961): 32–33. Also see Ovid Vickers, "Choctaw Names and Naming: A Diachronic View," *Names* 31, no. 2 (June 1983), who documents the way in which, during the "removal" of the Choctaws from Mississippi to Oklahoma in the nineteenth century, both teachers and missionaries renamed the Indians (pp. 120–21).

18. William Faulkner, *The Sound and the Fury* (New York: Random House, 1956), p. 71.

19. Henry James, *The Turn of the Screw and Other Stories* (Harmondsworth, England: Penguin, 1981), p. 120.

20. Charles Dickens, *Oliver Twist*, ed. Kathleen Tillotson (Oxford: Oxford University Press, 1966), p. 177.

21. A similar critique of (philosophic) knowing occurs from within philosophy (a critique that Nietzsche typically allows himself by renaming himself a psychologist—that is, by refusing to be a traditional philosopher): "The entire apparatus of knowledge is an apparatus for abstraction and simplification—directed not at knowledge but at taking possession of things." *The Will to Power*, trans. Walter Kaufman and R. J. Holingdale (New York: Random House, 1968), p. 274.

22. Lewis Carroll, *Alice in Wonderland*, ed. Donald J. Gray (New York: W. W. Norton, 1971), p. 132.

23. Ludwig Wittgenstein, *Philosophical Investigations*, p. 178e.

24. My revision is a direct importation from the world of the magic of naming: "In primitive thought, the personal name of an individual is not merely an attribute; it is an integral part of his self, his Ego. The Eskimos say that a man consists of three parts, his body, his soul, and his name, and of these the last mentioned alone achieves immortality." See Daniel G. Brinton, *Religions of Primitive Peoples* (New York: Negro University Press, 1969; originally published by G. P. Putnam's Sons, 1897), p. 93.

25. Stanley Cavell, *The Claim of Reason: Wittgenstein, Skepticism, Morality, and Tragedy* (New York: Oxford University Press, 1982), p. 409.

26. The famous phrase from Plautus comes from *The Persian*, line 625. It refers to a courtesan who appropriately gives as her name "Lucris," to which one of the characters responds, "That's a name and omen worth any price" ("*Nomen atque omen quantivis iam est preti*"). In short, the name advertises the use of the body, an example that recalls the paradigmatic act that names (or classifies) woman through reading her body, as in Lovelace's designation of Clarissa as "woman" or Humbert's designation of Lolita as "nymphet." Shakespeare's plays often use the Plautine model of the name as omen ("Portia" in *The Merchant of Venice* is an example of a name that works like "Lucris"), especially as part of the comic resolution of plays like *Cymbeline* (where the revelation of familial identity occurs through a telling name, and through the kind of bodily mark I have associated with the name). At the same time Shakespeare deepens and revises the convention, especially in such tragic versions as Lear's "My name is lost," or Coriolanus's "Only that name remains," or Richard II's "Alack the heavy day,/That I have worn so many winters out/And know not now what name to call myself," or in the complicated and well-known naming plot of *Romeo and Juliet* ("Oh, be some other name!").

27. The argument of my book has, of course, been based on why and how the name itself becomes unreadable and therefore situated at the center of a plot or series of plots—that is, why and how the name itself becomes the "Veiled Name." For an explanation of the ancient Jewish mystical tradition which calls the divine name "*ha shem hamphorash*" or the "Veiled Name," the name in need of interpretation, see Maurice Bouisson, *Magic: Its Rites and History*, trans. G. Almayrac (London: Rider and Company, 1960), p. 113. Nonetheless, because the name is a verbal sign, it always carries with it the sense of readability and intelligibility, and therefore functions as an especially serviceable (and dangerous) tool for knowing and mastering others. In Jewish history, for example, the deliberate veiling of

the Name of God—that is, its prohibition and mystification—occurred when the rabbis decided to circumscribe the uses and abuses to which the immense power of God's name could be put. See Ben Zion Bokser, *The Jewish Mystical Tradition* (New York: Pilgrim Press, 1981), p. 9.

28. *Othello*, ed. Alvin Kernan (New York: New American Library, 1963), IV.ii.70–71. The name "whore," like all classificatory names, erases the proper name, but whether it ultimately erases Desdemona's or Othello's name is unclear because of an interesting textual problem. I am referring to the line (spoken by Othello) that is read alternatively as "Her name, that was as fresh/As Dian's visage, is now begrimed and black" and "My name, that was as fresh/As Dian's visage, is now begrimed and black" (III.iii.383–84). The former reading tells a story familiar to the novelistic tradition. It is the story of Lovelace and Clarissa, the patriarchal Puritans and Hester, Tess and her two lovers, Marcel and Albertine, and Humbert and Lolita. The male assigns the female a value through naming, and in so doing he takes charge of the female's personal and generic names; in fact, by renaming her, he takes charge of her body (as is legally the case when he gives her his name in marriage), to the point of including every form of violation, even murder (as in the example of Othello and Desdemona).

29. My remarks on *Othello* are meant at least in part as an addendum to Cavell's brilliant reading of the play in light of philosophical skepticism (*The Claim of Reason*, pp. 481–96). To revise the traditional concept of body/soul, I have cited Iago's powerful speech to Othello: "Good name in man and woman, dear my lord,/Is the immediate jewel of their souls./Who steals my purse steals trash—'tis something, nothing,/'Twas mine, 'tis his, and has been slave to thousands—/But he that filches from me my good name/Robs me of that which not enriches him/And makes me poor indeed" (III.iii.155–61).

30. "She Unnames Them" appeared on page 27 of *The New Yorker* on January 21, 1985.

31. James Fenimore Cooper, *The Deerslayer* (New York: New American Library, 1980). References to this edition are given parenthetically in the text and indicate page number.

32. Ralph Ellison, *Shadow and Act*, p. 166.

33. Mark Twain, *Adventures of Huckleberry Finn*, ed. Sculley Bradley, Richmond Croom Beatty, E. Hudson Long, and Thomas Cooley (New York: W. W. Norton, 1977). References to this edition are given parenthetically in the text and indicate page number.

34. William Faulkner, *Absalom, Absalom!* (New York: Random House, 1964), p. 114.

35. Joseph Conrad, *Under Western Eyes* (London: Pan Books, 1975). References to this edition are given parenthetically in the text and indicate page number.

36. I am recalling the technical meaning of such a phrase in English law, especially as it is used in the tradition of the English novel. See my explanation of the phrase, as it is used in *Tom Jones*, in chapter 5, note 5, above.

37. These words are spoken by the title character in Tennyson's "Ulysses." This example is especially relevant because it reminds us of the ancient patriarchal hero who represents himself as "no one" on his way to establishing his right to his name. For a further explanation of the role of Odysseus in naming plots, see above, chapter 2, note 6, and chapter 5, note 5.

38. Fedor Dostoevsky, *Crime and Punishment*, trans. Jessie Coulson (Oxford: Oxford University Press, 1980). References to this edition are given parenthetically in the text and indicate page number.

39. In *Under Western Eyes* the self is consistently dissolved in various accounts of itself, so that the entire fictional model of *Under Western Eyes* literally translates "I" into "he." I refer here to the fact that the entire text is based on the English teacher's translation of Razumov's diary, a translation that turns not only Russian into English, but diary and confession ("I") into narrative ("he"). One could even argue that the nameless narrator's account of Razumov's life is really a confession of his own love for Natalia (once again told in the third person, as an account of another).

40. Thomas Hardy, *The Well-Beloved*, ed. J. Hillis Miller (London: Macmillan, 1975). References to this edition are given parenthetically in the text and indicate page number.

41. Charles Darwin, *On the Origin of Species* (Cambridge, Mass.: Harvard University Press, 1964, facsimile of the first edition), chapter 13, p. 420.

42. Thomas Hardy, *Tess of the d'Urbervilles*, ed. Scott Elledge (New York: W. W. Norton, 1979), p. 109. See my discussion of Angel's desire to make and produce Tess, and Alec's desire to "berth" her, above in chapter 7.

43. Emily Brontë, *Wuthering Heights* (New York: Holt, Rinehart and Winston, 1966), pp. 18–19.

44. I am referring here to the habit of one character designating another character as an "example," and thereby beginning to allegorize the plot of the novel from within the narrative itself. *Clarissa*, for example, begins with the trial of Clarissa as an example (which is a useful way of characterizing the trials which test her names: "daughter," "Clarissa," "Harlowe," "woman," etc.). Anna Howe writes to Clarissa, "Every eye, in short, is upon you with the expectation of an example." [Samuel Richardson, *Clarissa* (New York: Dent, 1978), vol. 1, p. 3.] And every new tragic circumstance of the story supplements and qualifies the way in which Clarissa serves as an example: "You will be as excellent an example as ever you hoped to be, as well as a warning: and that will make your story, to all that shall come to know it, of double efficacy" (2.280). For an especially ironic version of the woman as example, see the scene in which Angel Clare piously quotes to Tess the following passage from Paul just before she makes her confession: "Be thou an example—in word, in conversation, in charity, in spirit, in faith, in purity" (Hardy, *Tess of the d'Urbervilles*, p. 189); Tess has already feared the harm she might do as an "example" (p. 86).

Index

Note: Names that designate family members (such as parent and child or father and daughter) appear so regularly throughout this study that it was impossible to index them usefully.

263